Only Farmers Need Apply

Official Canadian Government Encouragement of
Immigration from the United States, 1896-1911

Harold Martin Troper

Griffin House
Toronto 1972

ISBN 0 88760 042 5

Published by Griffin Press Limited
455 King Street West, Toronto, Canada

Printed and bound in Canada by
The Alger Press Limited

Acknowledgements

Many persons have aided and encouraged me in the research and writing of this book. Thanks must go to both Professor Robert Adolph of York University and Professor David Smith of The University of Puget Sound for reading this work in manuscript form and saving me from many blunders, and Professor Patrick C. T. White under whom this work was begun as a doctorial dissertation at the University of Toronto. I am indebted to the staff of the Public Archives of Canada and the Reference Department, University of Toronto Library, notably Miss Mary McTavish for untiring patience in filling research requests, and the Canada Council whose financial support made two years of research and writing possible. I also acknowledge my debt to Dr. Ann Golden, Dr. Paul F. Sharp, Professor S. D. Clark, Mr. Howard Palmer, Miss Ann Wolfish, Miss Olive Lambert, Mrs. Minnie Sonnenreich, Mr. Bruce Bergman, Miss Lee Palmer and especially Miss Eydie Moll who not only encouraged and criticized with evenhanded sensitivity but also maintained good humour throughout.

Table of Contents

Anxiety and Change --- 1

Machine and Personnel --- 9

In the Field --- 33

The Unknown Failure -- 57

Selling a Country --- 79

The Other Lands --101

Closing the Door ---121

Conclusion --147

Notes ---159

Index ---189

To the memory of my father
who would have understood

Introduction

As Canada enters its second century few issues are as important as relations with the United States. Questions fundamental to Canada's continuance as a nation – Quebec and federalism, northern sovereignty, regionalism, economic independence and cultural development – are directly affected by the imposing influence of the American fact.

This influence is not new. Living with the colossus to the south has always been a central problem for Canada. Yet, while scholars have focused on the diplomatic, military and economic impact of the United States on Canada, relatively less attention has been accorded the historical patterns of social and cultural interaction between the two North American neighbours. Much remains to be written about movements of people between them.

Around migrating groups such as the Loyalists after the American Revolution, runaway slaves who moved from station to station along the underground railway, and recent Viet Nam draft resisters or military deserters, an overlay of popular misconceptions has grown intensifying the need for further objective analysis of their impact on the Canadian scene. But, the spin-off of folk mythology from these 'refugee' communities has given them a unique sense of self-perception and a source of common identity and unity as they integrated into Canadian society.

Unknown to most Canadians and Americans, additional tens of thousands of American settlers immigrated northward, not escaping the United States, but seeking economic opportunity in Canada. These settlers have generally eluded both the scholar and the mythmaker; their role in the development of Canada also remains unrecognized. It is hoped that for at least one period of Canadian history, an examination of the organizational structure and programme through which many of these settlers were brought into Canada will spur further study of American immigrants and of Canadian immigration history in general.

Anxiety and Change

A crucial episode in the history of Canadian immigration was played out during the fourteen years of Wilfrid Laurier's administration, 1896-1911. The many thousands of southern and eastern European peasants who crowded Canadian ports and settlers' trains en route to new lands in western Canada are well remembered.[1] Speaking before the Toronto Board of Trade in 1922 Clifford Sifton, Minister of the Interior under Laurier and initiator of an activist immigration policy, strongly defended the value of these European migrants. In retrospect he asserted, "I think a stalwart peasant in a sheepskin coat, born on the soil, whose forefathers have been farmers for ten generations, with a stout wife and a half-dozen children, is good quality."[2] But these European settlers were not the only new groups added to the Canadian community during this period. From farms throughout the midwest and prairie United States over half a million American citizens or residents crossed the forty-ninth parallel to take up new farms on the booming Canadian prairies.

This study is essentially an examination of this American migration northward during the Laurier years with special emphasis on the civil service structure assembled to promote the inflow. It details the Federal Government's role in encouraging Canada bound settlers and explores the internal workings of the civil service branch assigned to stimulate immigration. Special attention is accorded the efforts at publicity, the mechanics of American operations, personnel problems and the stretching of immigration legislation to exclude unwanted settlers, notably Negroes. The relationship of the Immigration Branch of the Department of the Interior to private interests, especially land

1

companies and railroads, as well as the Department's susceptibility to domestic political pressure in the hiring of personnel and use of public funds are also considered.

Previous historical research into American migration, and the activities of Canadian immigration authorities, has been encumbered by an over-reliance on the Dominion of Canada *Sessional Papers* as the single main source of primary material.[3] The *Sessional Papers*, inasmuch as they record the annual reports of the immigration authorities, are a valuable asset to research. One must realize, however, that they are essentially a product of self-evaluation and self-serving editors. As a result these reports are often edited to convey only that notion of immigration work the authorities wish to make public, and do not reveal much about those routine activities of the government organization which are essential for complete understanding.[4] Fortunately the recent release of previously unavailable immigration papers, letters and reports from the Laurier period has provided an invaluable new source of primary material.[5]

A cautionary note must be sounded as to the boundaries of this study. Primarily an examination of the American migration northward through the efforts of an organized government recruitment operation, it is not intended to explore the complex issues involved in any individual's or group's final decision to migrate northward except where such an analysis directly relates to the Immigration Branch's programme. Furthermore, in limiting itself to the area of immigration recruitment, this study does not directly consider the related but separate questions of immigrant settlement, adjustment and socialization once in Canada. While these important concerns are alluded to as each relates to official immigration work, they do not fall directly within the purview of this study and justly deserve individually separate treatment, for which, it is hoped, this study will pave the way.

Obviously movements of population do not take place in a vacuum. They are a result of shifting social and economic concerns, are prodded or restricted by political considerations, moulded by the self-restraint of cultural traditions and bound by the limits of geography. The American migration into Canada and the efforts of the Canadian government to spur this movement prove no exception. They were the offspring of a marriage between Canadian economic expansion and American agrarian land hunger during the first years of this century.

The *New York Times* marked the advent of the twentieth century with an editorial sigh of relief. While the newspaper looked to the future with an optimism born of economic revival, it remembered the nineties as hungry years which gnawed away at the national fibre.

> The country is yet steadily engaged in repairing the loss of tissue suffered during the lean years. It is making up through all its vast frame the low diet, insufficient nourishment and checked growth that were inflicted on it for some five years previous to 1897.[6]

As historians have noted, the financial disorder of the nineties was reflected in a sense of uneasiness. Robert Wiebe writes of an all pervasive and troubled national mood. "Anxiety, like the common cold, was a most egalitarian malady which in many respects ran the same course wherever it struck."[7] Richard Hofstadter has offered an analysis of the period based on what he has called a "psychic crisis", an era in which national expectation proved sadly out of joint with national perception. This domestic cognitive dissonance, Hofstadter contended, added impetus to the drive for imperial expansion resulting in the Spanish-American War.[8] Closer to the scene, Henry Adams, writing of his own experience from the prospective of 1918, remembered the American people in the nineties as "wandering in a wilderness much more sandy than the Hebrews had ever trodden since Sinai; they had neither serpents nor golden calves to worship."[9]

The American farmer was caught up in a tangle of economic uncertainty during this period. For two decades prior to 1896 he had been repeatedly buffeted by turbulent financial storms. Falling prices, indebtedness, loan sharking, railroad exploitation and corrupt or impotent state governments precipitated the rise of agrarian political protest in the Populist movement. Although their reform platform would greatly influence later reform groups, the Populists never recovered from the parallel blows of an unfruitful 1896 election alliance with the Democrats and a return of prosperity.[10]

The year 1896, which marked a downturn in the fortunes of the agrarian protest movement, saw an upswing in the American economy. Renewed prosperity quickly filtered down to much of the farm community. Encouraged by increased world demands for agricultural produce, farmers expanded their output and were often rewarded with improved market prices and inflated land values.

But, rural prosperity proved far from universal. The exhausting economic depression left a considerable number of farmers deep in debt or tenants on land they once owned. Bound by contractual debts or poverty, many farmers were unable to pull up stakes and move on as American pioneers had done in the past. Moreover, even those farm owners who sold out at a profit were finding it increasingly difficult to leap-frog westward to new lands. For rural America there grew a disquieting awareness that the frontier had ended and with it the end of an era in which good inexpensive land was available in seemingly unlimited quantities.

Well before Frederick Jackson Turner's famous speech of 1893 relegated the frontier to history, others were already concerned lest the closing of the frontier would mean changes in American lifestyle and values. For instance, popular jingoist Congregationalist minister Josiah Strong, author of the widely read essay *Our Country: Its Possible Future and Its Present Crisis,* reminded his many readers in 1885 that "the general welfare and contentment of the [American] people hitherto have been due, in large measure, to an abundance of cheap land." However, Strong was quick to caution, "When the supply is exhausted, we shall enter upon a new era, and shall more rapidly approximate European conditions of life."[11] While agricultural land was by no means unavailable, with homestead claims and private land sales brisk after the turn of the century, it was difficult to overlook the general feeling that the American land expansion was ending.

The gradual closing of domestic land expansion was balanced by a corresponding upsurge in urban development. To much of rural America, traditionally harbouring a distrust of cities, the rising spectre of Babylon challenged longstanding agrarian values and assumptions. Thomas Jefferson's Arcadian ideal had not lost its impact. Admonishing the new Republic to retain its strong agricultural roots, Jefferson hoped future generations would never "see our citizens occupied at a work bench or twirling a distaff . . . Let our workshops remain in Europe." In addition, Jefferson warned, "When [Americans] get piled upon one another in large cities, as in Europe, they will become corrupt as in Europe."[12]

This warning from the eighteenth century echoed across generations leaving many American farmers wondering what avenues still remained open to their own offspring. Uneasy over the lure of the cities, farmers found their sons denied that which Mark Twain's Huck Finn declared as his final option, to "light out for the territory ahead of the rest . . . ."[13] Furthermore, as domestic land values rose the farmer's temptation to sell high, move westward and buy cheap was increasingly frustrated within American borders. Yet, at this precise moment a path

4

into the virgin Canadian west was opening to replace, in part, the previously American route to land acquisition.

Prior to 1896, if the American farmer devoted even passing attention to the Canadian west, it was most likely as a frozen wasteland inhabited by Indians, fur traders and red-coated Mounted Police. As late as 1909 a Canadian immigration agent in Lexington, Kentucky reported ". . . I have found that very few people have heard or know anything about Canada except what they have seen in moving pictures such as Ice Harvest in Canada, Winter Carnival at Montreal, so it is quite natural for the people to believe that Canada is a country of Ice and Snow."[14] The recently ended depression had not been kind to Canada or its reputation. Reviewing the North American economic scene in 1895, W. C. Ford, director of the American Bureau of Statistics, claimed that "the depression in Canada has been more severe than in the United States."[15] Even an advocate of reciprocity in trade between Canada and the United States, Anthony Higgins, was forced to admit in 1893 that Canada floundered in a sorry economic state. He wrote of Canadians: ". . . today they do not grow. Trade and manufacturing are stagnant. Agriculture is depressed, and Canada has become a mere breeding ground for the United States."[16] Indeed, the seemingly endless stream of Canadian youth flowing southward into the United States to take up American lands had been such a pronounced fact of life in Canada that a witicism of the period held that "Canada's story begins in Lamentations and ends in Exodus."[17]

In 1896 after many years of broken dreams and frustrated hopes Canada found itself swept along in the tide of a world-wide economic upswing. For Canadians the international business revival was translated into one word – wheat.[18] Rapid European industrialization and urbanization, especially in Great Britain where no high agricultural tariff kept Canadian grains off the market, generated unprecedented demand for produce.[19]

Stretching westward along the lines of the recently completed transcontinental Canadian railway lay the vast Canadian prairie, potential wheat lands now ripe for development. Readily accessible by rail, the movement of settlers in and grain out was simple. But transportation was not the only technological advance stimulating western Canadian expansion. Agricultural techniques largely perfected in the United States, were freely copied by Canadians. Cultivation of vast areas was made more practicable with the chill-steel plow, self-binding reaper, new storage systems and a specially designed boxcar for hauling grain

5

in bulk. Methods of conservation and irrigation were also patterned on successful American models, and with minor variations, the homestead programme adopted by Canada was largely a replica of that in the United States.[20] One major Canadian innovation came too late to directly affect this initial period of settlement. The search for an early maturing wheat to overcome the threat of sudden frost only ended in 1911 with the general acceptance of Marquis wheat. This proved a factor in the later stages of agricultural development, after much of the west had already been settled.[21]

Before sod could be turned and seed planted, farmers had to be lured onto the land. The plains of what are today Manitoba, Saskatchewan and Alberta – the northern continuation of the American Great Plains stretching up from the Gulf of Mexico – have the best soil but the most severe and capricious climate of all inhabited parts of Canada. Summers are dry and hot, winters long and very cold. In addition to blizzards and the legendary chinook, early and late frosts added unpredictability to climatic extremes.[22]

This vast treeless expanse of land by 1896 was no longer isolated from the rest of Canada. The Prairies, locked in on the west by towering mountains and on the east by the seemingly impenetrable Shield, witnessed the completion of the Canadian Pacific Railway in 1886. With the subsequent demand for wheat the area suddenly boomed.

This timely union of economics, technology and geography in 1896-1897, which pushed the Canadian west into a long-awaited period of settlement, was complemented by the implementation of assertive immigration practices of a newly elected Liberal government in Canada. Official immigration policy was not initially changed; Liberal policy makers found little reason to tamper with existing statutory regulations. Canada had long recognized the desirability of increasing population, and the theoretical and legislative framework for encouragement of immigration was available. But in the light of changing economic conditions, aggressive immigration personnel with a new determination to attract foreign agricultural immigrants found it possible to translate theory into practice.

Canada's immigration law in 1896 was sufficiently flexible to permit a steady inflow of desired population while enabling the Minister of the Interior, responsible for the administration of immigration regulations, wide latitude in undermining the arrival of less welcome settlers.[23] To Clifford Sifton, appointed Minister of the Interior in 1896, immigration priority should be granted to agriculturalists who would populate and farm western Canada. Speaking to the Commons in 1902 Sifton explained that all government immigration work was directed exclusively toward encouraging settlement of rural areas.

> It has not, for many years, been the policy of the [Interior] department, either under the late government or under this government, to make any attempt to induce mechanics or wage earners to come to Canada . . . The test we have to apply is this: Does the person intending to come to Canada intend to become an agriculturalist? If he does, we encourage him to come and give him every assistance we can. But we give no encouragement whatever to persons to come to work for wages as a rule, and we give no encouragement under any circumstances to persons desirous of coming out to get clerical situations of any kind, the view being that we should have enough persons to fill situations of that sort.[24]

Whether seeking out potential settlers in the United Kingdom, Europe or the United States, the Canadian government's concern remained geared to the collection and absorption of agricultural settlers. Sifton, for instance, advised the Commons in 1899 that he had authorized Canadian immigration officials to employ the Alien Labour Act to inhibit the free entry into Canada of labourers or other urban-bound settlers from the United States. As he put it, "None but agriculturalists, we do not recognize the labourers at all."[25]

Heightened by the increasingly favourable world economic climate and renewed land hunger in the United States, in 1896 the Canadian west stood poised on the verge of rapid development. The only missing ingredient, or so it appeared from Ottawa, was the means of combining these two loosely related factors. To meet this challenge the Canadian government revitalized its total immigration operations. To a degree never previously attempted, the Canadian government welded the essence of its immigration policy to contemporary techniques of business – promotion, management and advertising know-how – each tempered by a keen awareness of political reality.

The American farmer remained a target of government activity. It is this government programme, the systematic initiation of a large scale movement out of the United States, and especially the institutional framework through which planning was transformed into activity, which this study explores.

7

Machine and Personnel
[IMMIGRATION ORGANIZATION]

The various elements which had coalesced by 1896 to create an atmosphere conducive to increased immigration from the United States found practical expression in the policies adopted by the newly elected Liberal government of Wilfrid Laurier. Prodded by growing western loyalty to the Liberal Party banner and pressing need for a national commitment to the full development of western Canada, population increase emerged as a basic domestic priority. The responsibility for translating general immigration policy into specific programmes for the encouragement of immigration fell under the jurisdiction of the Department of the Interior and its new Minister, Clifford Sifton.

Although the first federal seat Sifton would win was in the election of 1896, the new member proved a wise and logical choice for the Laurier cabinet. Sifton's political views, temperament and talents well suited a man who would guide the unfolding of a new era in western growth.

Sifton was born in London Township, Middlesex County, Ontario, March 10, 1861, but in 1875 his father, John Wright Sifton, moved the entire family west into Manitoba. Except for several years of study at Toronto's Victoria College, the younger Sifton remained in Manitoba and came to identify himself as a westerner. Here he studied law and eventually began legal practice in Brandon, Manitoba.

Sifton's eye, however, focused on politics, not on law. He had never been far from the political cauldron. His father, an active Liberal, was elected to the provincial legislature and chosen Speaker of the Manitoba House in 1878[1]. Accepting his father's political label, Clifford Sifton underwent his own electoral baptism by winning a seat on the

9

Brandon Board of School Trustees and in 1886 was appointed Brandon city solicitor and solicitor for the Western Judicial Board. Two years later he advanced into provincial politics, taking the seat in the legislature for North Brandon. In 1891 he joined Premier Thomas Greenway's cabinet as provincial Attorney-General, while simultaneously maintaining the ministerial portfolios responsible for education and provincial crown lands.[2]

His emergence onto the federal political stage in 1896 came at an auspicious moment for both the Liberal Party and western Canada. The opposition Liberals, long in the political doldrums, were entering an electoral battle from which they would emerge to form the government, while, at that moment western Canada was moving swiftly toward an unprecedented period of economic expansion. Sifton's energy in guiding the successful Liberal campaign in Manitoba as well as his impressive record in the provincial legislature brought his organizational skills to the attention of the new Prime Minister, Wilfrid Laurier. Sifton's biographer, John W. Dafoe, contends that Laurier singled out the young Manitoban for the federal Interior post well in advance of the Liberal triumph. But difficulties ensued. While others enjoyed the fruits of victory, the anticipated Sifton appointment remained stalled. While all other cabinet posts were filled by September, 1896, Sifton waited silently for over four months following the election. Having assumed the federal Interior position would be filled by Sifton, many western Liberals questioned the delay. Dafoe attributes the postponement of the appointment to active competition for the cabinet post from Sifton's fellow westerner, Joseph Martin.[3] However, it has been argued that the lengthy delay in appointing Sifton was a delay of his own making. Sifton was allegedly reluctant to assume the Interior post unless the new Prime Minister acceded to two demands. The would-be minister demanded that the new government turn its attention to resolution of the controversial "Manitoba School Question" and, more importantly, in terms of this study, allow Sifton complete freedom to organize western developmental programmes. Only by November was Laurier either willing or able to make the necessary guarantees and, accordingly, only then did Sifton join the federal cabinet.[4]

While Sifton showed a practical understanding of the necessity for reorganization within the Department of the Interior, he was more a technician than an original theorist. He was uncomfortable with experimentation and relied heavily on adapting tested techniques to Departmental needs. Fortunately for the new minister, the history of land settlement in North America offered countless precedents on which a programme of revitalized western development could draw. With his personal energy matched only by his commitment to western expansion, Sifton was to prove well suited to the task of co-ordinating the government's development programme.

Increased immigration was the backbone of Sifton's overall plans for western expansion. But Sifton also acknowledged the need for a well-founded federal government campaign to stimulate western Canadian development in conjunction with provincial authorities and private interests, especially railway and land companies. The central government's role, Sifton believed, was pivotal as it alone had the power and prestige necessary to generate systematic development. In order to spur growth, especially in the agricultural sectors, Sifton proposed reducing tariffs on manufactured goods and lowering railroad freight rates to and from the west. But, he realized, only increased population would sustain prosperity.

Sifton's support for relatively unrestricted entry of immigrants into Canada was not without qualification. When he accepted his cabinet position, immigration was officially forbidden to only three groups, the diseased, the criminal or vicious, and those likely to become public charges. Sifton, however, was not above stretching these provisions, as well as such legislation as the 1897 Alien Labour Act, to further prohibit entry to non-agrarian settlers. Although his vision may have been limited, the Minister's priorities were crystal clear. He wanted only those settlers prepared, experienced and strong enough to overcome the rigorous challenges necessary to build a productive agricultural economy on the Canadian prairies. No others need apply.[5]

It should not be suggested that this policy, even with existing controls, was unanimously endorsed in Canada as a whole or even in western Canada specifically. Opposition to the almost unrestricted inflow of foreign agricultural settlers grew in intensity as increasing numbers of immigrants disembarked at Canadian ports. As late as 1910, after a more selective immigration policy had already been adopted, the tone of a *Montreal Standard* feature article on new European immigrants reflected deep anxiety over the character of the foreign influx. Under one photograph of inbound migrants the caption read, in part, "They are bound for the West, and for the most part are inclined to be sullen and morose. Nearly every man carries a knife, but they are [sic] very seldom seen." Yet another caption read, "One peculiar characteristic of the people of this picture is their aversion to water – at least its external use."[6] Nevertheless, with the exception of small groups such as the Canadian Nationalist League, which held that western Canada should be maintained solely for settlement by Canadians, there was general agreement that increased immigration was desirable, or at least a necessary evil.[7] Opponents of open immigration generally favoured careful scrutiny of incoming settlers rather than closing off immigration entirely. In 1900 James R. Conn, a Presbyterian minister and supporter of immigration restriction, wrote an article for the *Queen's Quarterly* arguing that a greater emphasis on "quality" of migrants would not necessarily decrease "quantity". The more care taken in selecting the pieces of the Canadian mosaic, he argued, the greater the number of higher calibre immigrants who would find Canada attractive.

> A physician aims at the production of muscle through obtaining an abundant supply of blood and nerve. What Canada needs is superior brain and nerve tissue. If we look more to the quality of immigration the quantity would regulate itself satisfactorily. But by the unfortunate policy of filling up the country with a "hungry, poverty-stricken, skin clad population of wild eyed Asiatics and Eastern Europeans," we are adopting the surest means of keeping out people of real enterprise and progressive ideas . . . We cannot expect the best class of Anglo-Saxons to come in and mix with those inferior elements. Thus by a mistaken hope of present gain Canadians are forfeiting the best possibilities of the future; we are selling our birthright for a mess of pottage, and not a savoury mess at that.[8]

Immigration into Canada from the United States was generally viewed in a far more positive perspective. Though the spectre of "Americanization" of western Canada would periodically manifest itself in the Canadian and American press, Americans were generally recognized as being a desirable class of agricultural immigrants.[9] In 1910, Charles Alexander Magrath, then Conservative member of Parliament for Medicine Hat, lauded American settlers as "people of independent thought who understand the ways of this continent and its institutions."[10] Magrath's views were echoed in government ranks. In an article on immigration William Duncan Scott, a long time federal official in the service of Canadian immigration, outlined the Interior Department's position on the desirability of American settlers.

The people from the United States most readily adapt themselves to Canadian conditions. The greater portion come from the Northern and Western States, where climatic and agricultural conditions closely resemble those of the Dominion. As they are largely of the agricultural class and come to Canada to take up farming, they know the proper course to adopt immediately upon arrival. United States immigrants may be considered the most desirable for a number of reasons. They understand Canadian conditions so well that their success in the so-called dry belt of Alberta has been greater than that of the Canadian born; immediately on arrival they put large tracks under cultivation, and induce the railway companies to provide transportation facilities in the districts where they settle; they use the most recent machinery and labour-saving devices, and are thus an object-lesson, more especially to foreign settlers who, without this clear proof of the value of improved machinery, would be slow in commencing its use; and, lastly and most important of all, they employ upon their farms large numbers of the immigrants of all races, who yearly arrive without sufficient capital to commence operations at once on their own account, and who must seek employment with others until they have saved enough to begin work on their free homesteads.[11]

Scott went on to dismiss "Americanization" as a groundless and parochial fear. Indeed, as he put it, if it "means that the progressiveness of the American will be copied by the Canadian, the more rapid the Americanization the better." There was little danger of annexation, according to Scott, as Americans were quickly impressed by the innate superiority of the Canadian system of government and thereafter proved steadfastly loyal to it.[12]

Sifton was especially anxious that the promotional work among American farmers get underway quickly. However, on taking up his duties of office, Sifton found the existing immigration work of his Department in disarray. Speaking to the Commons in 1906, Sifton remembered the Department of the Interior as "a department of delay, a department of circumlocution, a department in which people could not get business done, a department which tried a man to death who undertook to get any business transacted with it." In view of the Department's "well known condition" Sifton made his first task grass roots Departmental reorganization and reform.[13]

Before turning to an examination of the reformed structure of the Immigration Branch and the character of its personnel, it is important to note the major impact Sifton's ministry had for homestead lands, the common denominator in all settlement programmes. No reorganization of the Department, no matter how well instituted could succeed unless land was readily available. Consequently, Sifton forced land grant railways to patent property which they had earned through track mileage construction but still remained unclaimed. This left the way open for the government to assign homestead lands unhindered by potential railway claims.

It has been rightly pointed out that Sifton did not originate the notion that Canada could profit by giving lands away. However, others before him had only paid lip service to homestead encouragement while taking no practical steps toward implementation of a far-reaching free land development policy in Canada. Sifton firmly established organized homestead settlement as a central tenet of the Interior Department's working philosophy.[14]

Turning again to his Department, Sifton not only found its operating procedures ineffectual, but he also discovered its personnel ill-equipped to deal with the particular complexities of organized western settlement. Shortly after his arrival in Ottawa, Sifton became aware that the previous ministry "employed in the department men who did not understand conditions of the country. There were men employed in the department who were as honest and well-meaning as it was possible for man to be, but who, not being acquainted with the conditions of the case, made the most absurd rules."[15] A transfusion of new blood was essential. Using the free hand granted by Laurier, Sifton introduced individuals into the immigration service who proved both sympathetic to the Department's objectives and acquainted with the characteristic needs of western Canada.

To accomplish his twin goals of structural and personnel reform Sifton reshuffled his Department into functionally cohesive work units. The Immigration Branch, a separate division within the Department of the Interior, was formed by uniting all immigration activity under one administrative umbrella. The activities of the Immigration Branch fell naturally into two main sub-divisions – the gathering of immigrants and their placement. The latter operation, generally outside the scope of this study, was centralized at Winnipeg and concerned itself with settlement of European settlers once in the country: their location, transportation and successful completion of homestead obligations. The former division, concerned with the actual recruitment of immigrants, was housed in the offices of the Department in Ottawa. As no comparable immigration structure operated under any previous ministry, Sifton constructed a new civil service section. He welded together an active corps of civil servants to encourage immigration into Canada where only a skeletal outline previously functioned.

While today one is often tempted to view civil servants as faceless mandarins, cogs in a mindless bureaucratic machine, this has never been the case in the sensitive area of immigration and certainly does not describe conditions at the turn of the century. Within the wide policy dictates established by the Minister, immigration personnel were often very individualistic in their response to immigrants and interpretation of policy. Racism, political prejudice, aggrandizement and insecurity were instantly reflected in discussions that affected not only other governmental personnel, but also the new immigrants as well. As a result, awareness of the general backgrounds of Immigration Branch personnel is an essential prerequisite to understanding the Immigration Branch's impact on both immigration policy and the immigrants.

Those appointed to organize and operate the fledgeling immigration service were, in large measure, "Sifton men". Often hand chosen by the Minister himself, the top Departmental and immigration officials were political allies and often fellow westerners. This is not to imply that they were not competent. On the contrary, the Ottawa chain of command was to show both resourcefulness and flexibility in dealing with settler recruitment. In appointing political friends Sifton guaranteed loyalty to the government's emerging immigration policy while rewarding allies for their support. The selection of westerners kept the appointees' natural geographic emphasis in concert with that of their chief.

Sifton's freedom to appoint those he wished to the civil service was not simply a result of the latitude allowed him by Laurier. In large measure it reflected the state in which the Canadian civil service found itself at the turn of the century. Each government department was divided into two administrative sections, the Inside Service and the Outside Service. In the Inside Service were all government employees in and around Ottawa, while those working outside Ottawa were lumped together as the Outside Service. This division was not arbitrary. The separation into two administrative divisions reflected differences in administrative function and control. The degree of control maintained by any government agency over the activities of its Outside Service varied inversely with a civil servant's distance from Ottawa.

Supervision and control over Immigration Branch personnel in the field remained a constant concern.[16]

Admission into the federal civil service was officially regulated by a Board of Examiners authorized to test each candidate and determine his general aptitude and employment suitability. Although the simple examinations were unlikely to give an acceptable applicant any difficulty, the Board's very existence was often ignored, or, at best, side-stepped by officials. It was not unusual for an appointment to be made by a minister and only later for the Board to be informed of the *fait accompli*. Although the Board had the privilege of calling Parliament's attention to such abuses, and often did so, Parliament proved reluctant to remove this pillar of the existing spoils system through decisive action.[17] The conclusions of a 1907 Royal Commission investigating the civil service noted that "the politics of the party were of greater importance in making appointments than the public interest of the Dominion."[18] Thus when Sifton began his term as Minister of the Interior, the most outstanding feature of the civil service was the role which patronage, political and nepotic, played in every aspect of the government's organization. Appointments, promotions, salaries, discipline, transfers and dismissals were all influenced by party and family affiliations. Such conditions were especially widespread in the Outside Service. Within such a loose framework, Sifton had no difficulty introducing whomever he pleased into Department of the Interior positions.

Dafoe argues that Sifton was less prone to reward his followers with civil service posts than were other members of the Laurier cabinet. The deluge of job-seekers, each of whom carried credentials proving past Liberal loyalty, that descended on the new Minister of the Interior was reportedly sufficient to fill all positions in the Department many times over, even if all personnel of the previous ministry were removed. However, Dafoe contends that the Interior Department witnessed no wholesale purge of existing employees. Most vacancies which occurred resulted from resignations of civil servants who were obvious supporters of the Conservative Party and feared for their jobs, or, perhaps, were merely unable to adjust to the new administration. Indeed, he points to cases where Sifton categorically refused to weed out known Conservatives in the Department's payroll even under pressure of local Liberal Party partisans.[19]

This is substantially correct. Of the twenty-three men listed as dismissed from the Department of the Interior during the new Minister's first few months at the helm, six were listed as removed for "active

16

political partisanship."[20] Such a small turnover on political grounds *per se* is far from a general housecleaning. Nevertheless, the lack of any policy for direct removal of existing employees did not preclude the use of patronage as a criterion for making new appointments. As the activities and staff of the Department of the Interior expanded the doctrine that loyal supporters should be loyally supported became a virtual dictum in filling the ranks. The young Immigration Branch was certainly not immune to the patronage infection. Indeed, as will be described, patronage became one of the few common bonds cementing Immigration Branch personnel into a unit. In the hierarchy of organizational interests, future survival and growth rank as basic considerations. In a new organization partisan political loyalty becomes an instant foundation on which to build security.

While ultimate responsibility for planning and operation of the Department of the Interior rested on the shoulders of its Minister, actual management of the Department was delegated to "his" appointed civil servants. Most important among these Departmental officials, and carefully chosen by the Minister, was the Deputy Minister. The Deputy Minister had broad powers and extensive responsibilities. He handled the actual day-to-day workings of the Department and, as one observer notes, "His is the responsibility (next to the Minister) if anything goes wrong, his the thankless duty of allowing the minister to take the credit if things go well . . . ." The Deputy Minister, being in direct control of continuing operational activities, had almost absolute control over transfers, salaries and promotions.[21]

Sifton's personal appointee to the post of Deputy Minister was James Allan Smart. Smart was born in Brockville, Ontario in 1858, where he operated a hardware business. In 1880, like the Sifton family before him, Smart migrated westward to Manitoba. A life-long Liberal, he was soon elected an alderman in Sifton's home constituency of Brandon. Smart went on to serve two terms as mayor of Brandon. During his interregnum as mayor, Smart sat as a member of the provincial legislature representing East Brandon between 1886-1888 and Brandon between 1888-1893. Smart and Sifton were cabinet colleagues with Smart serving as provincial Minister of Public Works. This association between the two Brandon Liberals continued in the federal Department of the Interior until Sifton's resignation from the federal cabinet in 1905.[22]

Subordinate to the Deputy Minister and charged with overseeing the co-ordination of existing programmes was a Departmental Secretary aided by an Assistant Secretary. It is difficult to establish the exact boundaries of authority granted the Secretary during the Sifton years; however, in 1919 a new Civil Service Commission published a job description for all civil service positions entitled *Classification of the Civil Service of Canada*. It is probable that in 1919 the Secretary carried out much the same duties as his predecessors. Under the direction of the Deputy Minister, the Secretary was charged with establishing and maintaining communication as required with other federal Departments, provincial governments or private agencies which had no special existing relationship with any division of the Department (such as the Immigration Branch). He was to keep personnel accounts and financial records in order while making note of anything taking place in Parliament which concerned the Department as a whole.[23]

Through 1899 the position of Secretary was nominally filled by John Richard Hall. He had been with the Department of the Interior since 1883, but his new Liberal colleagues successfully stripped him of responsibilities. While awaiting his official release on pension, Hall's duties were largely assumed by his assistant, Lyndwode Pereira.[24] The vacancy left by Hall's departure was immediately filled by a new Secretary, Perley George Keys, a Liberal who had been with the Department since 1878. At the time of his promotion Keys was in charge of the Ordinance and Admiralty Lands Branch and was touted as having "general knowledge of working [sic] of various branches of the department", which equipped him to deal with his new responsibilities.[25]

Unlike the ranking civil service positions within the Department of the Interior outlined thus far, those directly connected with immigration were relatively new. Responsibility for immigration administration had been transferred to the Department of the Interior only five years prior to the Liberal victory of 1896. Previously immigration had been the preserve of the Department of Agriculture. Under Conservatives from 1892 to 1896, the Interior Department organized immigration encouragement activities, but they had neither the independent structure nor the ministerial encouragement necessary to successfully support a far-ranging programme. It must also be noted that economic conditions in Canada, the United States and Europe, were far from favourable for Departmental immigration activity. In 1896 this all changed.[26]

Having chosen top Departmental aides and enthusiastically endorsed the principle of increasing population, Sifton turned to assembling a corps of Immigration Branch personnel who could direct government resources toward specific programmes for encouraging immigration.

A Superintendent of Immigration was duly appointed to head the new Branch. The duties of the Superintendent corresponded roughly to those listed in the 1919 Civil Service codification under "Secretary, Department of Immigration and Colonization." The Superintendent was responsible for personnel within the Immigration Branch. He prepared regulations, recommended immigration programmes and, in general, kept up to date on all details concerning immigration and colonization. His duties also encompassed co-operating programmes with provincial governments and transportation companies to better facilitate movements of settlers into the west and representing the Department in all matters concerning immigration. Finally, he assisted in drawing up all legislation which would have a direct impact on immigration activities.[27]

The first Superintendent of Immigration was Frank Pedley. Pedley was the only Maritimer in the Branch. Born in St. John's, Newfoundland in 1858, he attended McGill University earning a bachelor's degree in philosophy. He moved west, but only as far as Toronto where he earned a law degree and began practice in 1890. While in law school Pedley developed an active interest in politics. On accepting his Ottawa appointment he "was presented with a purse of gold by leading Toronto Liberals, in recognition of his service as past president of the Y.M.'s Lib Club."[28]

In 1902 Pedley transferred to the post of Deputy Superintendent General of Indian Affairs; his immigration post was reassigned to William Duncan Scott. Scott was especially well-informed on western Canadian development and experienced in both immigration organization and promotional work. Born in Dundas, Ontario in 1861, Scott followed what was becoming a well beaten track for Sifton appointees; in 1881 he moved to Manitoba, giving up his law studies in Ontario to take up work for the Canadian Pacific Railway still under construction. In 1887, Scott joined the Manitoba civil service as an Immigration Agent at Winnipeg. In 1895 he was transferred to Toronto where he continued with immigration work for the Manitoba Department of Agriculture. It is very probable that Sifton and Scott had close dealings prior to Sifton's entrance into the federal cabinet. As the minister in charge of provincial crown lands in Premier Greenway's cabinet, Sifton was concerned with settlement organization. Following the defeat of the Manitoba Liberal government in 1899, Scott joined the federal service as a Canadian Commissioner at international exhibitions, first assigned to the Paris Exposition of 1899. In 1903 he was promoted, replacing Pedley as Superintendent of Immigration.[29]

When Scott assumed his duties of office, he was free of one task initially performed by his predecessor. Pedley, who assumed the Superintendent position 1897, was also responsible for inspection of local government immigration agencies. As this was both a taxing and time-consuming task in its own right requiring lengthy periods in the field, the duty of inspecting agency offices in the United States was officially transferred to William J. White in 1899. White, like Sifton, Smart and Scott, was from Manitoba. Before the Liberal victory of 1897 he had been editor of the pro-Sifton *Brandon Weekly Sun*.[30] Brought to Ottawa by Sifton in 1897, White became Press and Advertising Agent for the Immigration Branch with special emphasis on public relations activities in the United States. In this capacity he maintained responsibility for organization and co-ordination of immigration agency work south of the border. His 1899 reclassification only served to formalize the administrative situation which had, in fact, already come into being.[31] As Inspector of Agencies in the United States, White continued to be responsible for the ongoing publicity programme in the United States.

During its first years of operation, the Immigration Branch employed a Secretary in Charge of Immigration responsible for immigration correspondence and liaison with other departments. The position was a holdover from the previous ministry and with reorganization it became an anachronism. When the Secretary, L. M. Fortier, retired, the post was dissolved and minor officials or clerks took over any of the Secretary's remaining duties.[32]

Although the Department's top Inside Service appointees showed the requisite history of loyalty to the Liberal Party, this was usually supplemented by other commendable qualities. As a group these ranking officials offered experience in administration, publicity, law, immigration recruitment, land development, personnel management and public relations. Largely westerners, new civil servants were familiar with local development and settlement requirements and sympathetic to regional demands. Sifton's Departmental organization and personnel remained largely untouched by his successor. Shifts in Departmental powers took place however, as a result of revisions in

20

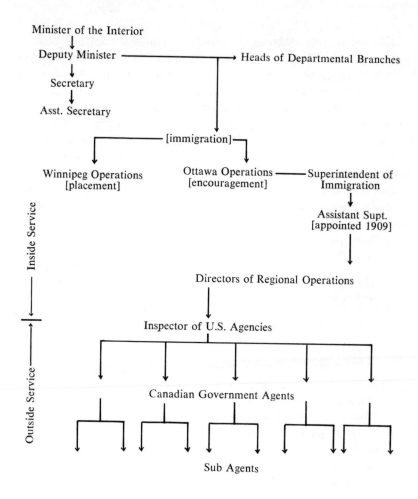

immigration legislation and a curtailment of ministerial discretion in making civil service appointments.

In 1905 Sifton left the cabinet in the wake of a dispute over the "Manitoba School Question."[33] The new Minister of the Interior, Frank Oliver, was also a westerner, from the rapidly developing territory soon to become the province of Alberta. Oliver was born near Brampton, Ontario in 1853. Attracted by journalism, as a young man he worked in the composing room of the *Toronto Globe,* then moved to Winnipeg where he joined the staff of the *Manitoba Free Press.* Lured still further west, Oliver moved to Edmonton. He tried storekeeping but was soon drawn back to the press. He founded and published the *Edmonton Bulletin*. A strong advocate of western development, Oliver was unwilling to confine his political concerns to the editorial page. In 1883 he was elected to the North West Council for the District of Edmonton and served a two-year term. In 1888 Oliver entered the territorial legislature where he crusaded for responsible government and local administrative reform. Attracted to federal politics, in 1896 he carried the seat of Alberta for the Liberal Party. Once in Ottawa, he established himself as watchdog for far western interests. He advocated railroad reform (even nationalization) and openly attacked Sifton's policy of "unrestricted immigration."[34] Oliver proved especially severe in his attacks on "Slav" immigrants.

> . . . there is nothing [the westerners] more earnestly resent than the idea of settling up the country with people who will be a drag on our civilization and progress. We did not go out to that country simply to produce wheat. We went to build up a nation, a civilization, a social system that we could enjoy, be proud of and transmit to our children; and we resent the idea of having the millstone of this Slav population hung around our necks in our efforts to build up, beautify and improve the country, and so improve the whole of Canada.[35]

Like most advocates of greater immigration restriction, Oliver was not opposed to continued encouragement of "quality" immigration. Well before entering the cabinet he placed on record his approval of continued agricultural immigration from Great Britain and the United States. It was in an effort, he claimed, to increase the desirability of western Canada as a home for Americans that he advocated strong restrictive legislation.

> As to the immigration that is coming from the United States . . . this is the largest immigration we are getting. The only immigration that could be more desirable would be that from the British Islands . . . Now I say these people are desirable, take them in mass, desirable in every way. They are people of intelligence, of energy, of enterprise, of the highest aspirations. They speak the same language, they worship in the same churches, they have the same political ideals, although they have enjoyed different political institutions. Moreover, these people are the strongest objectors to the ideal of indiscriminate immigration. They say they have suffered from that in the United States, and they will hold up both hands against such a policy in this country.[36]

On taking office Oliver quickly translated his personal misgivings over "unrestricted immigration" into legislation. He modified Sifton's policies in the direction of greater legislative restriction. The Canadian Immigration Act of 1906 and a subsequent Act of 1910 vastly expanded the powers of immigration personnel to reject entry into Canada by "undesirable" elements reaching Canada's ocean ports. The 1906 legislation also made medical problems, pauperism and "moral turpitude" grounds not only for exclusion but also for deportation. The government was granted powers to deny specified groups entry into Canada, although provision was made for investigation and appeal to the Minister. A money clause allowed for a minimum capital requirement to be set for certain classes. Possibly under pressure of rising American Negro interest in western Canada, this 1906 legislation was strengthened and extended in 1910. The Act of 1910 more specifically enumerated and defined prohibited classes and added race as a classification factor for immigration into Canada. Although appeals to the Minister were allowed, non-residents were denied recourse to the courts. It has been argued that the 1906 and 1910 acts were largely a formalization of the restrictive policies Sifton had long practised, especially with regard to non-agrarians. However, while designated employment was of no small consequence in gaining entry into Canada, the new emphasis on racial or ethnocultural restrictions went well beyond Sifton's pro-agricultural bias. More discretion in recruitment was consequently practised by government agents in Europe so that what previously seemed a straight and smooth path for prospective settlers developed bumps and winding curves.[37]

Meanwhile the American settler was little affected by these policy changes. A medical and character inspection was officially instituted at American border crossing points in 1908 but, at most, this proved little more than a minor inconvenience for the vast majority of white American farmers moving across the frontier. However, this nominal inspection was used as a pretext for the exclusion of black American settlers who tried to emigrate into western Canada. As the Department was prepared to inform Negroes, the exclusion of blacks, discused in a later chapter, was rigorously enforced after 1909. In a 1911 letter to the noted Negro leader W. E. B. Du Bois, Secretary L. M. Fortier outlined the government's attitude.

> There is nothing in the Canadian Immigration law which disbars any person on the ground of colour, but since col-

oured people are not considered as a class likely to do well in this country all the regulations respecting health, money, etc., are strictly enforced, and it is quite possible that a number of your fellow countrymen may be rejected on such grounds.[38]

The restrictive emphasis of new legislation and consequent administrative adjustments were Oliver's primary contributions to the Department's immigration organization. However, he was also inadvertently responsible for one important personnel change necessitated by his own appointment to the cabinet. When Sifton left the Department, his Deputy Minister, James Allan Smart, resigned.[39] The new Deputy Minister appointed by Oliver was William Wallace Cory. This first non-Sifton appointee was born in Strathroy, Ontario in 1865, but as a child moved to Manitoba. Cory studied law in Winnipeg and articled in the Attorney General's office where he became a clerk in 1889. As Cory was already clerk in charge of patent railroad lands for the federal Department of the Interior when Sifton was appointed Manitoba's Attorney General in 1891, the possibility of official contact between the two men was likely. Later that year Cory transferred to the post of Inspector of Yukon Offices for the Departments of Interior and Justice and in 1904 he was reappointed to the post of Assistant Commissioner of Yukon Lands. In 1905 Cory was elevated to the post of Deputy Minister.[40]

Except for carrying out the new duties required by the revised Immigration Acts, the general workings of the Immigration Branch remained substantially the same in character and methods under Oliver and Cory; in fact the introduction of Cory into the Department was the single major personnel change felt by the Immigration Branch's American operations (although by 1909 the increased activity of the Immigration Branch made appointment of an Assistant Superintendent of Immigration a necessity). The officials of the Immigration Branch, most appointed by Sifton, remained at their posts with no hint of discontent from either civil servants or their new master.

After 1908 Oliver was not able to wield the same wide power Sifton had so freely exercised in appointments to his ministry. Among the recommendations of the 1907 Royal Commission on civil service reform which found their way into the 1908 Civil Service Amendment Act was a permanent Civil Service Commission requiring supervised examinations for all admissions and promotions within the Inside Service. The Outside Service, however, remained beyond the reach of the 1908 legislation.[41] While abuse of the legislation was not uncommon within the Inside Service this reform was a signficant step toward substituting merit for patronage.[42]

The Department's Ottawa operations, its Inside Service, directed the overall programme of immigration recruitment. But it was government agents in the field, the Outside Service, who brought Canada's message to the potential settler's doorstep. From Ottawa, like the hub of a wheel, spokes radiated out to a series of salaried agents operating in different states and through them to sub-agents working on commission. While the local duties and activities of salaried agents and sub-agents will be dealt with in subsequent chapters, the overall organization, structure and personnel of the American field operations must be examined here as they relate to the establishment of a broad framework for immigration encouragement.

The defeated Conservative government had nominally supported immigration agents in the United States, but they were never more than marginally significant in government planning. A realization that the new government's undertaking was a radical departure from the past experience encouraged Canadian agents in the United States to request a new distinctive and effective title by which they would be known thereafter. White advised caution in selection of any official name.

> Being styled "Dominion Colonization Agent" was not favourable to [one agent questioned]. Not one [American] in ten – I think that is a safe average – has any idea what the word "Dominion" meant, while the word "Colonization" is immediately associated with some land company, and these are looked upon as one of the curses of the country. My opinion is that he should be styled "the Agent of the Dominion of Canada," or Canadian Government Colonization Agent might be acceptable. When it is learned that it is a government that is dealt with there is immediate change of front and a confidence shown that bears out the point I choose to make. It may seem a small matter, but my observations have led to this conclusion.[43]

The titles suggested by White were regarded as too long, but his objections to specific terminology were taken into consideration. Wishing to remain both simple and effective, the Immigration Branch chose the name "Canadian Government Agent" to designate its local salaried state immigration agents working in the United States.[44] Less than a year after Sifton inaugurated his new policy of immigration encouragement, there were seven Canadian Government Agents functioning. Much of their attention was initially focused on the Michigan stump-lands, lands originally cleared by lumber companies then resold to farmers, usually for dairying. Three offices opened in Michigan quickly followed by openings in other states.[45] By 1904 there were eighteen offices staffed by Canadian Government Agents across the American mid-west and prairies.[46]

The stationing of agents in the United States ideally required the selection of men who were prepared to move from area to area, experienced at organizing an office in unfamiliar surroundings and adept at initiating contacts with local residents. In reality these criteria, when met, were met by accident. One can only marvel at the measure of success achieved by men so ill-prepared for the duties they assumed. While no objective standard was used to judge a potential agent's talents or adaptability, political and nepotic patronage once again rank as the dominant factors in selection of personnel. The 1907 Royal Commission investigating the Civil Service warned that "politics enters every appointment" and once having entered, it stayed. The Commission noted, "in the Outside Service those who have 'political pull' use it for all it's worth; they pass by their superior officers and bring pressure to produce anything that may prove to their advantage."[47] Had they bothered to examine the Immigration Branch, the Commissioners might have agreed it was a classic case in point.

Just as in the Department's Inside Service, past experience and attitudes which immigration agents in the field brought to their work greatly influenced their interpretation of immigration regulations and the nature of their interaction with prospective settlers. While detailed biographical material on individual government agents assigned to the United States is scant at best, enough information can be pieced together to reveal a clear pattern of personal pressure applied to influence the selection of candidates. Indeed the Immigration Branch's Outside Service resembled a dumping ground for defeated Liberal politicians or unemployed members of political families. Unlike the Inside Service, there seemed little attempt to balance the necessity of appointing a competent agent against the political realities of the spoils system.

James A. Grieve, appointed Canadian Government Agent for Reed City, Michigan in 1897 was born in Mornington, Ontario in 1855, where he operated his own farm and local insurance business.[48] An interest in politics carried him into the Liberal Party and he was elected to the minor municipal position of Deputy Reeve for Mornington. In 1891 Grieve entered federal politics carrying the seat of Perth North. In 1896, a year of Liberal victory, Grieve suffered personal defeat at the polls but his disappointment was mitigated by appointment to an immigration post in the United States.[49] He had no background in immigration work, nor any other apparent experience of direct value to settler recruitment.

The Grieve appointment did not pass unnoticed by the opposition Conservatives. Nicholas Flood Davin, member of the Commons for West Assiniboia, assured Parliament that Grieve's employment was not "for the purpose of inducing immigration, but of rewarding supporters."[50]

Davin took care to point out that Grieve was not alone. Benjamin Davies, authorized to open an agency in St. Paul, Minnesota, was no less than half-brother of Louis Henry Davies, the Minister of Marine and Fisheries in the Laurier cabinet. Likely with some relish, Davin reminded the Commons that the Minister of Marine and Fisheries had been "one of the loudest denouncers of nepotism when he was on [the opposition] side of the house."[51]

The cases of Grieve and Davies were not unique.[52] As late as 1909 the opposition still hammered away at the government for employment of "immigration agents, most of them doing nothing, relatives of ministers, friends, brothers-in-law, ex-candidates . . . all over the United States . . . ."[53]

Like so many similar opposition attacks on patronage, this one levelled squarely against the Immigration Branch by Conservative member for Jacques Cartier, Frederick Debartzch Monk, did little more than irritate the government and its agents. In spite of a mild sensitivity to criticism, political and nepotic appointees stayed on. Edward T. Holmes, working out of Minnesota, was a brother of the Liberal Member of Parliament for West Huron, Robert Holmes.[54] Thomas Duncan, first employed by the Immigration Branch as an agent in Scotland in 1897 before transfer to Syracuse, New York in 1904, had served as a Liberal member of the Manitoba legislature together with Smart and Sifton.[55]

Some agents followed yet another route into the Department's employ marked by intercession at crucial junctures by well known political figures. One agent received his South Dakota appointment after Premier Greenway of Manitoba approached Sifton over the matter.[56] Previously the candidate had served as Special Immigration Agent for Manitoba in the Dakotas but following provincial budget cuts his employment was terminated. He immediately applied for a position with the federal Immigration Branch. Not offered a posting in spite of his obvious experience, a quality sorely lacking in most appointees to the Outside Service, he requested the Manitoba Premier intercede on his behalf. Premier Greenway apparently raised the appointment during conversations with Sifton in December, 1897 and a position as agent was offered shortly thereafter.[57]

After a much more blatant application of personal interference by an outsider, William Scramlin received an agency appointment in 1909.[58] Stepping in on Scramlin's behalf was John Gillanders Turriff, the Liberal Commons "whip" and a previous Commissioner of Dominion Lands from 1898 until his election for Assiniboia East in 1904.[59] Having for some unexplained reason become involved with Scramlin's request for government employment (Scramlin may have been Turriff's brother-in-law), Turriff demanded the Department hire the applicant. The Liberal member of Parliament wrote Superintendent Scott, "I enclose herewith a couple of letters requesting employment from Mr. Wm. Scramlin of Halbrite, Saskatchewan. Please meet his wishes to the full limit you can as I am anxious to get him at work."[60] The application was granted; Scramlin was assigned to North Dakota at his own request.[61]

Within the Canadian civil service, such obvious patronage was, of course, not confined to the Immigration Branch. However, the formation of a separate structure to encourage immigration with its demand for new state agents created a trough at which hungry Liberal faithful eagerly looked for a comfortable spot to feed. Obvious though patronage was, criticism of the practice fell far short of overcoming the formidable Liberal majority in the Commons; but, criticism could smart. In 1898 agent M. V. McInnes, Detroit, prodded agents to meet excoriation with determination. Twisting logic sufficiently to suit his needs, McInnes accused the opposition of playing politics with patronage.

> Why, with a Government alive to the importance of developing the resources of our great North-West heritage, should we not be able to send out thousands to settle in the great "Eldorado", who in the plenitude of the realization of their hopes, will bless the names of the agents to whom they owe a position of contentment and competence. I am sure that

the government is doing its share, and the Dominion expects every agent to do his share, so that they can point with pride to their staff, while the opposition will scrutinize with ruthless skill, any opening in our armour. Let our solid ranks of settlers in the West be our shield to ward and protect the Department from the unscrupulous assaults of disappointed politicians.[62]

Sifton, defending the Immigration Branch in the Commons, made no attempt to deny that relatives and political friends of the Liberal Party had found their way into American agencies. Indeed, on one occasion the Minister of the Interior proudly identified agent Davies as the brother of his colleague, the Minister of Marine and Fisheries, as if this fact alone would insure this agent's success in the field.[63] Again in 1901 Sifton came to the defence of Immigration Branch personnel. Instead of simply claiming past political allegiance to the Liberal Party was no reason to overlook a prospective applicant, Sifton proposed that it was this very history of partisan activity of job-seekers which tended to make them an asset to the work of the Immigration Branch, and he was not about to give up the practice in the face of Conservative attacks.

> I have had occasion to appoint a number of gentlemen to this [immigration] service who have rendered political service to the Liberal Party and in consequence of the fact that I have been bitterly assailed by non-gentlemen opposite . . . I do not regard the fact that a man has occupied a somewhat prominent position in the organization of the Liberal party and has been regarded as a capable, intelligent, experienced, and valuable man by the Liberal party, that that is any reason [sic] why he should not be appointed to the public service. But, other things being equal, I regard a man of that kind as likely to be a good public servant. I believe that the capability and intelligence which made him a valuable man in connection with political affairs makes a valuable public servant . . . [The opposition] will not be able to succeed in inducing me to cease the practice which they, no doubt, regard as very reprehensible, of appointing Liberals to office when there are vacancies to be filled.[64]

Patronage stayed. The attitude of the Minister of the Interior toward appointments of family or political allies, a long tradition of using the civil service to reward loyal followers and the exclusion of the Outside Service from reform provisions of the Civil Service Amendment Act of 1908 assured the continued importance of personal influence in governing the employment practices within the Immigration Branch.[65] Between 1896 and 1911 over thirty men held sensitive posts as Canadian Government Agents in the United States. While detailed background information outlining the manner in which they received their positions unfortunately is unavailable for all appointees, one can be sure that many of the state agents unaccounted for were hired more on the basis of loyalty than ability.

In spite of this lack of detailed biographical material, snippets of information reveal something of the variety in interests and talents reflected by immigration agents in the field. The majority of agents were originally from Ontario or western Canada; many lived for some time in Manitoba.[66] A few were once farmers and continued to own land but this was not common. One agent, for example, had operated a hotel in Brandon, the heart of Sifton's constituency.[67] Still other state agents were previously members of the Manitoba civil service and acquainted with top Departmental personnel from Manitoba.[68] Surprisingly, only one agent, M. V. McInnes, long in Detroit, had previous experience with federal immigration activities.[69] In 1890 he left a position as Traffic Passenger Agent for the Canadian Pacific Railway to enter the Department of Agriculture's small immigration programme. He moved to the Department of the Interior when responsibility for immigration shifted. He opened an immigration office in Detroit which he operated for several years before the Liberal victory.[70]

Among others who found their way into Immigration Branch employ were Canadians who had migrated to the United States during hard times. One such agent was remembered as "an old Manitoban now living in Dakota. When he was in Manitoba back in the eighties the bailiff was about the only man that had anything to do."[71] Work experience in the United States also differed from agent to agent. An exceptional candidate, originally from Alberta, was "formerly connected with the railway in Omaha. He was picked out [by the Department] as a man well qualified for the work and has done good work." Others were farmers or small merchants.[72]

Immigration personnel included the temperate and the tipsy. One agent, who passed the civil service examination in "precise writing" and applied for an agency post, wisely described himself as "a proficient bookkeeper and office man, accurate at figures, strictly sober and in excellent health."[73] He was hired, in part, because the Department recognized sobriety as no small blessing. Indeed, an immigration agent working in Edmonton was reassigned first to Indianapolis, then to Lexington, Kentucky, in hopes that a change of scene would help him sober up. As their agent was known to drink his money away, the Department doled his wages out in limited amounts. Requesting funds on one occasion, the agent pleaded, "I am completely busted. I will also inform you that I have not touched a drop of strong drink [in] weeks and have no desire to do so."[74] The Minister was personally concerned about the case and requested reports on the progress of the forced cure. He was informed, in part, "The letter [our agent] writes is in his own hand and appears to be well written, concise and intelligent. I should judge that he is coming along very nicely." His success in attracting immigrants was not mentioned.[75]

Since Sifton and later Oliver personified the link between political party and government policy, Liberal appointees found no personal contradiction between past allegiance and civil service employment. Indeed, personnel hired for both the Inside and Outside Service of the Immigration Branch by late 1897 had few common bonds except patronage which opened the door to government jobs and new loyalty to the Department which, they hoped, would prove the key to continued job security.

The reconstructed Department of the Interior and its immigration organization were a noteworthy achievement of governmental bureaucratic structure both in the speed with which it was accomplished and the smoothness with which it began to function. Here again Sifton, more an engineer than an architect, played the crucial role in sparking interest in immigration encouragement and outlining organizational goals.

It must not be forgotten that the institution of such a major immigration effort was undertaken in conjunction with related developments in other areas of government and the private section. Accounts had to be kept, propaganda written and published, transportation arranged, land surveys carried out and border immigration stations built. The effective co-ordination of the whole effort rested squarely on the new personnel, the functioning chain of command, and their ability to create and operate comprehensive immigration promotion programmes which would yield forth settlers from the day-to-day operations of agents in the United States.

In the Field
[AMERICAN OPERATIONS]

Domestic debate over the relative contributions of Canadian Government Agents to the movement of Americans northward into the Canadian west stimulated both the praise of partisans and the ire of critics. Sifton's immigration authorities readily claimed all credit for any increasing outward flow from the United States and contemptuously dismissed the work of the former ministry as negligible. Reviewing the activities of his predecessors, James Allan Smart, newly appointed Deputy Minister of the Interior, wrote, ". . . I have come to the conclusion that all previous immigration work done . . . has been wasted and that no real effort has been made to induce people to move, notwithstanding the fact there have been a number of Agents doing work, or purporting to do work . . . ."[1] The positive impact of the recently organized Immigration Branch was singled out for praise. Clifford Sifton strongly commended his state agents and reported that the Department had traced newly arrived "settlers almost altogether to places where our agents had been working." He contended that without his agents Canada "would not get one-third or one-quarter as many."[2]

Acknowledging the substantial impact of immigration agents, *Canadian Magazine* in 1905 described them as effectively engaged in "missionary work on a business basis."[3] This image of a businesslike Department co-ordinating a network of dedicated salesmen was also adopted by internationally known American journalist Frank George Carpenter.[4] Writing for the *New York Herald in* 1906 Carpenter was especially impressed by the magnitude of the government's enterprise.

> [Canada] has inaugurated an immigration campaign bigger
> than any ever backed by any government, and it is now
> working in the United States just as a wholesale dealer
> works his territory. It has our country divided up into
> districts, and there are immigration agents at every center,
> with instructions to drum the neighbourhood for pioneer
> farmers . . . [the agents] have mapped out the territory,
> just as a book publishing firm lays out the field which it
> expects to sell . . . [the propaganda material used is] more
> like our patent medicine almanacs or advertisements, and
> show the effect of this country upon the settler "before and
> after taking."[5]

The assertion that Canadian Government Agents played the pivotal role in steering American settlers northward to Canadian lands did not go unchallenged. In 1897 the General Passenger Agent for the Canadian Pacific Railway criticized the newly appointed agents for readily scoffing at past efforts before producing positive results of their own. As he put it, the typical agent "denounces everything done by his predecessors, and promises wonders."[6] But, even as the tide of immigration flowed northward, members of the Conservative opposition in the Commons rejected government attempts to claim credit for determining the quality, quantity or direction of this movement. In 1903 Edward Frederick Clarke, opposition member for Toronto West, argued that the generally acknowledged closing of the American land frontier created population pressures that quite naturally followed the path of least resistance into Saskatchewan and Alberta. If any group merited special mention for instigating the movement, Clarke contended, it should be the "American land speculators who have bought large blocks of land in the territories and are advertising in whole page advertisements in newspapers of the United States the superlative advantages of our North-West as a country for settlement."[7] Conservative Thomas Simpson Sproule, member for East Grey, also charged that public funds expended on immigration agents were wasted; American economic conditions predetermined that many farmers would be "coming whether we spent money among them or not." No government encouragement was deemed necessary.[8]

If, as the opposition charged, land companies, including the powerful Canadian Pacific organization, were already doing all that was necessary to stimulate awareness of Canada among land-hungry American farmers, why were government agents kept in the United States at all? Conservative member for Leeds, George Taylor, looked no further than patronage for his answer. As Taylor explained, "The government might recall every peddler it has out in the name of this immigration service, it might stop every dollar of this expenditure on printing and advertising, and still the people would come in. The government is simply throwing away the people's money."[9] In actual fact, while patronage was not the *raison d'être* of the agency system, the Department's obvious use of political or family favouritism in filling immigration posts supported opposition attacks. In 1907 George W. Fowler, Conservative member for Kings and Albert, once again charged land companies, not government agents, were the central force around which any practical immigration organizational work should focus.

> The minister of the Interior, Frank Oliver stated that . . . the labours of his agents in the country to the south of us, were largely responsible for the great influx of settlers from the United States into Canada. I take exception to that statement. To my mind the fact is that the much abused real estate agents are responsible for the greater part of this valuable immigration. They have done five times more than all the literature which has been distributed by the government and the labour of its agents . . . .[10]

In retrospect the influence Canadian Government Agents had in promoting the American outflow was neither as insignificant as the Department's critics charged, nor as pervasive as the Immigration Branch would have had the Canadian public believe. Somewhere on the middle ground, individual immigration agents worked with varying degrees of personal dedication and success to promote the resettlement of American farmers on the Canadian prairies. While the impact of promotional activities by private land interests should not be minimized, government agents played a distinctively special role in encouraging Americans to emigrate.

As critics always were ready to point out, Canadian agents owed their appointments to rampant patronage, both political and nepotic. Few had previous experience in either immigration work or land settlement ventures. Thus, any positive agency results might be seen as a triumph over rational expectation. However, this conclusion neglects the total framework of immigration operations. In spite of their inexperience and local autonomy, Canadian agents were far from isolated in the field. They were supported by a well financed publicity campaign, guided by a centralized bureaucracy in Ottawa, aided by a network of related governmental settlement activities and, perhaps most importantly, recognized by American farmers as the officially appointed agents of the Canadian government. This last factor must not be overlooked; it was of immeasurable importance in paving the way for the novice agent. The Canadian Government Agent represented himself as the personification of Canada's land settlement policy with one object – orderly national development. To this end he offered free homestead lands of good quality, or when called upon, information on private lands for sale. Private land interests, increasingly mistrusted by more wary American farmers, could offer neither free lands nor the authority of officially appointed government agents. Reviewing the success of the Canadian immigration undertaking, the American magazine *Outlook* in 1911 acknowledged the value of impartiality in land dealings. The magazine reported that "the Canadian Government, and not some private transportation company with selfish interests to serve, decides upon the character of the [immigration activity and] propaganda."[11] This point was not lost on either the potential settlers who turned to Canadian Government Agents for advice and guidance or the agents themselves who vigorously protected their reputation from tarnishing assault.

Nevertheless, while new agents were not unsupported raw recruits thrown into the heat of battle, individual success or failure was directly related to the ability of each agent to respond independently to shifting local conditions. No amount of prestige, land hunger or institutional leadership could completely overcome personal ineptitude. The frequent necessity for instant decisions, the problems of coping with specific local issues and the demands posed by periodic lapses in communication with Ottawa and fellow agents, made self-assured independence of action essential, but a characteristic not common to all agents. In the final analysis, the productive output of each agent depended on a delicate combination of local initiatives tempered by administrative guidance. William J. White, Inspector of United States Agencies, recognized the need for this balance. In visits to agencies in 1899, during which he offered organizational assistance to agents as requested, White noted that it was "impossible to define any particular line which [agents] should work, but each agent had adapted himself to the surrounding conditions in which he found himself."[12] This, he allowed, was not only to be expected but also to be encouraged.

In organizing a revitalized network of state agencies after 1897, planners in the Immigration Branch initially theorized that immigration agents could most productively begin recruitment among those farmers suffering financial difficulties, especially tenant farmers. In preliminary instructions issued newly appointed agents in February, 1897, agents were advised to locate their offices "in a small agricultural town as near as possible to the centre of a district where the crops had for a few years, or many years, been bad."[13] The following year Superintendent of Immigration, Frank Pedley, pointed out the propaganda value of unexpectedly heavy precipitation in western Canada. He advised agents to place special emphasis on promotion in "burnt out districts" of western states where drought had destroyed crops.[14]

However, the poverty which heightened a farmer's interest in possible northward migration also hobbled his ability to move. It has been argued, that the northward flow of population was actually "motivated by economic distress" especially among tenant farmers. Americans escaped tenancy, according to this thesis, by taking up farming on free lands in Canada.[15] However, this farm to farm "safety valve" theory remains unsubstantiated. While there were undoubtedly tenant farmers among the thousands of Americans who came into Canada, the reserve capital required to finance a move, even to free homestead lands, effectively eliminated most poor American farmers. Indeed, the agent in Kansas City claimed in 1898 that farm tenancy was the "one fact" which "for this year at least would seriously operate against results."[16]

Nor did farm ownership ensure mobility.[17] This fact was clear to White as early as 1898. He observed that repeated crop failures, drought, hot winds and short crops made the accumulation of reserve capital necessary for "farm-making" almost impossible.

> The people residing [on unproductive lands] have become worse off each succeeding year until at present they have not sufficient means to permit their removal to some other district. They were among the most anxious people visited and showed a strong desire to secure new homes in Western Canada. Their cases while pitiable are such that nothing can be done with them, although it is believed they would soon become producers and consumers.[18]

Agents in the United States were not long in conceding the truth of White's economic analysis. In 1900 one agent observed, for instance, that the inability of local farm owners to sell their farms during a period of drought kept them tied to their land, unable to migrate.

> Land was selling rapidly and at a good figure until the effects of the drought [became] so apparent. Many who "thought they had sold" found later that the parties "got frightened and backed out." – It is a mistake to think the poorer the conditions and prospects are – the greater the emigration. Indeed the reverse is true – as all or nearly so must sell before they can leave. – The rains have greatly improved the prospects in many portions of the state. With improved conditions I hope to duplicate the [good] results of the last five months.[19]

Prolonged drought was but one factor affecting a farm owner's ability to sell or a tenant farmer's ability to lay away enough capital to finance migration. As the agent in Grand Forks, South Dakota, reported in 1903, the very possibility of "financial uncertainty in the United States" was enough to evaporate interest in "the movement to western Canada, in some of the districts where we were getting large numbers of settlers."[20] Since the Canadian government only financed promotional activities and provided no direct financial support to settlers, the courting of poorer farmers soon stopped.[21] Finding few assets in adversity, by 1900 the Immigration Branch astutely transformed its inability to resettle poorer farmers and tenant farmers into an element of positive planning. White declared that the programme of settler recruitment was consciously geared against the poor.

> I would like to impress upon [the Minister of the Interior] the fact that only the best class of settlers is looked for, and the instructions to the agents are to give close attention to these as possible. It is safe to say that not one of the pauper class has gone in from the States; on the contrary many have gone in with considerable means. The reports of the department will show that some who have taken up lands this year had as much as $50,000 each, others even more than that, while no inconsiderable number had from $2,000 to $10,000 each.[22]

Agents quickly realized that wealthier farmers proved more promising candidates. In his report to the Commons Committee on Agricultural and Colonization in 1901, the Superintendent of Immigration noted state agents were "making an inroad on the best class of farmers, who are coming into Canada and finding out that they can make a safe investment for their money."[23] Perhaps reflecting the prosperity of many American farmers who sold or rented their land before moving to Canada, cash purchases of farms from Canadian railroad or land companies were brisk.[24] Some farmers "surrounded themselves with every social comfort and [made] not only their own settlement attractive, but [added] values to the lands which surrounded it."[25] Nor were free homestead lands neglected. It was not uncommon for American settlers who purchased farms to also homestead a piece of land which bordered their new property. In this fashion it was possible to acquire large holdings at minimal cost while "still [putting] considerable capital investment into expensive farm equipment which they brought with them into Canada or purchased on arrival."[26]

An exact picture of settler finances may never be known. Immigration statistics for the Laurier years are notoriously unreliable and those reporting wealth are, if possible, even more untrustworthy.[27] The Immigration Branch relied on estimates submitted by its agents and, as indicated by agent William V. Bennett, Omaha, in his procedural outline, these could be speculative at best.

> In estimating the amount of Capital – they took with them – I arrived at the total in this way, – They usually tell how much they have to go with – Then I find out how much stock [and] chattels [sic] they have. Then basing an estimate on same as follows – Horses $50.00 per head. Pram Wagon and Harness at $100.00. Full car of Immigrant movables at $1000.00 – I find the 237 people [sent in 1897-1898] have taken with them into Canada in Money and Chattells [sic] a valuation of $116,475.00.[28]

The majority of American settlers who entered Canada were not extremely wealthy. Nevertheless, they were far from impoverished. Many considered the purchase of Canadian lands or the completion of homestead obligations as a wise investment of both time and capital. The sale or lease of American farms generally ensured migrants the capital necessary to purchase and equip sizable farms in the Canadian west.[29] However, one group attracted to the Canadian west were neither tenant farmers nor farm owners in their own right: farmers' sons, often sponsored in the move northward by their families.

The Jeffersonian belief in the intrinsic value of agrarian life had long been rooted in American tradition. However, at the turn of the century this was being challenged. The highly idealized picture of the honest yeoman on his own land was giving way to a counter image of the country bumpkin, especially in urban centres. Apostles of agrarian life were confronted by the spectrum of rural youth being attracted to the urban Sodom.

The magnetism of urban life was intensified by the seeming end of the frontier. A farmer with mature sons was finding it increasingly difficult to place his offspring onto nearby farms or to find good empty American lands to which his sons could migrate. Urban migration, a process well under way, was to many an undesirable alternative.[30] The 1910 American census noted that in many rural areas the mean age of residence was already greater than that of nearby urban centres "partly by migration from country to city – and consequently the age distribution of the total population of a given class in a state or division is much affected by the proportions urban and rural [sic]."[31] The availability of fertile lands in Canada offered a natural alternative for parallel rural mobility. What is more, the sale or renting of the family farm could mean enough capital to move the whole family northward and thereby acquire a series of contiguous farms for each member.[32] A 1902 article in the *American Review of Reviews* emphasized this very point.

> Now that land can no longer be had in the United States for the squatting on, and when even railroad lands bring big prices in the open market, the temptation which such a country [as Canada] offers to the progressive American farmer is great. If he has money, he can buy a good improved farm in western Canada for very much less than his own holding will bring. If he has a wealth of grown boys, he can obtain free of cost to himself, and for every boy over eighteen years, a farm of 160 acres ready for the plow, and by united effort they can double their holdings by the yield of their labor in two or three years.[33]

The Immigration Branch became increasingly aware of the attraction Canadian lands held for farmers' sons.[34] In 1898 White described landless farmers' sons as "some of the most practical of the young men of the Western States, men possessing a reasonable amount of capital to begin with."[35] In his 1909 essay on Canadian immigration, *The Sowing,* Emerson Hough pointedly emphasised that farmers' sons came to Canada with financial means.

> They did not largely come from exhausted New England and the over-crowded East, but most largely from the choicest farming sections of the western United States. They

come, not because they were poor, *but because they were too rich to stay home,* – because they had money with which to buy land and operate it. Not one of these needed any sort of help.[36]

Agents began courting farmers' sons almost immediately.[37] In many cases agents convinced both father and son that a joint move to Canada would hold the family together. As a result requests for advice on farmer-son ventures were common. The agent in Watertown, South Dakota, received a letter from a prospective settler reading, in part, ". . . we are situated to take homesteads [sic]. I have four sons old enough to take land. We are farming out here [Pierpoint, South Dakota]; but the land is too high in price to buy a large enough farm for myself and the boys." As a result the family had decided to move elsewhere in an effort to preserve the family unit.[38] The agent in Mt. Pleasant, Michigan, reported that one farmer in his region after touring western Canada, was so impressed with Canadian lands that he acquired "three-quarters of a section of land about fourteen miles from Leduc [Alberta], and at once made arrangements for moving out his family, also his sons and their wives and families; [and] there they are now . . . ."[39] Yet another settler who moved from Minnesota "to Dauphin [Manitoba] with his six sons [all of whom were of age for homesteading], took a train load of ten freight cars" in order to move the family's effects.[40]

Farmers' sons were not the only group designated for special promotional efforts. In their search for prospective settlers, Canadian agents discovered that hyphenated Americans, especially ethnic and religious groups facing the joint dilemmas of holding landless offspring on farms and resisting outside pressure to assimilate were fertile ground for immigration activity. Canada seemingly promised not only good free or cheap lands but also continued ethnic or religious cohesion within new or existing group colonies.[41] Examples are plentiful.[42] The Mountain Lake, Minnesota, Mennonite community, gave limited support to migration by the group's younger members after it was assured that settlers could be integrated into existing Mennonite settlements in Alberta and Saskatchewan.[43] The Immigration Branch also made special arrangements to encourage Mormon settlement of the dry lands in southern Alberta where it was expected that Mormons would soon "demonstrate what it was possible to do with unoccupied lands . . . where irrigation is applied."[44] Scandinavian-Americans in the northern, midwest and prairie states were wooed by a specially appointed Swedish speaking agent who worked out of Ottawa.[45] Another agent was shifted out of the Department's Edmonton offices into American immigration encouragement partly in the hope that his German speaking ability could be put to good use among discontented German-Americans in search of new lands.[46]

Delegates of American ethnocultural groups, with the exception of Orientals and Negroes, were encouraged to visit the Canadian prairies as guests of the railways and the government.[47] Special interest was paid to the German-Baptist Brethren, commonly called Dunkards, who had previously organized 'daughter colonies' for their co-religionists in the Dakotas and Minnesota. In 1901 they indicated an interest in Canadian lands. The government's agent in Indianapolis explained that "many people who have moved from [Indiana] to Dakota have not found that country what they expected it to be" and after a delegation of Dunkards visited Canada, a new colony was organized.[48]

Many of the non-American born settlers who moved north had not become American citizens. Some were originally Canadian farmers from Ontario who had immigrated south in the seventies and eighties only to return during the Canadian land boom. They were joined by Scandinavians, Germans, southern Italians and English settlers. During the fiscal years 1908-1910, the United States Commissioner General of Immigration reported that 67,301 aliens departed from the United States for Canada.[49] Canadian records indicate a total inflow of approximately 222,000 American residents during fiscal years 1908-1910. This means that approximately 33 per cent of all settlers from the United States for this period were themselves immigrants into the United States.[50] It is not clear what percentage of this group, if any, came to the United States intending to migrate to Canada.

Surprisingly, Canadians farming in the midwest and prairie states were not subject to special repatriation efforts. Agents were instructed to seek out and encourage Canadians to return home, but few agents devoted any energy to the task. One suspects that while Canadians were generally open to government promotion and often returned amidst showers of patriotic rhetoric, agents knew Canadians returned only if it suited them. They returned not because they were homesick but because they wanted Canadian land just as much as did their non-Canadian neighbours.[51]

In spite of the responsiveness of restless farmers and the anxiety of American ethnic communities, the agent's duty was not merely to act as a directional guide, pointing land-hungry Americans northward.

Although conditions were ripe for the development of Canada fever, especially under the impetus of a well organized promotional campaign, it was the agent's task to spread the fever by initiating contact with prospective settlers, first through propaganda to heighten interest followed by personal contact to turn interest into commitment. These activities required local bureaucratic support.

The hub of a Canadian Government Agent's activities was his agency office. In 1897 three offices opened in Michigan, but by 1904 a shift in emphasis toward prairie states found eighteen offices dotting the American great plains.[52] Initially each office functioned as a one man operation. In his annual report for 1898, the Inspector of American Agencies observed that the Department's policy was to operate as few offices as possible with each "agent attending to such work for which other provisions had not been made . . . ."[53] However, as interest in Canadian lands mushroomed the volume of inquiries made to agency offices sharply increased. Agents soon complained that the necessity of keeping offices open every day, answering letters and interviewing visitors, made it difficult to travel into the field. One agent discovered his work load increasing so rapidly that in 1898 he requested permission to hire his wife "to attend to correspondence and advise people who came in for information." After verifying the urgency of his predicament the Department allowed their agent's request.[54] But, this request was but the first of many. Demands for competent office assistance or new efficient office equipment began to flood the Immigration Branch. The agent in Kansas City complained that being tied to his office desk, especially answering simple requests for promotional literature, made it increasingly difficult for him to meet commitments on the road.[55] In Grand Forks the agent was so swamped with office work that he pleaded for a full time typist just to handle mail inquiries.[56] Another applied for funds to buy a bicycle in order to get around town.[57] Bowing to the advance of technology, in 1907 an agent in Pittsburg requested permission not only to purchase his stenographer a new typewriter but also to install a telephone in his office. The telephone, he contended, would save him from walking "all over town six or eight times a day on office business."[58] The Department allowed for a typewriter, but no telephone.[59]

In an effort to fill the growing demand for assistance, newly appointed agents were assigned to an apprenticeship in established agencies before moving to an office of their own.[60] But the number of agents in training was never sufficient. By 1904 the Department conceded that agents required permanent local staff if offices were to operate efficiently. As White explained to William Duncan Scott, Superintendent of Immigration, it was proving less expensive to employ local help in offices than force agents to neglect field work for lack of staff.

> With an assistant in the office the agent has the opportunity of getting out amongst the people and interviewing many of them personally. This is found to be a very good means of securing the direct attention of settlers. Another reason for having an assistant is the great necessity which arises from the fact that in the offices . . . correspondence is large, running from 25 to 30 letters per day, and it is necessary that replies should be sent to each of those correspondents. This in itself, if properly attended to, would occupy a large portion of time of the agent. Apart from this there are a large number of personal inquirers to whom attention must be given, and as your experience will show, a great deal of time is consumed in this way.[61]

Despite the time consuming demands of office operations, activities in the field still took up the majority of agents' work days. The fifteen salaried agents, active during the fiscal year 1901-1902 spent about two-thirds of their time on the road personally meeting and encouraging farmers to consider Canadian lands.[62] The Department correctly reasoned that reaching farmers in their homes, at farmers' meetings or agricultural fairs was a far more productive tactic than relying solely on responses to a bombardment of promotional publications, although publications effectively paved the way for most direct contacts.

The systematic mailing of promotional literature to potential settlers was the first step in arousing interest in Canada. Such mailings required lists of addresses. At first methods of gathering lists varied from agent to agent but soon only those procedures which proved efficient became generally accepted. Addresses of persons replying to government newspaper advertising were carefully gathered, these respondents already indicating a positive interest in Canadian migration. However, in order to blanket an area with promotional material, massive mailing lists were needed. On opening a new office agents collected copies of voters' lists, membership rolls of local and state farm organizations and, where accessible, tax assessment lists.[63] Names and addresses were also gathered at state and local agricultural fairs and from farmers who had already committed themselves to

44

Canadian migration.[64] During the first year of Immigration Branch activity, before the Department's newspaper campaign was in full swing, some 25,000 addresses were collected in Minnesota alone.[65]

Once names and addresses were collected and a packet of government propaganda publications sent to each prospect, state agents systematically visited every corner of their jurisdiction to follow up the mailings. Backed by lantern slide shows, small exhibits and more promotional material, meetings, lectures and parties were organized enabling agents to reach farmers in their own homes or meeting halls.

Field trips were but part of an agent's seasonal operation. Agents set aside winter and early spring, the farmers' slack seasons, for travelling assigned territory meeting farmers.[66] Late spring and summer found the same agents organizing and leading parties of immigrants or tours by prospective settlers into the Canadian west. Canadian Government Agents were also encouraged to make personal visits to western Canada to keep abreast of changing conditions. Long absences from western Canada would leave them, as one agent warned, "completely out of touch with the progress of settlement."[67] Organized railway excursions continued into the harvest season, "when the country is seen to best advantage." But autumn was also fair season and agents, who began entering exhibits at fairs in 1897, turned their attention once again to gathering names and reaching out for personal contact with farmers.[68]

When recruitment efforts were rewarded with committed settlers, the state agent significantly assisted smooth migration often playing mover, travel consultant, land agent and reassuring friend. Extremely important, he issued a Settlers' Certificate to each settler. This Certificate entitled the settler and each member of his party to a railway ticket at a special minimal rate of one cent per mile from border crossing point to Canadian destination. The Certificate also enabled the Department to tabulate immigration statistics as each Certificate carried the settler's name, previous address, names and ages of all those in the settler's party and their proposed destination in Canada.[69]

Family units were not always able to travel together, the senior male member or an elder son setting out earlier to establish a homestead. White declared it the duty of salaried agents to assist divided families to reunite at the earliest possible date. It was not unusual for local agents to make all arrangements for such families to travel northward. Much like a commercial moving agent, "the agent himself renders very valuable assistance to the settler, visiting his home and

45

also at the depot on leaving and assisting him arrange his car, selecting his route and in other ways making it easier for him to move to
his new home."[70] Nor was it unusual for agents to accompany settlers
to their new homes or, at least, to border crossing points, especially
when a large group was moving. This was partially a defensive
manoeuvre. Agents justifiably feared that competing American land
company agents might lure away settlers on route.[71]

In addition to the increased local office assistance, the Immigration
Branch felt that its agents might need more immediate aid to reach
into every corner of their jurisdiction. In the preliminary plans for
American operations, planners envisioned that state agents, acting at
their own discretion, would choose local residents to aid in the Department's work. These sub-agents, as they were called, received financial
bonuses based upon the numbers of settlers they could prove to have
sent to Canada. Each was granted a specific ethnic or geographic sub-
section of an agent's jurisdiction within which to operate, hopefully
under the watchful eye of the local salaried agent. In actual fact the
sub-agent system never lived up to expectation, and, in part because
of a lack of guidance and direction, it was silently phased out after
1903.[72]

Agents were quick to realize that while their initial employment
may have been the result of patronage, security and advancement
within the Branch was a product of performance. Salaries, for
instance, were set on the basis of seniority or, more importantly, on
"the merits of the work of the different agents."[73] Speaking before
the Commons in 1902 Sifton assured the house that agents were
"paid according to their capacity and ability to do work. If salaries
are raised it is because of satisfactory and efficient service . . . ."[74]
Among individual agents in the United States, salaries might vary as
much as fifty per cent at any given time.[75] The yardstick used to
measure the relative achievement of state agents was immigration
returns. This was to strain harmonious inter-agency relations as each
agent became a jealous protector of his own settlers and guarded
against incursions into his jurisdiction by his brother agents. White,
somewhat removed from the fray, was fully aware of this competition
although he understated its intensity. He observed in 1904, "The
work of the agents has been continuous and very satisfactory. It has
been a personal matter with them, and a healthy rivalry exists, as to
which one shall secure the greatest number of settlers."[76] This
"rivalry" was often marked by open antagonism and overt obstruc-
tionism. Settler piracy almost became an art.

46

Salaried agents kept a wary eye lest their fellow agents lift original Settlers' Certificates from migrants on route to Canada, only to replace the original Certificates for ones of their own. In 1901 agent William V. Bennett, Omaha, accused his brother agents in St. Paul, Des Moines and Grand Forks, North Dakota of deliberately engaging in Certificate substitutions in order to inflate their immigration returns.[77] On a trip to the Canadian border Bennett claimed to have met settlers originally processed at his agency office only to find them now carrying Certificates of other agents. He reissued his own Certificates, taking care to forward the disputed Certificates to Ottawa with a personal protest.[78] While the case was never pursued, inter-agency bitterness continued to run high.[79]

Similar friction was quick to develop when more promising states were divided between two competing agents. Accusations of settler poaching flew freely. Agent Bennett, Omaha, having ceded six eastern counties of his state to his brother agent in Des Moines, Iowa, in a territorial reshuffling, protested that the Des Moines agent was using the re-allotted counties as an open door to the whole state.[80] In Wisconsin the state was divided between Thomas O. Currie, Milwaukee, in the south, and James M. MacLachlan, Wausau, in the north. MacLachlan accused Currie of deliberately mailing out promotional material over the whole state claiming to be the only authorized agent for Wisconsin. Currie followed up the mailings by conducting interviews in MacLachlan's northern half of the state. What was more, Currie was not above telling prospective settlers that the Wausau agent was "working under him, and had to report to him in all things." As a result of such underhanded tactics, MacLachlan found it difficult to "work in harmony with [Currie] in the interests of the work," and the state's immigration activity suffered.[81] Again, in North Dakota, agents in Grand Forks and Minot, repeatedly accused one another of usurping all credit for joint undertakings.[82] One continually accused the other of lying, or as he euphemistically observed on one occasion, "I believe I was on the same train as [a fellow agent] where he claims to have located certain settlers and I am very inclined to think that he draws strongly on his imagination."[83] Other cases of inter-agency friction were not uncommon.[84]

Job security also seemed threatened when a sub-agent began to eclipse the state agents under whom he was working. In 1900 the sub-agent working almost exclusively among Mennonites of the Mountain Lake, Minnesota region, proved so successful that he requested and received permission to expand his operations to include Mennonite communities in South Dakota. In a rare show of inter-agency co-operation, the two agents overseeing South Dakota immigration activities from offices in Watertown, South Dakota and St. Paul, jointly protested the incursion.[85] In defence of his new assignment the sub-agent claimed to have received a number of letters from Mennonites in South Dakota requesting his assistance in moving to Canada. As he explained, "I only thought that while I was able to speak to [Mennonites] in their own language, I could induce a number of them to start for Canada . . . but I do not want to have hard-feelings to either" of the salaried agents.[86] But "hard-feelings" there were.

In this case the Immigration Branch ruled against its salaried agents.[87] As a seeming gesture of compromise, the sub-agent was forced to submit all Settlers' Certificates he issued in South Dakota to be countersigned by the Watertown agent. The salaried agent thus, could protect himself against possible encroachment into non-Mennonite areas of the state.[88]

By 1903 the Mennonite sub-agent's success in South Dakota encouraged him to request still further territorial expansion. With the Department's blessing, he began to "look up districts of Pennsylvania, New York, Ohio and Indiana where there are large Mennonite communities." While the sub-agent welcomed the additional territory, with each new addition he trod on the delicate toes of another salaried agent.[89]

The tensions generated by a policy of evaluating each state agent's achievements almost exclusively on the basis of an immigrant head count created an atmosphere in which agents knowingly turned a blind eye toward deceptions connected to the issuing of Settlers' Certificates. Agents were well aware that they could issue Settlers' Certificates to unauthorized persons and find these Certificates eventually tallied in immigration results. Canadian railroads charged that some agents were not above issuing Settlers' Certificates to tourists. This gave visitors to Canada a subsidized one cent per mile rate on travel in Canada while inflating the issuing agent's statistical standing.[90]

In border areas, especially Michigan, Canadian railways contended that they were victims of yet another ploy designed to boost statistics of individual agents. With agent complicity, it was a simple matter for Canadians desiring to travel westward as settlers to slip across the border, acquire a Settlers' Certificate as a migrating American, and thereafter travel in Canada on the reduced immigration train fare. In

1905 the Canadian Pacific Railway accused the Detroit agent of deliberately bolstering his sagging returns with this all too transparent ruse. The railway threatened to reject all Certificates issued in Detroit unless the practice was stopped immediately.[91] The agent sheepishly denied all knowledge of the practice.[92] However, while the railway never stopped honouring his Certificates (perhaps the railway's warning proved enough to make him more cautious) railroad complaints against deliberate padding by other agents continued to reach Ottawa.[93]

The Immigration Branch and its salaried agents proved especially sensitive to conflict with the railway companies in both the United States and Canada. The Department recognized that the co-operation of transportation companies was important for the smooth movement of immigrants. Where good relations were lacking in the United States, usually as a result of competition over settlers' or a railroad's endorsement of private state land sales, an agent's work was made far more difficult. Co-operation with Canadian lines, however, was generally easier as both government and railroads made common cause in encouragement of immigration and combined in joint programmes to promote the settlement of empty lands.

Nevertheless, there was much friction between a corps of Canadian Pacific company land agents working in the United States and the homestead-promoting Canadian Government Agents. Often rejecting co-operation, coexistence was difficult at times.[94]

The Canadian Pacific, for instance, was reluctant to share an advantage its agents had over government agents – free rail transportation in the United States. It was not uncommon for North American railroads to extend one another's employees the courtesy of free transportation. To save on the costs of travel for its agents in the United States, in 1897 the Immigration Branch approached the president of the Canadian Pacific, William Van Horne, in the hope that he would intercede on the government's behalf in acquiring free annual passes. Van Horne refused even to forward the government's request to the American lines. He claimed that such a request would, if granted, violate the American Interstate Commerce Law. The statute called for a $5,000 fine on persons found guilty of granting discriminate favours to one "consignor or consignee" or to an "officer or agent of such a corporation."[95] While Van Horne admitted that, to his knowledge, "this law is violated a dozen times a day," he would not accede to the Department's request for assistance.[96] It may be that Van Horne had other plans in mind. If the government's agents could be integrated into the Canadian Pacific's American operations, authorizing Canadian Government Agents to deal in Canadian Pacific lands, it probably would have meant the granting of the railroad passes. Such a scheme, when proposed by the Canadian Pacific, was rejected.[97] The Immigration Branch had no desire to see its agents tempted by the possibility of royalties from the sale of railroad lands. This effectively would have undermined their position as spokesmen for free homestead lands. Equally important, the government could not afford to have its agents compromise their neutrality by joining the ranks of one land company as opposed to any other. Thus, when a similar scheme was proposed by the agent in Detroit, it too was rejected.[98]

As part of an overall government economy drive in 1900, agents were advised of "the great necessity that exists for the utmost economy with respect to expenses" including "travelling expenses."[99] At the same time the Immigration Branch tried once again to squeeze free passes from American railway lines through the intercession of Canadian railroad authorities. The Superintendent of Immigration took the government's case to James M. Lyons, General Passenger and Ticket Agent for the Intercolonial Railway of Moncton, New Brunswick. As bait for the Intercolonial, the Superintendent hinted that the largely maritime railway might somehow "share the traffic arising from so large a movement of population," although no specific promises were made.[100] Lyons, knowing that it could do the Intercolonial no harm to endear itself to the Department of the Interior tried to convince the General Manager of the Intercolonial Railway to accede to the government request. Lyons suggested an agreement might be hammered out whereby the Canadian Government Agents could function as quasi-Intercolonial personnel and "canvas for regular and tourist business and look after the distribution of . . . time folders and advertising material" in their respective jurisdictions.[101] No conflict of interests over land sales existed. The proposal was rejected by the General Manager, who, Lyons was sorry to report, felt the Intercolonial Railway did not have the necessary influence with American lines to acquire the requested passes.[102]

As Canadian railways could not or would not co-operate in securing free transportation for Canadian Government Agents, the Immigration Branch turned directly to individual American railroads in order to secure passes and, more importantly, negotiate special ticket rates

50

for settlers on route to the Canadian border. Although individual agents were encouraged to make whatever local arrangements would most benefit their settlers, White was placed in overall charge of formal liaison with American lines.[103] In districts where local railroads had no land of their own to offer settlers, or were not acting in concert with private real-estate interests, the Immigration Branch often succeeded in negotiating for passes and reduced rates on settlers' tickets.[104] Even in an area where an outflow of population at first appeared detrimental to local railway interests, it was possible to make special arrangements with the lines concerned. As a steady movement of population seemed determined to reach the Canadian west, railroad "management soon became aware that people were about to leave whose passage money might be lost to the railroad company" if forced for financial considerations to travel by wagon.[105]

Those American railroad companies willing to co-operate, however reluctantly, with Canadian authorities objected to having their roads used as mere feeder lines for the Canadian Pacific or the Canadian Pacific's subsidiary, the Soo Line. A meeting of agents from the Central Passenger Railroads held in Chicago in December, 1897, decried the practice of sending settlers not over the quickest route to the Canadian west, but on the shortest route to a Canadian Pacific or Soo Line depot.[106] The agents contended that more American lines would be willing to concede special rates to Canada-bound settlers if the practice was stopped.[107] In turn the Canadian Pacific and Soo Lines also charged Canadian agents with discrimination. In 1906 the Soo Line accused the St. Paul immigration agent of working in the interests of the Great Northern and Canadian Northern railways. A railway spokesman went so far as to employ a Pinkerton detective agent to spy on the St. Paul agency.[108] The Pinkerton agent, masquerading as a prospective settler, approached the office requesting a quick, inexpensive routing to western Canada and was advised to travel the longer Great Northern-Canadian Northern roads.[109] In defence of his agent, White explained to the Superintendent of Immigration, that the agent was not acting for or against any particular transportation company, but, rather, in the interests of his settlers. As White observed, "if there are advantages in competition and the agent used his judgment in the matter of moving business," the Canadian Pacific-Soo Line must offer better service and not just shorter mileage before an agent would feel bound to send his settlers over their line.[110] Nevertheless, White took the precaution of warning agents to show more impartiality in selection of railway transportation lest railroad interests remain irritated.[111]

If the Department's agents were deliberately showing partiality to one railroad over another, there proved no consistency in their choice of favourite. In 1911 it was the turn of the Canadian Northern to accuse the Immigration Branch and especially the agent in Syracuse of a pro-Canadian Pacific bias.[112] The Department once again advised agents to act with impartiality.[113]

In its efforts to acquire low freight and passenger rates to the Canadian border, time continued to work in favour of the Immigration Branch. Increased migration forced recalcitrant railways, especially those with no land interests of their own, to give the Department special settlers' rates rather than lose the haul of settlers and goods. The railways were quick to learn that increased northward migration did not necessarily mean a loss in productive population. Rather, it signalled a turnover in land ownership or departure of landless farmers' sons. Experience changed railway attitudes. As early as 1898 the Kansas City agent reported that he was able to offer excursion rates reduced from $53.50 to $26.95 on trips from Kansas City to the Canadian border.[114] The following year the agent in Mt. Pleasant, Michigan, noted that he was optimistic about securing special rates from the Michigan Central and Flint and Père Marquette railroad.

> Think better arrangements can now be made than formerly as to special cars [and] the Railroads appear to be willing now to help along with the work. Formerly they were rather inclined to do us all the injury they could as they thought taking people out of the state was not in their interests. Perhaps now they see they are going away and may as well try to get a piece of business out of it.[115]

The Immigration Branch continued to have limited success in prying concessions from American lines. In 1901 White advised the Minister of the Interior that permission had been granted by several railways for use of their ticket offices and passenger stations as distribution points for Canadian immigration literature.[116] Furthermore, some lines had already allowed their employees to double as Canadian sub-agents.[117]

American railways, in some instances, had their own special reasons for co-operating or even fomenting the movement of settlers out of their territories and northward to Canada. In Oklahoma, for instance, the Southern Pacific Railway was instrumental in encouraging black land owners to sell their property and migrate, potentially to Canada, in order to soothe racial anxieties of white settlers moving into eastern Oklahoma.[118] Similarly, in 1902 the Union Pacific informed an immigration agent in Nebraska that it would readily participate in any programme of encouraging ranchers along its line to move northward into Alberta. The Union Pacific, the agent explained, "want to get [ranchers] out so the land can be divided up for settlers." The Omaha agent warned the Immigration Branch it might be unwise to reject the railroad's offer out of hand. "The Morgan interests, or Hill interests do everything possible to stop the movement to Canada and if the Harriman interests go against us it will hurt and it looks now that we had better stand in with our friends."[119] The Immigration Branch advised its agent to co-operate cautiously in the Harriman controlled Union Pacific scheme.[120]

In general, however, the Department preferred to remain free of encumbering entanglements with individual land companies or railroad land promoters. This resolve was periodically tested. Individual agents were accused of accepting secret commissions for working in the interest of private Canadian land companies. If such accusations were true, they would compromise the agents' position as spokesman for free homestead lands and undermine the neutrality of the Immigration Branch in dealings with other land companies.

Formal co-operation between land companies and agents was not ruled out. For instance, it was common for an agent, when asked about specific lands or "improved lands," to refer persons to Canadian land companies. There was, of course, to be no payment for this service.[121] However, rumors and complaints that individual state agents functioning as quasi-agents or secret agents of private land firms persisted. In 1909 a representative of the Milwaukee Land Exchange informed C. J. A. Dalziel, president of the Imperial Development Company, Winnipeg, that an agent in Milwaukee was deliberately preventing settlers from examining the Dalziel company's lands.[122] Bringing the issue before the Department, Dalziel contended that this case was "only one of a number of incidents that our company could place before you of a similar conduct on the part of Dominion Immigration Agents, which has caused considerable trouble and consequent loss."[123] In his defence, the Milwaukee agent accused the land companies of deliberately keeping settlers away from government agents who, in turn, could give an impartial appraisal of

53

competing land company properties. As a general rule, he declared, land companies were prone to "misrepresent and lie about the country and . . . use any means in their power to separate intending settlers from their hard earned money . . . ."[124] Nevertheless, government agents were repeatedly cautioned against showing favouritism to one land company over another, or even making special arrangements with land firms for specific groups.[125] A suggestion by an agent in Spokane, that would have allowed the representative of a local land company *carte blanche* in promising Settlers' Certificates to Canada-bound clients was vetoed by the Immigration Branch.[126] The proposition was rejected even though the land salesman in point was described as, "a Scandinavian and [had] a connection with his country people and [was] able to meet a great many of them that otherwise would have [had] no possibility of meeting."[127]

As the Immigration Branch and many of its agents were generally wary of land companies and involvement in private promotional undertakings, they were understandably uneasy over the emergence of a united land company publicity service, the Western Canadian Immigration Association, founded in 1904 by prominent dealers in Canadian lands, including many Americans.[128] The W.C.I.A. publicly advocated the co-operation of all Western Canadian commercial interests in a "harmonious, systematic and effective effort to attract desirable population and investment capital."[129] In actual fact the land promoters merely planned to pool a portion of their promotion funds with money solicited from public or private agencies, thus increasing resources available for advertising Canadian lands, or at least advertising private lands for sale in the Canadian west. What appeared on the surface as a useful adjustment to government operations was in reality – a front for a land company publicity campaign designed to inflate land values.[130] Some people were fooled. Accepting the fledgeling condition of land companies at face value, the *Manitoba Free Press* declared, "The men who have launched this business undertaking mean business, and the interests of this country cannot be better served than in strengthening their land."[131]

The Immigration Branch however, was not fooled by the Association's organizational facade. They quickly labelled the W.C.I.A., its leadership and advertising campaign as an obvious threat to all government immigration activities. Because the Association presented itself as the honest broker of western development while secretly boasting private lands, it not only seemed to be appropriating the

Immigration Branch's duties, but was undermining the whole home-stead programme.[132] In a fruitless attempt to scuttle a federal grant to the organization, authorized for political considerations, White exposed the W.C.I.A. to his superiors.[133]

> This Association is of no use whatever in assisting to get settlers. On the contrary, it has worked altogether in the interests of real-estate men and speculators by booming Canadian lands in City papers, and raising land values beyond the paying power of a great many. In getting settlers in, the City press is no assistance whatever. Look at [W.C.I.A.] statements of expenditure [sic]. Who audits these accounts? The salary of the Secretary for three years has been guaranteed by men who, along with the Secretary are the only ones apparently anxious to keep the Association in existence. The work of the Department covers every field of getting settlers.[134]

The W.C.I.A. proved short-lived. First shaken by its inability to sustain momentum or meet publicly stated goals, by 1908 the organization crumbled and dissolved. The hostility generated by the W.C.I.A. within the Immigration Branch exemplified the antagonism felt toward possible poachers on the government's immigration preserve, and, indeed, toward all who would interfere with its long-range programmes for short-term private gains.

While Canadians still debate the delicate balance between the roles of government and private initiatives in guiding national development, there can be little doubt that at the turn of the century Sifton and his Department's business-like approach to the encouragement of immigration were laying the social and economic foundations of western Canada for years to come. Tempered by contemporary political reality, the American operations of the Immigration Branch harnessed a commitment to increased agricultural immigration to already proven promotional techniques. Within this framework, Canadian Government Agents confronted the strains of patronage, inexperience, inter-agency rivalry, mistrust of private developers and the unpredictability of agro-economic conditions. The degree to which they overcame these handicaps while maintaining or expanding productive promotional activities determined their degree for success and eventual contribution to the development of western Canada.

The Unknown Failure
[SUB-AGENTS]

To encourage prospective American settlers to move into Canada, the Immigration Branch hoped to extend the reach of its local salaried immigration agents through employment of sub-agents working on commission. The territories assigned local agents were large; travel was time-consuming and transportation not always available. As a result the Department felt local agents would need the assistance of sub-agents to initiate and maintain contact with potential settlers. Just as the local agents were to act as the arms of the Immigration Branch reaching into the United States, so the sub-agents were to be its fingers – flexible, sensitive and immediate.

Expectation often proves a far cry from reality, and accordingly the sub-agents fell short of the goals assigned them. To the Department's disappointment, what might have evolved into a useful supplement to agency operations was never able to overcome personnel and administrative difficulties. Hampered by Departmental red tape, exploited by outside interests, misrepresented by land companies and abused by many of the sub-agents themselves, the system of employing commissioned sub-agents was forcefully revamped twice in only six years. In the wake of the second reorganization in 1903, the sub-agent programme was reduced in priority, thereafter commanding secondary importance. While the sub-agent system was still organized and functioning after 1903, any results it produced were viewed apart from the mainstream of immigration work.

The decision to introduce a large number of commissioned sub-agents into the Department's American campaign was made early in 1897. The previous ministry had also employed commissioned agents in the United States, but the new organization, as restructured in 1897, was far broader in scope than the earlier experiment. Initially local agents were instructed to choose reliable and energetic individuals living in their territory who could readily undertake immigration work for the Department. Each sub-agent appointed was guaranteed remuneration based on the number of persons he could prove to have been directly responsible for sending to Canada as settlers. The initial instructions sent local agents regarding sub-agents stated that "The Sub-Agents shall be paid by commission the amount of which will be $2.00 per head for every man and $1.00 for every woman or child conditionally on the parties emigrating to Canada."[1]

Immediately one agent protested that the commission payments were too meagre and certainly "not enough to get a boom on." With such a small per capita commission, he asserted that any attempt to persuade competent men to assume the sub-agent position would undoubtedly prove futile.[2] The Assistant Secretary of the Department disagreed. In a note to Deputy Minister James A. Smart, the Secretary protested that sub-agents were "fairly well paid for the work they do by their present commission." If more money was allotted to immigration work, it could be better spent in granting each settler a cash rebate after he completed his three year homestead requirements. Support of farmers already in Canada rather than of sub-agents in the United States could be an added inducement to settlement and "even though [the rebate] might be small, it could not but be appreciated by the settler." Under a system of cash refunds to settlers, he argued, it might also be possible to induce the Canadian railways to contribute funds thereby defraying government expenditure.[3]

The Secretary's proposals found no perceivable support in the Department and it was decided to increase the commissions offered to sub-agents. Bonuses announced only one month earlier were increased and a new classification for persons under eighteen years of age was added. "For each man over eighteen years, $3.00; for each woman over eighteen, $2.00; for each person under eighteen years, $1.00."[4]

The discretion to employ sub-agents and their selection was left largely in the hands of local agents. The local agent was free to subdivide his territory in any way he chose among several sub-agents, each of whom would have predefined boundaries. These boundaries were not always geographic. Some sub-agents were employed to best advantage not in overseeing a territory but in circulating among the members of a specified ethnocultural group. For example, the sub-agent in Mountain Lake, Minnesota, was appointed on the strength of his ability to work among the large German-Mennonite community of Minnesota.[5] He was himself a Mennonite and as a child had joined the large exodus of Russian Mennonites who migrated to the United States and Canada.[6] Offering similar promise, John W. Taylor was designated sub-agent at Salt Lake City. His was considered a choice appointment. He was a dedicated Apostle of the Mormon Church, a member of the Church's twelve man governing body.[7]

After selecting a suitable candidate, the local agent supplied Ottawa with the name and address of his choice. The Department in turn confirmed each sub-agent's appointment by letter. There was more form than substance to this exercise. There is no evidence to indicate that before the reorganization of 1903 the Immigration Branch refused to confirm the appointment of any designated sub-agents.

Each sub-agent was issued a book of numbered Settlers' Certificates used to confer settler status on prospective immigrants. As with those issued by salaried agents, at railway crossing points settlers exchanged these Certificates for reduced railroad rate certificates. The Canadian railways, in turn, collected the Settlers' Certificates and relayed them from central assembly points to the Department's office in Ottawa. Here they were tabulated, each sub-agent receiving due credit and a cheque for the appropriate amount.[8] State agents, of course, received no commission.[9]

Each sub-agent was instructed to maintain a duplicate record of Certificates issued. When his commission was paid, he was supplied with a master list noting which settlers had been processed by the Immigration Branch. It was thus possible for a sub-agent to account for those settlers he claimed to have sent yet were still outstanding on his account. In order to collect a commission on a settler who had travelled overland, or for other reasons did not have his Certificate processed in Ottawa, the sub-agent was compelled to prove the alleged settler had in fact migrated to Canada. Sub-agents were required to submit the name, destination and the probable time of arrival at the frontier for each settler claimed but unaccounted for. The Department then attempted to trace missing settlers through local customs or postal records.[10] In one case, where the Department expected a large group of settlers to cross the border by wagon-train, customs officials were instructed to collect Certificates and forward them directly to Ottawa.[11]

Most men selected as sub-agents or commissioned agents, as they were sometimes known, were local farmers. But preference was initially given to railroad employees. Ticket agents and station personnel of American railways were considered the most desirable class of sub-agent as they proved to be generally informed on the migration sentiment among area farmers. Nor was it unusual for railroad men to supplement their incomes through participation in various promotional or colonization schemes offered them. Clifford Sifton noted that American land interests had long used Canadian railway employees, especially in Ontario, to further American land sale projects. Speaking before the Commons, the Minister of the Interior observed that he was ever ready to follow a good example.

> I tried to work out very much the same plan that the American railways have adopted in the province of Ontario so successfully for a great many years. The American roads, through the agencies of the Canadian railway agents in the province of Ontario, sent thousands of people to the western states. Having familiarized myself with the way in which that is done, I tried to apply that in western states, and so far, I think, with considerable success.

Sifton informed the Commons that William J. White, Inspector of American Agencies, had undertaken an extended tour through the American northwest in the hope of assisting local agents persuade railroad personnel to join the new sub-agent organization.[12] A form letter issued over the signature of the agent in Detroit was mailed to over one hundred railway employees throughout the midwest in July, 1897. After detailing the quantity and quality of free homestead lands available in western Canada, the bonus offered for each settler dispatched and the potential influence the railroad employee possessed with prospective immigrants, he extended to each individual the "proposal to act as agent in [his] district."[13]

The response to this invitation is unknown. However, in a report to the Department the agent did note the appointment of a number of railway personnel across the midwest. Included among the lines covered were: The Ohio Central; Detroit, Toledo and Cincinnati; Ann Arbour; the Cincinnati, Hamilton and Dayton; the Columbus, Hoking Valley, Toledo Railroad; the Buckeye Route and the Baltimore and Ohio Railroad. With respect to these lines little opposition was voiced by railroad management as, for the most part, these roads had no land of their own to sell. They may well have appreciated their personnel's moonlighting activities, knowing it might potentially increase company carrier business. It was the railroad, after all, which would carry settlers and their goods to Canada.[14]

The railroad sub-agent had substantial success in stimulating migration to Canada. His first hand knowledge and understanding of local farmers' problems and his opportunity to act in an advisory capacity to land-hungry farmers made him an effective recruiter. One immigration agent was so pleased with the achievements of railroad employees that he saw no reason for searching out any other class of sub-agent. With only three months' experience in the field, he claimed that the railroad men working in his territory were "with one or two exceptions the only class of [sub-agent] that [were] of any use . . . ." All other sub-agents, he complained, "think they should get a salary for doing nothing . . . . The people all goes [sic] to the R.R. Agents for information. So I would strongly advise the appointment of nothing else but R.R. Agents as our [sub-agents]."[15]

Agent McInnes, Detroit, praised the railroad personnel with equal fervour and better grammar. Upon request he was granted permission to appoint men on the Grand Rapids, Indiana and Michigan Central Railway.[16] Much, he hoped, could be anticipated from the appointments.

> . . . we can get, from this portion of the States, twice the number of settlers we otherwise could do. The Ry. Agts., are by far the best class of men for us, securing settlers, distributing advertising matter and getting up little parties [of settlers]. It is their profession, and they depend on the commission they earn for a living, and as a general rule they are hustlers.[17]

Where interests of the American railways conflicted with those of the Immigration Branch, especially over land promotion, the companies did not greet the utilization of their railroad personnel as sub-agents with any sympathy. As a result local agents were forced to look elsewhere for possible appointees. In the main most of the non-railway sub-agents recruited were local farmers who previously expressed interest in western Canada. Often the prospective sub-agent first came to a local agent's attention by responding to Departmental advertising. Farmers or small rural businessmen particularly suited to work with specific minority groups were in great demand and it was possible for such appointees to eventually expand their base of operations to include other settlers with whom they came into contact.[18]

Sub-agents left on the Department's rolls from the previous ministry proved to be of little value. The new agent arriving in Reed City, Michigan, was supplied with the names of twenty-six such men who lived in his territory. Having written each for an accounting of recent immigration activities, he received only six replies. The local agent lamented that "these were of such a nature that [he] at once concluded that they with two exceptions were agents in name only." Retaining the two sub-agents who gave good account of themselves, he was required "to start as if no work had been done in the field."[19] On yet another occasion, he observed, "I find the [sub] Agents who had been appointed formerly are – least those who I have met – simply no good, doing nothing and not trying to [sic] so it will be necessary for me to travel over the whole field and get new men."[20]

From the introduction of a renovated sub-agent system in 1897 numbers of appointees continued to climb until 1903. In July 1898 there were 179 sub-agents authorized to work in eighteen states. In Michigan alone agents supervised seventy sub-agents.[21] By 1900 the number of sub-agents had increased to 270 in twenty-three states.[22] Reorganization of the sub-agent network in 1900 reduced the number of men in the field to 236.[23] However, the following year the number of sub-agents jumped to a new high of 276 in twenty-four states and territories with one agent assigned to working among Hungarian farmers wherever he might find them.[24]

It would be inaccurate to conclude, as one magazine article did, that sub-agents acted in harmony, unity or with equal vigour. Exaggerating the number of sub-agents in 1903 the *Overland Monthly and Out West Magazine* claimed that the United States had been invaded by "an army of 370 men, commissioned to bring under the flag of Canada every substantial American who [could] be induced to quit his own country."[25] This description coincides more with Departmental hopes than with actual fact. A tabulation of results produced by sub-agents during the fiscal year 1901-1902 indicated that one sub-agent was alone responsible for sending almost one third of the 3,822 settlers on whom a bonus was paid. While this agent managed to send nearly 1,200 settlers, his success must be contrasted with the dismal results of others. Some sub-agents sent no settlers. The average number of settlers sent by agents who received a commission (that is to exclude sub-agents who received no remuneration) was only seventy-eight. However, in actual fact the majority of sub-agents sent no more than ten to fifteen settlers into the Canadian west.[26] In comparison to work by local agents, the sub-agent effort was small indeed. Government figures list 26,388 Americans having migrated to Canada in 1901-1902 and commission was issued for only seven per cent of the total.[27]

Some local agents, lamenting the inability of sub-agents to initiate the desired mass movement, began to search for alternate structures to help stimulate migration. In Kansas, for instance, the local agent created quasi-sub-agents by forming what he called Free Land Clubs. In towns across the state, Saturday, the farmers' day in town, proved a propitious occasion for the agent to hold organizational street meetings to publicize free Canadian homesteads. Farmers who expressed interest in Canadian land were encouraged to form clubs with their own local executives. In turn, clubs were encouraged to hold regular meetings and light social gatherings for both membership and the community at large. The salaried agent often attended club functions and used them to meet farmers. Those converted to Canada were encouraged to participate in further settlement work. As the agent observed, each Free Land Club was organized "having in view the distribution of literature, and a grand knowledge of the country, through the members of such organizations, whose secretary, by virtue of his position, becomes an agent."[28] Of course, no commission was paid for the immigration work of the club's executive. The agent, thus, created an organized structure which gave him both a means of meeting and influencing farmers and a virtually complete sub-agent system in his state at no cost to the Department.

While the majority of local agents continued to rely on official sub-agents for assistance, the agent in Watertown, South Dakota, experimented with a second alternative. He found that farmers who had been sent by the Department to see western Canada as visiting delegates often sustained the enthusiasm necessary to influence their fellow farmers. Preferring returned delegates to sub-agents, he explained his position for the Department.

> . . . I would say my reasons for not appointing sub-agents are: (1) I realized from the outset that unless good trustworthy men were secured they would do more harm than good. Having no special interest in the welfare of the

country beyond the commission they received, they would run a class they wanted to get rich of [sic] – and a class *we do not want* . . . . (2) I have been particular to send the best available men as delegates [to visit western Canada]. Those of them who returned "delighted with the country" I gave them to understand we would expect them to help in every way possible because of the concessions given them as delegates. In this way I have received the best kind of help and in a way which did not cost the Department one dollar. I feel such men have great influence upon their neighbors – and will accomplish more real good than those only interested in dollars and cents they get out of it.[29]

The introduction of returned farm delegates in place of sub-agents was little more than a natural extension of the already widespread utilization of delegates within the Department's publicity programme. Rather than leave delegates to function as tools of the publicity effort – writing reports, giving lectures on their first hand observations and possibly setting an example through their own migration – the South Dakota agent brought them into the recruitment programme as his unpaid sub-agents. He prided himself on the calibre of his delegates and boasted, on one occasion, that he had enlisted "not only the warm interest but active assistance of four prominent and influential men in the districts in which they live." Among them was "an ex-member of the State legislature."[30]

The efforts to by-pass the official sub-agent structure were exceptions, but exceptions which indicate the existence of a slowly maturing dissatisfaction with the formal sub-agent organization. Nevertheless, for a time sub-agents generally continued as the rule in assisting local agents in their work.

The jurisdiction of officially appointed sub-agents was similar to that of the state agent although, of course, on a more limited scale. It must be remembered that most sub-agents depended on their commission only to supplement their incomes and were usually employed elsewhere. Remaining directly responsible to the agent from whom he received his appointment, each sub-agent was encouraged to work independently, doing all in his power to focus attention on Canada. Like the local agent, the sub-agent distributed literature, held meetings, attended local fairs and organized groups of farm delegates to visit Canada. He might even tour the Canadian west himself in order to gather added insight into the area being promoted. Sub-agent J. H. M. Parker, Duluth, made two tours of western Canada.

In 1901 the Department encouraged him to visit newly opened areas with other sub-agents and in 1902 he led fifty-seven Norwegian-American settlers and eleven farm delegates on a tour of the Canadian prairies.[31]

On the whole, as the *Overland Monthly and Out West Magazine* noted, it was the sub-agent's "duty to penetrate the farming communities" as best as he could in the cause of increased migration to Canada.[32] However, the sub-agent was only too aware that he was only paid for results. He had to issue Settlers' Certificates to *bona fide* American settlers before he could personally profit from his own activity.[33]

The meagre returns noted for 1901-1902 were representative of the entire sub-agent effort. Local agents, however, hoping to stimulate increased activity among their appointees occasionally tried to encourage them to work harder with incentives to supplement their regular commissions. For example, agent McInnes, Detroit, offered his better sub-agents a party on rails. He promised these more productive sub-agents a gay, all expense paid excursion from Detroit through western Canada.

> I intend to have the train decorated and everything made comfortable for the trip. All [sub-] agents who secure ten settlers for this excursion will be furnished with free transportation for himself [sic] over the Canadian West and return. As I intend to be with the party, you can rest assured that the [sub-] agents will have a jolly good time, as well as a profitable one.[34]

The success of this scheme is unknown. However, the excursion, consistent with so much of the Immigration Branch activity, required the co-operation of Canadian railways, specifically the Canadian Pacific. It was this need for continuing harmony with the railways which precipitated the first reorganization of the sub-agent system in 1900.

Friction between the Immigration Branch and the Canadian Pacific over the sub-agents erupted immediately. The railway maintained its own land and colonization agents in the United States, including those stationed along the "Soo Line," the Canadian Pacific subsidiary. The government's sub-agents charged that the railway's agents were systematically stealing their settlers. After "working up a party" of immigrants, it was possible for a sub-agent to be deprived of his duly earned commission as railway land agents in the United States ignored Settlers' Certificates issued by sub-agents and directly offered settlers the railway's reduced rate certificates. As a result sub-agents had no means of claiming credit for their work.

Hinting that the Canadian Pacific's agents were using this deception to artificially inflate their work figures at the expense of sub-agents who promoted the migration, the Departmental Secretary conferred with railway officials in an effort to stop the practice.[35] Although the company did not offer to withdraw the right of its agents to issue reduced rate certificates in the United States, the General Passenger Agent for the Canadian Pacific proposed a compromise. He suggested that in addition to placing the settler's name and the address of the issuing office on the railway's reduced rate certificate, the point from which the settler originally started for Canada should also be entered. This, he contended, would allow grounds for any realistic claims a government sub-agent might have to collect bonuses still unpaid on settlers whom he claimed responsibility for sending.[36] Though it did not find it wholly satisfactory, the Department agreed to the compromise as the only means of keeping friction with the railway at a minimum. Nevertheless, the Immigration Branch appreciated that this concession would entail both delays in payment of commissions and continued complaints from sub-agents.[37]

In 1900, rather than phase out its own operations in the United States, the Canadian Pacific suggested that the government's agents and sub-agents be integrated into the company's work. The railway proposed that sub-agents be authorized to act as agents in the sale of company land. The offer was flatly rejected.[38] The Immigration Branch could not allow its agents or sub-agents to work for the sale of private lands of one firm to the exclusion of others; nor was it pleased with the prospect of having its sub-agents take a vested interest in the sale of company lands. If sub-agents were known to be tools of a land company, it could not help but undermine their credibility as spokesmen for free Canadian homestead lands. But, if the Department did not want its sub-agents to act as agents in the sale of Canadian Pacific lands, the Canadian Pacific was equally adamant that the Immigration Branch not employ American railway personnel as sub-agents. The Canadian Pacific demanded that these railroad sub-agents be weeded out of the government employ. Although the Canadian Pacific reserved the right of its own agents in the United States to engage in colonization activities it was not prepared to have its employees compete with those of other railroads, notwithstanding the latter's claim to be carrying out a government commission. The Passenger Traffic Manager for Canadian Pacific telegraphed his displeasure to the Department and demanded immediate dismissal for all sub-agents also on the payroll of American railroads.

> We object to agents or representatives of other railways or transportation companies issuing certificates in connection with settlement of North West, the Danger is too great of demoralizing our regular business. Trust therefore, you will have all these appointments cancelled. This question was thoroughly gone into between this company and the Department a few years ago and our objections were then recorded and which we still hold.[39]

Just over two weeks after receiving the Railway's telegram the Immigration Branch discontinued the use of American railroad personnel.[40] This first sub-agent reorganization had the effect of forcefully removing the most productive sub-agents and raising an outcry from some of the salaried agents.[41] However, the Department could only explain "that as matters stand it is clear that such appointments cannot be made, and the existing rule [against employment of American railroad personnel] must be adhered to, at least for the present time."[42] The Immigration Branch needed harmony with the Canadian Pacific more than it needed the discharged sub-agents. However, their removal was to prove a substantial loss.

The numerical gap created by the forced departure of railway employees from sub-agent ranks was quickly filled by local farmers. In a single stroke, a local agent in Minnesota, collected twenty sub-agents from among farmers who responded to newspaper advertisements.[43] But, in discharging railroad personnel and opening the door to farmers the sub-agent system suffered a marked decline in productivity. This change of personnel was not the only cause of continually disappointing returns. It remains to be explained why most farmers proved poor promoters, what external forces hindered the system's smooth operation and what internal factors joined in steering the sub-agent system toward eventual failure.

Many farmers appointed as sub-agents indicated a previous interest in Canadian lands. But even if this interest was maintained, it provided no guarantee that a sub-agent would not face disillusionment once confronted with the actual task of gathering settlers. The undertaking often proved more difficult and less rewarding than anticipated. Except for railroad sub-agents, ejected from the service in 1900, most did not have the time, training, talent or ambition necessary to organize large scale migration. In many cases all that could be expected was that a sub-agent might issue a Settlers' Certificate should he happen upon a farmer already planning to move his family northward. Presumably some farmers may have accepted the post for its prestige. Beside the apparent honour of being asked to serve as a Canadian government agent or the chance to earn a few extra dollars, the new sub-agent could hope to see his name in local newspaper advertisements or on letterhead stationery, and even take an all expense paid vacation in Canada. While not all sub-agents were unproductive, the majority accomplished so little that one cannot help but question their motives for accepting the appointment.

When a sub-agent did organize a party of settlers and successfully moved them to the Canadian west, the financial reward was often long delayed. To be sure, sub-agents were given to understand the procedure used to verify commission claims was complex. However, slow processing of Settlers' Certificates as they passed from hand to hand before final tabulation in Ottawa left many sub-agents feeling deceived or neglected. An agent in Ohio was not alone in attributing a quick breakdown of sub-agent morale to inefficient payment procedures. He complained that two sub-agents under his supervision received no commission after hard work and lengthy waits.

> Now this I do not think is right. After arrangement is made and they are properly appointed, the Government behind the appointment. And they have faithfully done their part, and made great sacrifices, they should have their money. [sic] [44]

Other sub-agents, finding their patience severely taxed, joined in the outcry. In April 1902, sub-agent Parker, Duluth, claimed his commissions were four months in arrears. "There is certainly," he charged, "neglect or mismanagement somewhere."[45] Further delays only increased his antagonism to alleged Departmental incompetence.

> It certainly looks very bad. It is impossible for me to keep my bills paid when you treat me this way. I am positively ashamed to be obliged to tell people when I owe that the Canadian Government do not [sic] pay me promptly . . . I have worked faithfully for the past six years and have done as much for immigration as any one of you.[46]

Long delays might have been reduced by streamlining the method of verifying commissions. However, the checking process undertaken before payment was finally authorized was further complicated by the failure of many bonus claims to be validated at all. When no Settlers' Certificates reached Ottawa, the Department had to await proof from other sources that a settler had indeed taken up residence in Canada. Sub-agents complained their Certificates were being stolen. A common accusation made was that other Canadian agents or sub-agents lay in wait along the settlers' route and secretly exchanged the original Settlers' Certificates issued for one of their own. The same thing was said about the Canadian Pacific agents.[47] Furthermore, as some railway agents at the border were ready to issue reduced rate certificates to any settlers who crossed into Canada, it was common for farmers carrying Settlers' Certificates not to turn them in even though they had the Certificates in hand. In each of these cases Settlers' Certificates never reached Ottawa to corroborate a sub-agent's own record. Performing the function of a central counting-house in payment of commission, the last link in the chain, the Immigration Branch was careful not to assume responsibility for payment of dubious claims. The Superintendent of Immigration explained.

> In any case where commissions have failed to reach sub-agents the fault has been, not with the Department, but it has been due to the non-presentation of the certificate by the holder, or the non-receipt of any return from the Railroad Company, Customs officials, or Dominion Lands or Immigration officers, showing that settlers had arrived.[48]

Complaints of slowness or non-payment of commissions continually harrassed Department officials. A process for validating questionable claims consumed additional time. Letters from the Immigration Branch were mailed to postmasters in areas where a supposed settler was thought to be farming. Only on receiving word that the settler had indeed been located was payment issued. Although this cumbersome procedure helped a little, some sub-agents still thought they were being cheated.

While the demand for faster payment on weaker evidence grew stronger among concerned agents and sub-agents, pressure in the opposite direction was exerted upon the Department from the House of Commons. Opposition from Conservative members, expressing concern for unwarranted payments, compelled Sifton to assure members of the Commons that bonus cheques were only extended upon the receipt of absolute proof. In 1898 he confessed that the difference between commission claimed and commission paid was "several thousand." The minister explained to the Commons ". . . it is a difficult thing to work out, but there is little danger of our being defrauded."[49] Sub-agents were not always confident of the same guarantee.

Not all problems arose from complaints of sub-agents against the Immigration Branch. The Department had good reasons to be discontented with the activities of its sub-agents. For instance, it was feared that some were issuing Settlers' Certificates to persons not falling into the settler category. The temptation to issue Settlers' Certificates to tourists or, more importantly, land speculators was difficult to resist. The results were both fraudulent commission claims and irritation of Canadian railway officials who felt duped into issuing non-settlers with reduced rate certificates.[50]

Of far greater concern was an obvious conflict of interests developing among the ranks of government sub-agents. Individual sub-agents were often approached by representatives of land companies with holdings in western Canada who offered to make them land agents. When such offers were made directly to the Immigration Branch they could be rejected. The Canadian Pacific had not been the only land company to present the government with an offer to integrate immigration promotion with land sales. In 1900 the firm of Osler, Hammond and Nanton, a well known and respected Canadian business house active in the sale of western lands, approached the immigration agent in Detroit regarding the use of his sub-agents. He and his sub-agents were offered a commission of three per cent on all land sales "traceable to [them] and made from [their] individual efforts without the assistance of local [company] representatives." In any case where land company agents and government agents "joined forces to bring about a sale the commission was to be divided."[51]

The agent referred the matter to the Department.[52] Refusing to become involved in land sale schemes or to sanction the use of its agents in such undertakings the Superintendent of Immigration, instructed his agent that such arrangements were not in the best interests of the Department and must be rejected. Promoting lands for private companies was, the Superintendent warned, "a class of work in which it is thought advisable that agents should not engage."[53]

In reality Departmental pronouncements proved ineffectual in combating a steadily enlarging body of conflict of interest cases within sub-agents' ranks. Furthermore, the Department realized its innate impotence. It simply did not have the authority necessary to control the unsavoury ventures of individual sub-agents who used their government appointment as a lever in land sales. While restraint was hopefully maintained over salaried agents, the Immigration Branch was admittedly powerless to frustrate the private exploits of men working on commission.

The Haslam Land and Investment Company of St. Paul, active in the sale of lands in southeastern Saskatchewan, encountered unexpected competition in the person of a Departmental sub-agent. The company bitterly complained that one of its land salesmen had taken a client to arrange for a Settlers' Certificate only to have that same settler offered lands of another company in the Indian Head District of Saskatchewan by the government's agent. Since the Haslam firm professed to be spending over three thousand dollars each month on land promotion, it was not prepared to allow allegedly neutral government appointees to pirate its clients for other land companies. Preferring to conceal the identity of the culprit in this case, the company contended this incident was not unique. The company threatened that if such practices were not stopped it would "simply have the matter brought up in Parliament."[54]

The Haslam company received little satisfaction. Confessing that such incidents did take place, the Immigration Branch transferred blame from agents to sub-agents. The latter, the Department admitted, were not confined by the rigid control exercised over salaried agents.

> . . . our regular agents are not allowed to do a land brokerage business. It may be that you have reference in your letter to our sub-agents, who you probably understand are appointed on a commission basis and who occupy an entirely different position from the salaried agents. The Department does not pretend to exercise the same control over the local commission agents as it does over those who are regularly appointed by and under salary from the Department.[55]

Although aware that its ability to restrain sub-agent land dealings was limited, the Department was equally cognizant of the pernicious impact such widespread activities were having on the total sub-agent programme. The temptation of unscrupulous individuals to use a Canadian government appointment in secret alliance with land promoters was matched only by the desire of land companies to cajole sub-agents into such agreements on the promise of easy money. White cautioned that continued profiteering at the expense of land-hungry settlers would undermine the integrity of the whole Immigration Branch and reduce the ability of honest agents or sub-agents to speak for homestead lands. But, White warned, the infiltration of quasi-land agents into Department ranks continued to be actively sought by land companies.

> [Sub-agents and land agents] are conflicting, and in order that the land companies may have a special boom [one] can easily understand how it will help their own business to be able to advertise that they are Agents of the Dominion Government. This is really what they want rather than the remuneration by way of commission from the Department.[56]

Among the chief offenders was sub-agent Parker, Duluth. It was found that Parker was using Departmental stationery to promote the settlement of private lands in Stavely, Alberta, seventy miles south of Calgary.[57] The Department might not have discovered Parker's embroilment with land company sales were it not that White, on an inspection tour through Wisconsin, accidentally ran across one of Parker's leaflets. The Immigration Branch knew only too well that its neutrality in land promotion stood compromised so long as one of its sub-agents gave Stavely "strong and personal endorsement, the main reason of course being that he [was] handling land in that district . . . ."[58] While no direct disciplinary action was undertaken, tolerance for such conflicts of interest was beginning to wane.

Minor reforms were advocated. White recommended that all Settlers' Certificates issued by sub-agents be countersigned by local agents. This procedure would add considerable delay in some cases, but would hopefully prevent excessive exploitation of Certificates by known speculators. It would also expose any sub-agent promoting the private lands of one region to the exclusion of others. There was no reason, White claimed, why the Immigration Branch should be required to support the activities of secret land agents or non-settlers.[59]

> The Sub-Agents will be issuing certificates to all sorts of persons to go into Manitoba and the Territories and we will simply be paying commission on men who are going to speculate. Under the circumstances I would suggest that it would be well to be careful in appointing sub-agents to see that men are all of the proper class.[60]

Instituting a closer watch on the issuance of Settlers' Certificates or more careful selection of future sub-agents only skirted the major problems. The Department still would not have firm control over the activities of its sub-agents nor would it be able to rid itself of land company infiltrations. Indeed, White warned, the Department was already becoming a battle ground between competing land interests. If any one land company seemed to be favoured, or gained influence among sub-agents "the jealousy of a dozen other land companies would be aroused."[61] While land companies active in the sale of western Canadian property had their own agents in the United States, it was an undesirable boon to have company agents able to cloak their activities under a mantle of government authority. This prize only spurred infiltration and continued infiltration would ruin the entire sub-agent system.

While the sub-agent programme was proving itself of dubious value except to land companies, Conservative member of Parliament for Lexington-Addington, Uriah Wilson, demanded that sub-agents be entirely eliminated. Government money, he felt, was "being thrown away" when private land companies were promoting the American migration at their own expense and with far greater success.

> [American settlers] are coming as a result of land com-
> panies. The land agents are the people who do all the work
> and the commissioned agents are the people who get all the
> money . . . After the land companies have induced people
> to come to their country to buy land these commissioned
> agents come along and reap the benefits of that work and
> the people of Canada are the poorer for it. I think it is
> folly for the government to spend so much money in the
> way they are spending it. I think it would be wise if the
> Hon. Minister would abolish altogether the system of
> employing agents on commission.[62]

Wilson would have been surprised had he known that notwithstanding his praise for land company activities, his demand for an end to the sub-agent system had supporters within the Department. The agent in Watertown, South Dakota, had early labelled the sub-agent scheme as one "nuisance" he could well do without. He contended that he would rather do all his own work than have the assistance of sub-agents who only could be goaded by "mercenary motives" often above and beyond the commission they received.[63] Other salaried agents echoed this position. Looking back over six years of sub-agent activity, one concluded that "speaking generally they are a failure." In his estimation only one in ten made any effort to fulfill the Department's commission. "The great majority will issue certificates to parties when they come across them by accident or otherwise will not put themselves out to solicit business." Without alluding to the problem of land companies, he continued, "There should be a weeding out . . . I think a goodly number might be quietly dropped and the work could go on just the same."[64] The agent in St. Paul had already taken it upon himself to prune the dead wood from among his sub-agents. Sifting out those who could be depended upon to conscientiously support the government's programme, he discharged the others.[65]

By 1903 it was becoming obvious that sweeping reforms were required if the sub-agent system was to survive in some form. Problems continually bore away at the structure's foundations. Sub-agents discouraged by Departmental inefficiency in paying claims joined ranks with those who had long been sub-agents in name only. Land companies vied with one another for commissioned agents and threatened to discredit the entire American operation. Dissatisfaction with the bonus system was further illustrated by a growing reluctance of local agents to continue the use of sub-agents in their territories. However, if these difficulties were not in themselves enough to dictate a revamping of the sub-agent system, the Department's own statistics finally clinched the issue and made reform inevitable.

A jump in the number of sub-agents from 179 in 1898 to 291 in 1903 indicates that in spite of the removal of railroad personnel in 1900 it was not difficult to find men willing to accept the name of sub-agent.[66] Statistics, faulty though they are, support the inescapable conclusion that the gulf between name and substance was abysmally wide. Even the accomplishments of the few who took their work seriously were marginal at best, with only one in four sub-agents performing functions deserving of compensation.[67] Of those who did

TABLE I: Number of agents paid commission; highest commission; lowest commission; average commission among those receiving a commission; total expenditure on commissions: 1896/97 to 1903/4.

Year	No. of sub-agents receiving commission	Highest commission	Lowest commission	Average commission	Total
1896/97	22	$ 296	$3	$112	$ 2,462
1897/98	44	$1,472	$3	$ 82	$ 3,615
1898/99	58	$1,026	$3	$ 52	$ 3,017
1899/00	67	$2,303	$3	$ 96	$ 6,410
1900/01	78	$4,559	$3	$152	$11,863
1901/02	50	$1,896	$3	$158	$ 7,903
1902/03	77	$2,833	$3	$194	$14,917
1903/04	74	$3,107	$3	$195	$14,428

receive commissions, the majority processed only a handful of settlers, sometimes only one or two settlers per sub-agent. It was common, as we have seen, to find one outstanding sub-agent responsible for sending a large percentage of settlers. For example, in 1901-1902 the Salt Lake City sub-agent received bonuses for one third of the nearly four thousand persons on whom such bonuses were issued.[68]

With the exception of a few individuals, by 1903 the sub-agent system was bankrupt. It had failed to produce either an immigration boom or a credible reservoir of local good will. In the spring of that year hopes for the survival of an unreformed sub-agent system appeared as bleak as its past performance. The continuing absence of encouraging results, the steady bickering over payments of commission, the complaints of salaried agents and the danger of usurpation of sub-agents by land companies continually racked Departmental policy makers.

Furthermore there was a growing confidence in the general abilities of salaried agents to competently fulfil all duties in the United States. As a result the Department finally moved to institute a second radical reorganization of the sub-agent system. The Superintendent of Immigration informed the Deputy Minister of the policy changes.

> I have decided that our whole work in the United States, outside of the regular salaried agents, must be reorganized. It seems to me that the system which was workable years ago regarding the Local Sub-Agents is unsatisfactory in our work today. Of course, when we first attempted to stir up the interest in Canada in various portions of the United States it was a good plan but I think that its usefulness is very largely gone now and I think we ought to have a reorganization on better lines. You might have a conversation with Mr. White as to what is to be done. In the meantime the Agents should be advised that appointments of Local Sub-Agents are to be cancelled at the end of the month of June. [1903][69]

The Superintendent was diplomatic in admitting the sub-agent programme a failure, but his intent was clear. The Deputy Minister endorsed the withdrawal of sub-agent activity and applauded the shift in emphasis toward the more promising work of local agents. White and the Superintendent quickly organized a procedure for phasing out the sub-agent system. Sub-agents were mailed a letter informing them that their employment with the Department would be terminated as of July 1, 1903. Simultaneously each local agent was instructed to supply Ottawa with a list of those sub-agents worthy of reappointment. In any such cases evidence to justify retaining the individual was also requested. Done quickly and quietly the change of policy would assure the continued success of work performed by local agents and acceptable sub-agents. "By this means," the Superintendent explained, "we will be able to get rid of a lot of old wood who have never done anything and we can weed out the land agents who are simply using the certificates to send speculators up who have no intention of becoming settlers."[70]

Oddly one sub-agent did so well that he priced himself out of a job. Commissions earned by William Ritchie, Grafton, North Dakota, had grown so large that his jurisdiction could be assumed by a new salaried agent at a substantial saving to the Department. Thus, at least for Ritchie, there seemed no premium on excellence.[71]

The reorganization of the sub-agent system was raised in the House of Commons. Sifton led members to believe the change of policy was not an outgrowth of any inherent weaknesses in the Department's programme but a direct result of its strength. He attributed the partial elimination of sub-agents solely to the improved capacity of local agents to cope with activities heretofore delegated to sub-agents. Deeper problems could not be completely hidden. Sifton was forced to concede, "all the sub-agents were removed, their appointments cancelled. Since that time some forty or fifty of them who were considered to be of some value, were re-appointed."[72] Predictably, the Minister made no mention of the wider concerns raised by sub-agents: their general inability to supplement the local agents, to spur immigration work or the inability of the Department to prevent abuse of the appointments it had authorized.

TABLE II: Total American Settlers; Total upon whom bonus was paid and per cent upon whom bonus was paid 1904/05 to 1911/12.

Year	Total U.S. Settlers	Total on commission	Per Cent on whom commission was paid
1904/05	43,543	3,681	8.45
1905/06	57,796	3,134	5.48
1906/07	34,659	2,561	7.39
1907/08	58,312	2,226	3.82
1908/09	59,832	2,647	4.42
1909/10	103,798	1,872	1.80
1910/11	121,451	2,965	2.44
1911/12	133,710	3,613	2.70

After 1903 only the skeletal framework of the previous sub-agent system remained. Departmental support for the experiment was never revived again. Local agents dutifully complied with instructions and returned lists of those sub-agents whom they wished retained. On the basis of these recommendations qualified and trustworthy sub-agents continued to be employed but with decidedly less enthusiasm. Commission payments plunged.[73] While numbers of settlers entering Canada steadily increased for the next ten years, sub-agent contributions continued to decline.[74]

Not all sub-agents accepted their dismissal with equal grace. The Department tolerantly, if not wisely, kept J. H. M. Parker, Duluth, on the sub-agent rolls for an additional five months on a probational basis. His continued employment hung on his promise to avoid involvement in the activities of private land companies.[75] White soon discovered that Parker was violating that trust.

> . . . he is going through the country under the auspices of land companies and my opinion is that no concessions should be granted him. I think that better work is accomplished by the regular agents without stereopticon views, especially when [the sub-agent] has no greater abilities than Mr. Parker has.[76]

Parker's removal was approved and a telegram confirming the decision was sent.[77] However, Parker refused to close down his office and, in turn, attacked the Department. He charged, "I have been working for your department for the past eight years and have during that period found every detail dissatisfactory inasmuch as the department used me as the tool to further the interests of other agents, who are incompetent to carry on the business on their own merits." Pointing to an unspecified group of personal supporters, he declared he would not accept the Department's fiat but intended to keep his office open under the name of Canadian Land and Immigration Office.[78] Parker proved as good as his word. In co-operation with private land interests he continued to present himself as a government agent. For the next seven years the Department informed everyone known to have approached Parker on business that he was no longer authorized.[79]

Appreciating Departmental sensitivity to bad publicity, Parker was quick to carry his grievances to the press. On the basis of an interview with Parker the *St. Paul Globe* carried an article under the headline, "Canadian Money Is Being Wasted, Dominion Agent Tells of Immigration Frauds Practised on His Government."

Hundreds of thousands of dollars has been expended by the Canadian Government in securing settlers for the Dominion from the United States . . . and a goodly portion of the money has been wasted. I could take one third of the amount and double the immigration. This deplorable state of affairs is due to the fact that out of the seventeen Canadian government agents now located in the United States only five are doing active work. The others are simply drawing the salary that is paid them by the government and the work that is being done through their office is the work of sub-agents from the government for immigrants sent into the country.[80]

Finding himself chosen as one of Parker's five active agents, salaried agent M. V. McInnes, Detroit, pointedly disassociated himself from his admirer. He branded Parker a "disappointed and disgruntled bag of hot air." McInnes continued,

I wish it to be understood that I consider it no compliment whatever to have my name coupled with such a blockhead [as Parker]. His endorsement is no certificate of efficiency or good character and I felt particularly displeased when I saw my name in print in such noxious conjunction.[81]

Another agent happened into Parker on a trip to Winnipeg and reported to White, "I am surprised that there are no more inmates in some of the asylums in Minnesota for the incurable."[82] However, Parker's article, reprinted in the *Toronto Telegram,* coupled with a letter received from him by Conservative critic Uriah Wilson, gave the opposition party a springboard for attacks on the Department's American activities, especially over alleged waste of money and the use of politically motivated criteria in selection of local agents.[83]

The Parker episode aside, after 1903 the impact made by the sub-agent structure was marginal. Delegated to a subordinate status, sub-agents no longer merited the attention paid them earlier. It was to the credit of local agents that they were able to disguise the collapse of the sub-agent system and save themselves much embarrassment.

Selling A Country
[PUBLICITY]

A co-ordinated advertising campaign was crucial to sell the country and establish the credibility of Canadian Government Agents in the United States. Without an organized sales effort by the Immigration Branch, it is doubtful whether individual agents would have sparked more than marginal interest in Canadian lands among potential American settlers.

The only group of prospective settlers openly solicited in the United States were white farmers, especially those of the prairie and midwest states.[1] Fortunately for the newly organized Immigration Branch, the methods of reaching this group were readily available. A long tradition of North American land promotion offered numerous precedents upon which the Department's publicity campaign could draw.

The propagandist must be as ready to re-educate the misinformed as he is to educate the uninformed. This was true of the Department. He was immediately confronted by many farmers who had long assumed that Canada was little more than a frozen wasteland. Travelling through his assigned territory an agent in Michigan reported having met "hundreds [of farmers] who had never heard of western Canada spoken of except as a region of perpetual snow."[2] Even the Canadian agent at Syracuse, in the heart of the New York State snow belt, complained that except for their visions of unending winter "though close neighbours, the people have known very little about even eastern Canada, and absolutely nothing about our western country."[3]

Consequently preliminary advertising deliberately focused on spreading flatteringly "factual" information about western Canada while challenging "misconceptions" about its climate. A 1903 American magazine article reviewing the Department's work in the United States contended that the whole publicity programme "was done with the object largely of disabusing the American mind of the belief that western Canada is a land of frosts and snows." At least for the campaign's early stages the article was correct.[4]

As a small but increasing stream of settlers began to flow northward into Canada, the Department was gradually able to shift away from such basic educational concerns. While never completely abandoning the battle against the climatic hobgoblin, especially in the face of hostile propaganda from competing American land interests, stress increasingly accorded the achievements of American settlers already farming the Canadian prairies. This accent on social and economic progress eventually became the central theme of the publicity programme. Drawing on the immigrants' successes, the Department's message proved artfully simple – what one American settler has achieved could be duplicated or surpassed by others.

The time and money expended on promoting American emigration had an important side-effect in which the Department took great pride: it converted the American press as well as the American settlers.

By judicious manipulation of its advertising budget the Department generally guaranteed press co-operation, including an editorial moritorium on adverse reports from the Canadian west. In one case the government went so far as to reward an American newspaper's continued support for the overall Liberal Party programme, especially advocacy of reciprocity in trade between the United States and Canada, with large homestead and immigration advertisements.

Newspaper provided one way to reach potential settlers. There also was: pamphleteering, exhibitions of Canadian produce and guided tours of western Canada. Co-ordinated from Ottawa, these interrelated promotional tools were already well-worn sales techniques when ably adapted to fit Canadian needs.

Many American farmers were first informed of the existence of Canadian homestead lands by reading their newspapers. While newspaper advertisements and promotional material issued by private land-companies were familiar to most farmers, those of the Immigration Branch had a tone all their own. Rather than promote specific lands, they praised national development and promised completely reliable and official government information on request. This tactic had two

80

objectives. First, it was designed to distinguish the Department from private promoters, especially among farmers justifiably sceptical of private land company pronouncements. Secondly, it exposed land seeking farmers who, in answering an advertisement, became subject to more direct promotional methods available to the Department. Therefore, the newspaper campaign was designed more to elicit a response than to sell a product.

The first promotional tool introduced following expansion of activities in the United States was large scale advertising in the rural and agricultural press. Initially no co-ordinated system of advertising was instituted. In a preliminary organizational circular sent to local agents, each agent was advised to advertise as he pleased in the local press of his area. The Department asked only that advertisements be accompanied by a cutout coupon which could be filled in and returned by those interested in further information.[5] But it was soon recognized that such local sporadic advertising was insufficient to promote the large response desired. State agents working independently tended to use newspaper advertising to announce a specific local event such as a public meeting rather than as part of an overall promotional programme. As a result a centrally organized and co-ordinated newspaper campaign became essential.

Almost immediately the Department negotiated a contract with the Western Newspaper Union of Chicago to blanket the midwest and mountain states with newspaper advertising. The Western Newspaper Union represented a grouping of over 2,700 local weekly newspapers for which it solicited advertising. With a combined weekly printing of over half a million newspapers, the Union claimed a readership of well over seven million people. The Union's operation was simple. It printed double page "patent sheets" which integrated news of general interest or miscellaneous reading matter with the commissioned advertisements. Mailed to the local press in bulk, the client papers published local news on the blank pages of the sheet. They then inserted the whole sheet as the newspaper's centre leaves.[6]

The desire to further expand this newspaper advertising programme brought the Immigration Branch into formal contracts with two other newspaper unions, the Chicago Newspaper Union and the A. N. Kellogg Newspaper Company.[7] By 1902 advertising companies were handling Canadian publicity in more than 7,000 local and agricultural newspapers.[8]

It was felt that the key to reaching every interested farmer was constant repetition of the government's message. William J. White, in charge of the American press campaign, praised patience. Success, he advised, would only come with time.

> The advertisement of one year may not induce a man to move, but when he sees the same advertisement inserted in the same paper the third year he becomes impressed with the fact that the advertiser has an article that is useful, stable and has merit. He will begin to enquire, and if satisfied will change his location.[9]

The texts of newspaper advertisements were drawn up by the Department in Ottawa, and one differed very little from the next. Inserts were kept in constant rotation with older advertisements periodically being replaced by new releases. Each insert was between two and three inches in height with a small flag proclaiming "160 Acre Farms In Western Canada Free." Copy usually extolled the general fertility or productivity of western lands. Claims were sometimes exaggerated. One advertisement made the assertion that lands of western Canada were sufficient "to support a population of 50,000,000 or over."[10] But, most statements seemed more reasonable. It was common to hold out the promise of twenty-five bushels of wheat or a gross return of $16 per acre. As homestead lands began to fill and American settlers often sought additional lands, box advertisements began to include notes on the availability of private lands, perhaps to be bought in conjunction with a homestead claim. All inserts closed with addresses of the Department in Ottawa and a local agent or sub-agent whom interested parties were encouraged to contact for further information.[11]

Press advertising was published on a seasonal basis. Obviously anxious to get the best return on the dollar, the Department wisely held off advertising during the farmer's busy summer or harvest months. Nor was advertising published during the Christmas season. Instead, advertising appeared during winter when farmers had long cold nights to devote to reading newspapers and dreaming of new lands.[12]

Individual agents were still allowed to advertise when they judged it necessary. Reaching a foreign language group or the opening of a new agency demanded special arrangements between specific newspapers and agents. In Salt Lake City, for instance, the sub-agent made extensive use of newspaper advertising in the Great Basin during his first year of activity.[13] In contracting for a short-term run in the local press, an individual agent was more apt to pay for advertisements out of his local operating budget than have the costs covered directly from Ottawa. However, the bulk of total advertising expenditure in the press remained paid out under contract with the newspaper Unions.

The Unions functioned merely as middlemen. The Department retained total discretion as to which of the Unions' clients would or would not receive advertising. As a result the local press remained on guard against offending Canadian sensitivities and often censored items which might annoy Canadian officials. In 1904 the Department claimed that its advertising, together with other activities undertaken to curry favour with the press, defused an overt attempt by anti-Canadian land interests to organize a press campaign. The Department, as White explained, had expected opposition to its work "and we have had it; but, I am pleased to say that it has been greatly checked owing, to a large degree, to the fact that our opponents were unable to find willing co-operation in the newspapers in which the department advertising is carried on."[14]

A local newspaper reluctant to jeopardize advertising its revenue by attacking Canadian migration usually proved receptive to articles and features relating to the Canadian west or the activities of local agents. This free coverage "for which nothing was asked in return" except continued advertising, was recognized as valuable supplement to the formal advertising campaign.[15] Local agents were encouraged to grant interviews or write articles for newspapers in which the Department advertised. One agent reported that of the seven local newspapers in which he placed small advertisements in 1897, three carried articles outlining his activities. The impact of these articles, he claimed, far outweighed that of his formal advertisements.[16]

The establishment of cordial relations with the American press was but a by-product, albeit an important one, of efforts to stimulate farmers interested in western Canada to reveal themselves to the Department. If the success of the press campaign can be correlated with the number of inquiries received, then it was, indeed, a success. At times a staggering one thousand letters a day arrived in Ottawa.[17] Still more letters were received by individual agents. During the fiscal year 1904-1905 alone, the eighteen agents in the United States received 70,948 letters, most asking for information about the Canadian west.[18]

Newspaper advertising prodded the curious and the land hungry to request the additional information about Canada promised in the advertisement. By identifying themselves they became the target of a propaganda blitz specifically designed to convert interest into immigration. Reinforcing an already exposed curiosity, the Department mailed each would-be settler a packet of specially prepared promotional pamphlet material.

American farmers were already well-acquainted with the bottomless bag of tricks available to land promoters. When previously buying land or even considering new lands, no farmer needed suffer for lack of colourful reading material. Long after moving, many were still being barraged with unsolicited railroad or land company publications extolling the marvels of this or that tract of land still on the market. Consequently, in spite of increased demand for farm lands, the lavish claims of many land promoters did little to appease a natural scepticism.

Nor were promotional publications new to the Canadian government, the provinces or Canadian railroads. Well before Confederation, the Province of Canada had conducted an official campaign to encourage immigration, and literature designed to stimulate the movement of people was published.[19] With little sucess, this work was continued by the young Dominion.[20] In far larger campaigns, Canadian railroads had long advertised their saleable lands. This promotional work paralleled that of the government.[21] Thus, in 1896 the Immigration Branch did not need to look far afield for time-tested publications and techniques.

The Department's literature had two advantages unavailable to promoters. First, the Immigration Branch focused on its role as the spokesman for an overall programme of national development. It was not a promoter of specific private land holdings. As a result, its publications could be viewed as a non-partisan service to settlers interested in Canada, leading them not into temptation but delivering them from swindle. Secondly, in view of the neutral role assumed by government, each publication maintained an air of authority and official truth. This could not help but soothe many farmers legitimately sceptical of land company claims. After all, would a government that invokes the name of Queen Victoria be dishonest?

Clifford Sifton, realized the importance of preserving the general confidence of the American farmer in the credibility of Canadian publications. He avoided the earlier naive representation of Canada as a utopia and substituted something closer to the truth. Sifton warned his ministry's publications to "impress the ordinary farmer with the sense of reality, in contrast with the usual advertising methods in which glowing statements are printed while there is no guarantee of their genuineness."[22] While it was both difficult and undesirable to weed all misrepresentation out of propaganda material, the Department remained far more cautious than many previous governments or land promoters.

An evident concern of early publications was the familiar need to break the cameo vision of Canada as Kipling's "Our Lady of the Snows."[23] An 1899 pamphlet, *Western Canada,* cleverly reminded prospective settlers that many of the most fertile regions of their own country were once labelled "the Great American Desert," unsuited for agriculture. "It was said that fruit could not be grown; that it was not possible to raise cattle successfully; and that farming operations could not be carried on with any degree of success. But," the pamphlet continued, "long since it has been demonstrated how erroneous these ideas were." The conclusion was obvious. Canada had been misrepresented too. In fact, it was suggested that dry weather made the Canadian cold not just tolerable but bracing. One was more likely to get sick from overeating than overexposure. In some areas the climate was so mild that "the soft maple tree has been known to grow more than five feet in a single season."[24] This stretched the truth, the imagination and, of course, "the soft maple tree."

This seventy-seven page pamphlet, like many which followed, went on to detail immigration, customs and homestead regulations as well as offer an invitation for further correspondence. This pamphlet also specified that the non-agriculturalist was neither needed nor wanted in Canada. "Clerks, shop assistants and persons desiring situations, are advised not to emigrate unless proceeding to appointments already secured or to join friends. Any demand for labour of these kinds is fully met on the spot."[25] Only farmers need apply.

The increased presence of Americans on the prairies, as migrants and visitors, generated a patent medicine style of promotional literature for American distribution. Pamphlets were published containing the personal observations and comments of visiting newsmen or prospective settlers reviewing the Canadian west and its climate as a possible cure for farmers' ills. Not surprisingly, all printed testimonials were of a positive nature. Among the largest collections was the 1899 *Delegates Reports and Settlers Experiences in Western Canada.* The 144-page booklet was filled with letters of new settlers or those who had recently visited the west and were planning to migrate. Identifying each settler by name and address, the booklet was highly regarded as an example of Americans speaking to Americans.[26] Similarly, newsmen and editors of American newspapers who took part in organized tours of Canada found excerpts from their articles reprinted in Departmental pamphlets. One such publication was ponderously entitled *Symposium Of Ideas And Prophecies On The Canadian West By The Members Of The National Editorial Association, And What They Said In 1900*.[27] Leaving little to chance, the Department also published a small pamphlet, *Reliable Information For Use Of United States Newspaper Editors Visiting Western Canada*, just in case an editor might need a little guidance as to what to write about his visit or his hosts.[28]

After 1903 a shift in emphasis took place. Rather than continue to stress elementary facts about Canada, the Immigration Branch set new importance on publicizing agricultural productivity and commercial prospects in western Canada.[29] With the influx of Americans well under way, promotional material generated an optimism based on statistical analysis of the nation's actual achievements. Pamphlet titles reflected the new approach: *Great Growth of Western Canada; Prosperity Follows Settlement in Western Canada; The Canadian West, Strides That Have Been Made in Recent Years; Canada Land of Opportunity* and *1905 The Biggest Crop In The History of the Canadian West*.[30]

Though most promotional pamphlets had a short life and were quickly replaced by new or updated entries, two publications survived year after year of revision and republication. Starting in 1897 an illustrated *Atlas of Canada* was published for American circulation by Rand, McNally of Chicago.[31] The atlas also appeared in several foreign languages for European immigrants in the United States, and steady demand eventually brought copies into libraries, elementary schools and clubs as well as private homes.[32]

In 1906 the Department first issued its magazine-like pamphlet, *The Last and Best West*, the title soon shortened to *The Last Best West* with the text slightly enlarged.[33] *The Last Best West* was undoubtedly the Department's slickest promotional publication. It blended photographs of the west, a light readable text and detailed maps of the prairie provinces into an effective piece of propaganda. A question and answer section was designed to cover most areas that would interest an American. For example:

Is it well to carry a revolver?
ANSWER: It is against the law to do so without a special license, and it is most unusual and almost unnecessary to do so under ordinary circumstances.[34]

It is not surprising that *The Last Best West* made use of American mythology: the agrarian ideal, the Horatio Alger tradition and log cabin stereotype. Each of these elements was extended across the border as if by osmosis.[35] However, Immigration Branch publications were not content to advance the Canadian west as merely a natural extension of the legendary American frontier. Where it was practicable, the Department played up the theme that the border acted as a barrier on the north side of which lay an ordered society, characteristically unlike the traditional American wild west. Without actually identifying the United States, one Departmental pamphlet proclaimed, "Respect for law and maintenance of order are very prominent features of life in Canada, as distinguished from other new countries." The red-coated Mounted Policeman was an ideal symbol of Canada's orderly and peaceful western settlement.

Sharing the same continent with the United States, Canada also claimed the advantage of initiating western development at a point which had taken United States over a century to reach ". . . as the 19th century was the century of the United States, the 20th century is the century of Canada . . . . The United States is the America of achievement, but Canada is the America of opportunity."[36] However the Department was not above adapting the most traditional American patriotic rhetoric to describe Canadian institutions. Reminiscent of Lincoln, one pamphlet explained that Canadian democracy "ensures a government of the people, for the people and by the people, to a degree not surpassed by any nation on earth."[37]

While the Immigration Branch relied heavily on distribution of its own publications in the United States, one major exception was the yearly Harvest Edition of the Sifton owned *Manitoba Free Press*. Purchased in large quantities, it was shipped in bulk to local agents for circulation in late autumn and early winter "when farmers have plenty of leisure and inclination to read uo [sic] these publications."[38]

Judging from the response of land seekers, the Department's pamphlets were effective for their limited purposes. They were primarily designed to further whet the appetites of prospective settlers already hungry for good land and offer Canada as a possible means of gratification. In order to meet this objective promotional pamphlets had to appear truthful to overcome the general scepticism of land seekers, factual to offer settlers reliable information and seductive to entice still further contact.

Though they appear heavy-handed today, the hard sell never obscured the persuasive intent of the publications but often paved the way for later visits by local agents or sub-agents.

As another element in its publicity campaign the Immigration Branch participated in exhibits of Canadian agricultural goods at state and county fairs across the United States.[39] These annual events had increasingly become a focal point in the social and economic life of rural America and by the turn of the century their organization and structure had become stylized. Although the annual agricultural fair has been described as the one way "show window" of the farm community, it is more correct to see it as a two way window.[40] The farmer enjoyed not only the opportunity of displaying his rich produce, but also of exposing himself to social and technological changes.

Agricultural fairs, always important annual events, were well attended. It was not unusual for ten per cent of a state's population to visit the state fair grounds each season. Iowa, which had a population of 2,224,771 in 1910, averaged an attendance of 231,538 at its state fairs between 1908 and 1911. Minnesota, with a population of 2,075,708 in 1910, averaged 311,125 state fair visitors between 1906 and 1910.[41]

A major feature of every fair was the collection of exhibits and displays by agricultural institutions, government agencies, civic groups and commercial organizations. Display booths promoting a specific cause or product often were able to attract large numbers of curious farmers who seemingly came to the fair quite prepared to be cajoled, informed, entertained or even seduced by quick talking exhibitors.[42]

Realizing the potential value of advertising booths the Department began entering fair exhibits as early as 1897. Its first venture took place at the Nebraska State Fair in Omaha. The exhibit was not undertaken alone. All Canadian fair representation at the time was within the jurisdiction of either the Department of Agriculture or the separate provinces. In Omaha the Immigration Branch worked with the Province of Manitoba. The Department arranged for exhibition space, literature and agents to man the display, while Manitoba set it up.[43] Premier Thomas Greenway of Manitoba personally agreed to authorize assembly and shipment of the exhibit to Omaha in time for the opening.[44]

Fairs or exhibitions which attracted national attention were assigned special priority. At the 1898 Trans-Mississippi and International Exposition in Omaha, co-operation between the Immigration Branch and the Department of Agriculture was required to construct and man a Canadian booth. Urging the federal Minister of Agriculture, Sidney A. Fisher, to join the proposed inter-departmental advertising venture, the Deputy Minister of the Interior prophesied that such an exhibit would be "productive of very considerable results."[45] The prediction seems to have been borne out. An official Canadian display was arranged. A section devoted to immigration work managed by the local salaried agent reportedly did "more to advertise Canada and especially the N.W.T. than all the balance of the work . . . done in the last two years."[46]

In continued co-operation with the Department of Agriculture, the policy of entering exhibits at agricultural fairs expanded from year to year. In 1898 it was decided to enter displays not only in Nebraska but also in Minnesota, Michigan, Kansas and South Dakota.[47] Simultaneously the Department instructed local and sub-agents to enter their own exhibits at local or county fairs in their jurisdictions and three portable exhibits were constructed for their use. During the fall fair season some local agents took to the road travelling the "circuit" like side-show barkers.[48] It was not long before agents were organizing their own effective displays. A salaried agent boasted that in a single season agents could "become artists in the way of exhibiting land produce from actual experience," and the Department did not have to pay outside designers.[49]

Careful preparation and presentation of agricultural and immigration displays brought a positive response not merely from farmers but from the local press as well. It was common for a Canadian exhibit to receive special coverage in the local press, especially if the Department was also an advertiser. Sometimes enthusiasm for the quality of an exhibit spilled over into enthusiasm for lands it promoted. Reviewing the Canadian booth at the 1899 Tri-State Fair in Toledo, the *Toledo Record News* went so far as to "advise the young men, who are looking for homes and a future to visit [Canada] where there is health and wealth and plenty of it."[50]

The very popularity of Canadian exhibits at state or local fairs sometimes became its own greatest enemy. By 1903 pressure from American land interests opposed to Canadian immigration activity forced rejection of Canadian applications for booths at some county fairs.[51] However, in areas where the impact of local competition was not so great, the Canadian exhibitor was a sought-after addition to a fair's attractions and revenue.[52]

One of the largest Departmental undertakings was at St. Louis. In 1904 St. Louis, then the fourth largest city in the United States, marked the centennial of the Louisiana Purchase with the Louisiana Purchase Exposition, commonly called the St. Louis Exposition. Canada was well represented. A Canadian pavilion was constructed under the supervision of Colonel William Hutchinson, Commissioner of Expositions for Canada. The Immigration Branch recognized the giant fair as an excellent opportunity to reach farmers from areas where no agent had yet operated. The St. Louis event promised to draw visitors from all across the country. If expectations can be measured by preparations, it is noteworthy that the Department authorized an initial shipment of 200,000 pieces of immigration literature to the fair grounds and ordered publication of a new pamphlet written specifically for fair visitors.

The Department's efforts were housed in a large room within a separately constructed Canadian pavilion. Here literature was easily distributed, interviews held and even arrangements for migration to Canada formalized. The immigration section was manned by two agents while a third agent, stationed in the main agricultural exhibit room, directed likely prospects to the immigration room.[53] So important was the selection of proper agents to supervise the Department's work in St. Louis that the Inspector of American Agencies demanded minimum standards for general experience, personality and physical condition be applied to their selection.

He wanted:

> . . . men who are well posted on Western Canada and able to discuss Western Canadian possibilities without reference to hard books, and to speak from their own experience and knowledge. They should also be men of good presence, easy to approach and having a talent for making acquaintances. Another requirement and an essential one would be that they be physically able to withstand the somewhat hot weather which may be expected during the time of the Exhibition. For a portion of the period, some of our agts. who are accustomed to the Southern climate should be used in the work.[54]

White, while personally visiting the Canadian exhibit, used the fair as a springboard for initiating or broadening good relations with the local press. He organized a reception for the Minnesota Editorial Association at which Canadian liquor played no small part in producing a light and friendly atmosphere. White seemed satisfied that he had drowned any future "adverse criticism in the Minnesota press" of Canadian immigration activities.[55] The exhibit itself received good press coverage. The *St. Louis Republic,* for instance, published a full page feature entitled "Canada at the World's Fair" in a Sunday edition.[56]

Although the Department never doubted the value of its effort at St. Louis, in one area the immediate effect was unexpectedly negative.[57] The immigration figures for 1904 showed a decline in the numbers of settlers entering Canada not only from Missouri but from the neighbouring states of Indiana, Iowa, Kansas, Nebraska and many of the southern states. This was attributed in part to the election year and, in part, to the fair, both of which monopolized the enthusiasm of many farmers who, it was said, would not consider moving to Canada while the excitement lasted. This may be a questionable assessment, but the following year the trek northward was renewed with increased vigour.[58]

In review, the Department was satisfied that fairs offered an excellent vehicle for reaching American farmers. They allowed for large scale face-to-face contact between agents and potential settlers in an exhibit which itself dramatized the productivity of western Canadian lands. One agent reported that a visit to the Canadian agricultural booth "was a revelation to many who had been told that our North West was too cold to produce sustenance for man or beast."[59]

As a social event the fair may well have made many farmers more responsive to Canadian propaganda. It was often occasion for a family outing making a farmer's wife or older sons equally ripe for Canadian promotional work. Thus, the fair enabled agents to reach beyond the head of the household to other potential converts.

In addition to promotional techniques bringing knowledge of Canada to American farmers, the Immigration Branch instituted programmes which actually brought Americans to Canada for a first hand look. These undertakings were of two distinct varieties – visits by groups of prospective settlers and visits by touring newspaper associations.

American newspaper associations had long been organizing spring and fall excursions for their membership but the first such visit to western Canada took place in 1898. A joint invitation for a trans-

Canada rail tour was extended to the Minnesota Editorial Association by Clifford Sifton and the President of the Canadian Pacific Railway, Sir William Van Horne. The visit of the Minnesota group was regarded such a success that it was followed later that same year with a tour by the Wisconsin Editorial Association.[60] The fostering of cordial relations with the American press and the publication of numerous flattering articles as a direct result of these excursions seemed ample reward for any effort the Immigration Branch exerted in connection with these visits. Indeed, almost immediately, the visits by newsmen and editors became routine.

The precise cost of these press tours cannot be determined. As close co-operation between railroad and government was a prerequisite of any such undertaking, special financial arrangements existed during the initial stages of the programme. Before the tours of 1906 no costs, except those for small incidentals, were recorded in the *Reports of the Auditor General*. However, in spite of any agreements which might have previously prevailed between government and railways, by 1906 the government was being forced to subsidize the cost of rail transportation.[61]

The Department was displeased with the necessity of paying for railway service on ventures felt to be mutually beneficial. A second visit by the Minnesota Editorial Association in 1908 was almost aborted in the wake of demands by the Canadian Northern Railway for the payment of transportation costs. Writing to the railway's Superintendent of Publicity, White expressed shocked disappointment at the railroad's position:

> I do not think it is reasonable, nor fair, that the government should be asked to pay for hauling this train. The Government already spends vast sums of money in the development of the country in which your road is interested, and to be asked to further tax itself does not seem to me to be right. It is only just that your company should do what it can and everything that it can to further a cause, which will be instrumental in the development of the country tributary to your system.[62]

It is unknown whether White received any satisfaction from the railway in this instance; however, if this battle was won, the war itself was lost. The following year the government authorized payment of $1,137.87 to the Canadian Pacific and $2,233.30 to the Canadian Northern to cover the costs of a visit to Canada by the Michigan Press Association.[63]

Perhaps in an effort to recoup some of its cost, or to get the best possible promotional mileage out of the excursion vehicle, the Department worked out a method whereby press associations would cover the costs of their trips through "free" advertising. Newspaper associations were pleased with such arrangements. In 1906 the secretary of the Illinois Press Association and editor of the *Jerseyville Democrat* complained that he was only sorry he could not convince the American railroads over which the group travelled *en route* to Canada to accept free advertising in exchange for expenses as had been done in the Dominion.[64]

The Michigan Press Association wanted to guarantee themselves a trip and were willing to begin advertising well in advance of their excursion. The association's vice president and editor of the *Battle Creek Journal* outlined his delegation's proposal to the Immigration Branch.

> We would put [the tour] on a bona fide business basis and agree to pay dollar for dollar in advertising for every dollar expended, [sic] in fact we will go even beyond that and see to it that such matter as you supply us will appears [sic] in all the papers of the association whether represented on the trip or not . . . In this case we will promise you the best kind of advertising and for each dollar which will be expended you would get two or three in the best publications in the state, most of it in advance of the trip.[65]

To ensure that the desired copy would be in the hands of Michigan newspaper editors well in advance of the group's departure for Canada, White was invited to visit Detroit to make final arrangements. It was recommended by the association that publication begin during the winter months as "This is the time when it should be of the greatest service and there is nothing in the way of preventing starting it."[66]

The grand tours undertaken by most press organizations were similar even where size of delegations varied. The government ably accommodated both small groups and those as large as the 600-member American Editorial Association's 1899 delegation representing over 1,000 newspapers.[67] Special press trains which wound their way across Canada at harvest time generally had sleeping car facilities and commissary cars although, on occasion, accommodations could be juggled with the size of the group.[68] Naturally, most of the time on the tour was spent on the prairies, especially in areas where good crops could be found and transplanted Americans were available to sing the praises of their new homes. Nevertheless, tourist spots were not neglected. Pleasure stops were arranged at Banff and Lake Louise. In large centres sight-seeing tours and entertainment were provided. A 1906 Pennsylvania press delegation stopped in Winnipeg at fair time where it was prearranged for the "City Council and Exhibition Board to give them a trip on the Winnipeg Electric Street Car lines around the city, and leave them at the exhibition, where the industrial fair was in progress. It being American Day they were entertained to a complimentary luncheon in the Director's Building."[69]

If tours suffered from one major defect it was that press groups were constantly being rushed. Perhaps deliberately not enough time was spent at any one spot to ensure the newsmen anything more than a cursory impression of the community. Towns *en route* had their own complaint. They often provided visitors with free meals and were upset when visitors "had time only to eat the meal provided and then rush on [to] some other place in time for another meal, and then from these elsewhere." A slower pace was often requested.[70]

Whether a newsman ate or, as was likely not uncommon, drank his way across Canada, the most important result the Department expected from the tours was a sizeable output of articles which each visitor was to write. Explaining the small expenditures connected with early visits by press delegations, Sifton assured the Commons that visiting editors

> . . . will go back to their homes and give favourable reports about what they have seen. Of course, this is the best kind of advertising. It does not cost much, and it is the very best kind of advertising we can get, because when the editors are writing from the result of their own personal observations, they are much more likely to impress the people than if ordinary advertising were presented to them.[71]

Usually the articles were favourable to the Canadian immigration effort, but not always. In 1903 the Illinois delegation disappointed their hosts when unfavourable articles appeared in the *Chicago Times*.[72] As a result the Department made special efforts to "guide" editors toward meeting government's expectations. Special information booklets and press releases were supplied both during and after visits. Indeed, it was possible for a newsman to totally avoid work by regurgitating press releases supplied by the Immigration Branch instead of writing his own articles.[73] In one instance the Department reported having received assurance from tour members that in future all adverse reports about Canada would be "blue penciled" and those who wrote the negative articles would be reported to the Immigration Branch and never again be allowed to make the trip across Canada.[74]

On returning home editors were reminded by letter that the Immigration Branch looked forward to receiving copies of all material they published on their Canadian visit. Here, too, guidance was offered. Newspapermen were advised that while it was interesting to mention the majestic beauty of the Rocky Mountains or the peaceful quiet of Lake Louise, most attention should be paid to the fertility, productivity and prosperity witnessed on the prairies, especially the success of American settlers.[75]

Not all editors would comply with the Department's outline but most made an effort to do so. The editor of the *Shelby Sentinel* of Shelbyville, Kentucky, wrote White a most unusual apology for the newspaper's seeming inability to meet the Department's requests promptly.

> I have already up in type my first installment to my paper, and, I could not therefore follow the lines set forth in your letter. In next weeks [sic] issue I hope to get to the kernel of the subject. When I arrived home, I found my office in uproar, with every member of the force drunk except my lady stenographer. I took some time to set matters aright, and I could not then give my Canadian trip the attention that I hope to.[76]

Many articles on the tours and stories on the west appeared in American newspapers. The Department collected, edited and republished them for wider American circulation in pamphlet form and they made convincing propaganda material.[77] But, as was so often the case, the newsmen did more than tell Canada's "story to millions of people through the agency of the pen."[78] They established or maintained contact with the Department and its programme. They remained open to more articles about Canada and, according to White, fought off attempts to have their journals used in any anti-Canadian press campaigns.[79]

The prospect of having Americans proselytizing Americans encouraged the Immigration Branch to underwrite a programme of farmers' excursions into the Canadian west. Such tours were not an original innovation. Once again, the Department was adopting a time tested land sales technique long employed by American land interests, especially land grant railroads.[80] In the early nineties this promotional device was brought to Canada by the Canadian Pacific Railway.[81]

Practical operation of the farmers' tours was uncomplicated. Agents working among a group of farmers encouraged them to select a few of their number to act as the group's delegates for a visit to the Canadian prairies with all expenses paid. As it was felt that the degree of a delegate's eventual impact on his community was directly proportional to his social status in that community, agents prided themselves on seeking out already influential farmers as delegates. A salaried agent in Michigan was especially pleased with a delegation he sent out in 1899. He noted, "they were without exception, practical farmers, most of them having served as municipal officers in some capacity in their respective townships."[82] An agent in South Dakota was able to send out a recent member of the state's legislature among his delegates.[83] In the case of ethnocultural groups, agents attempted to convince influential members of the community's leadership to tour possible colony sites or visit persons of that group already in the west.[84]

Often accompanied by the government agent who organized the trip, small groups of farm delegates explored the Canadian west during the early autumn. They were encouraged to examine government and private land offerings and meet with transplanted Americans. The railroads provided transportation and were often rewarded with the sale of property to land-hungry farmers. If a farmer did not pick a homestead site or buy a piece of land for himself, he might well have done so for his son. Sales of land to delegates were brisk and in many delegations few farmers "returned [home] without having bought or homesteaded land."[85]

The Department often integrated delegates into the ongoing promotional work in their home communities. As part of the agreement under which they visited Canada, returned delegates wrote a report of what they had seen and done. As with the articles by newsmen, the farmers' reports were collected, edited and published in suitable form for distribution in the United States.[86] The majority of such reports were simple accounts of the productivity and prosperity witnessed on the prairies. One aimed at Canadian farmers in the United States was overly florid.

> 'They will go Westward where the star of empire takes its sway.' 'Soon the East must bow to the West for she holds in her hands the keys to the graineries of the world.' In conclusion we [delegates] want to thank you one and all for the many acts of kindness extended to us; from the highest government or railroad officials to the humblest

homesteader in his little shack. Every one gave us a warm hand of welcome, not only to us but to one another also. They made us think of the good old Roman days as told by Lord Macaulay, where the rich men helped the poor and the poor men loved the great. O yes, Canadians, come home, where as good a farm awaits you, almost for the asking, as rests beneath God's sunshine. The Flag that floats o'er England's seas lives and loves you. And to you who were born under other suns she extends a welcome on the same terms as her own children. Come and share her peace and prosperity.[87]

Returning delegates were also encouraged to submit articles on their findings to their local newspapers and to give lectures to farmers' groups. Public meetings organized by agents saw delegates, as if at a revival meeting, commit themselves to Canadian migration and encourage others to follow suit.[88] In question and answer sessions the returned delegates were especially effective in combating misconceptions about Canada, especially with regard to its climate.[89] Agents might also fit returned farmers into their sub-agent network or have them act as quasi sub-agents receiving no bonuses for their work. Many of those who accepted the formal sub-agent position reportedly used their commission to finance their own migration. Still others acted as "distribution agents" for Departmental literature.[90]

Numbers of delegates varied from year to year and delegation to delegation. In 1902 alone there were 465 delegations that made their way across the prairies.[91] However, at least one agent foresaw the delegation system becoming increasingly less effective as knowledge of western Canada became more widespread. In 1904 one agent recommended less reliance upon the delegate tours, claiming that the momentum of existing immigration was enough to make this promotional tactic unnecessary except in newly opened agency areas.[92] Since agents in the field set up the tours, each could judge the effectiveness of the farmers' excursions on his work and then decide for himself whether the programme was required in his territory. The programme itself was not discontinued.

While it is difficult to measure with accuracy the degrees to which the Department's overall publicity campaign affected the American migration, it is probable that the effect was considerable. For consumption outside the Immigration Branch, the Department was eager to attribute any increased interest in the Canadian west to its own activities. Appearing before the Commons Committee on Agriculture and Colonization, the Deputy Minister indicated that "during the months of the year when the department withdraws its advertisements interest in Canadian lands shows a sharp decline."[93] However, he was conveniently confusing the facts. The actual reason the Department withheld its advertising during certain periods was because of an anticipated decline in interest while farmers devoted their attention to more immediate concerns such as the harvest. Nevertheless, the Deputy Minister tried to leave the impression that there was a quantifiable correlation between the Department's publicity and immigration statistics. This, of course, cannot be proved.

More realistic was the observation of committee member and Liberal Member of Parliament for Kent West, George Stephens, who saw the advertising of the Department as analogous to the promotional work of any business firm.

> A business man advertises his business, but he never knows, he never did know, and never will know, exactly what effect that advertising had on the increase of his business. If his business increases, he naturally thinks it is because he advertises; and I have no doubt that will be the case with regard to immigration.[94]

Accepting this business analogy, a few conclusions can be drawn. The Department was appealing to a selective clientele, although even within the desired group the Immigration Branch claimed that quality rather than quantity was considered a major concern. Propaganda was selectively geared toward encouraging white American farmers to migrate from farm to farm. There was no emphasis on any change in their style of life. While publicity could not be confined entirely to the agricultural class, the major inducement to migration, free or cheap land, guaranteed that migration would be self-limiting. Non-farmers could and did take advantage of the land offerings in the Canadian west, but advertising was never designed to foster their emigration.[95]

Advertising tactics, while not original, were flexible. When the Department adapted techniques of publicity to meet changing needs, the alterations were generally in emphasis rather than in method. For instance, while the simple educational tone of earlier publicity was replaced by production figures as immigration increased, the means of reaching farmers remained the same. As White noted in 1906, continued success was reason enough not to tamper with the established programme.

> It has not been considered advisable to make any changes in the method of advertising. The plan adopted in the early

stages of the work, which has brought the number of settlers up from less than 1,000 to nearly 60,000 in the space of nine years, has been considered good enough to adhere to. No other plan can be submitted that would be more effective.[96]

In the final analysis the publicity campaign of the Immigration Branch did not create demand, it merely guided it. In spite of the need to compete actively with American land interests, the Department was promoting a product for which there was an already existing demand. Land hunger did not have to be artificially stimulated or maintained. The Department was faced only with making Canadian lands a credible alternative to land offered elsewhere and in this the Immigration Branch was successful.

THE ONLY DRAWBACK.

UNCLE SAM: (Looking over Canadian West with Mr. Bull) THEY SAY ITS A FINE LOOKIN'
COUNTRY. JOHN. BUT DURN IT ALL. YOU CAN'T SEE IT FOR THE WHEAT.

Dept. of Interior, To Canada:
For Investment, *Ottawa 1903.*

UNCLE SAM — WHERE THERE IS MONEY TO BE MADE
YOU'LL FIND A YANKEE.

ON THE MARCH TO
WESTERN CANADA.
(FROM PHOTO)

THOUSANDS
OF
U. S
SETTLERS
MOVED
TO
WESTERN CANADA
IN 1902 &3

Dept. of Interior, To Canada:
For Investment, *Ottawa 1903.*

ON THE MARCH TO WESTERN CANADA FROM
CRAWFORD, NEBRASKA.

PRAIRIE SCHOONERS MOVING NORTHWARD
INTO CANADA.

EMIGRANTS LEAVING COTTONWOOD CO.,
MINNESOTA, FOR WESTERN CANADA, 1902.

Public Archives of Canada

TRAIN LOAD OF SETTLERS AND THEIR EFFECTS,
WHICH ARRIVED IN CANADA FROM SOUTH DAKOTA.

Public Archives of Canada

BLACK SETTLERS, ATHABASCA LANDING, ALTA.

TYPICAL AGENCY OFFICE

The Other Lands
[COMPETITION]

Amid the excitement of the 1893 Columbia World Exposition in Chicago the American Historical Association met to hold its annual convention. Among the scholarly papers delivered to the gathering was historian Frederick Jackson Turner's "The Significance of the Frontier in American History." In what could be interpreted as an eulogy for the American frontier, Turner submitted an analysis of American development based upon the nation's birthright of unsettled land. As Turner put it, "The existence of an area of free land, its continuous recession, and the advance of American settlement westward, explained American development." By 1893 land resources no longer appeared inexhaustible, and Turner lamented that the frontier had vanished. An era had ended ". . . four centuries from the discovery of America, at the end of a hundred years under the Constitution, the frontier has gone, and with it has closed the first period of American history." Turner was not yet prepared to predict what would act as the new catalyst for national development in post-frontier America.[1]

In his Chicago address Turner did more than merely report the conclusions of his research or express a personal uneasiness over the frontier's passing. He added scholarly substance to an already developing sense of national urgency over the future course of American growth. The apparent end of the frontier and the closure of its settlement "safety valve" posed potential problems which others had already acknowledged. Typical was the *New York Herald* in 1891. Reporting a land rush in Oklahoma, it suggested possible dangers which lay in wait for a nation which could no longer offer its people the security of unoccupied land.

> That there should be a rush for these acres is not surprising. What would happen in France or England or Belgium or Germany if twenty thousand homesteads were to be offered, practically without price to first comers? These countries are crowded. Life is a constant grind, food is difficult to get, wages are low. A million acres of free gift would set the people wild. And we have reached that state in our history when it sets us wild also. Seventy-five years ago land was to be had, almost anywhere, for the asking. But the people have mightily increased in number and what spare acres we once had have been mostly taken up.[2]

While Turner was not alone in reflecting a growing uneasiness over the future course of American development, it was in fact too early to read an epitaph for the frontier. As one historian has suggested, there may have been a "psychological" closing of the frontier but there had not been a "material" closing of the frontier.[3] Farms were still available. In large pockets across the western half of the nation land still lay open to settlement. Private lands awaited the right price and public lands required only those ready to fulfil homestead obligations before ownership was granted. The lure of lands in western Canada was thus not unchallenged. Vested interests determined to fill empty American lands or hold the restless American farmer at home continued active in promotion of American real-estate.

Between 1896 and 1911 territory which previously lay unoccupied, often dismissed as undesirable for farming, was pushed onto the public market. Indeed, as late as 1900 the American public domain still contained over five hundred million acres of unclaimed land.[4] Between 1868 and 1897 a total of seventy million acres of land was settled under the Homestead Act of 1862; but between 1897 and 1917 land applied for under the 1862 act and supplemental legislation established claim to another one hundred million acres of the public domain.[5] Perhaps, in part as a response to growing fears that the nation would face a prolonged domestic crisis if the areas open to settlement had truly disappeared, Congress supported schemes granting farmers easy access to remaining American lands. Historian Paul W. Gates suggests that the American tradition of free land remained so powerful a part of the national mythology that Congress dared not ignore the demand for settlement lands. So long committed to a policy of free land, congressmen were "reluctant to believe that the era of free lands for farms was over after 1900."[6] Rather than allow a momentary dilemma to become unchecked anxiety, re-examination of available homestead lands was encouraged.

Much of the land which federal and state governments now earmarked for settlement had long been ignored as marginal, unproductive tracts on the "Great American Desert." Semi-arid regions previously regarded as too dry for farming were re-evaluated. A growing pressure for irrigation resulted. With continual prodding from western states which viewed irrigation as a partial panacea for retarded economic development and from landowners who managed to juggle the rhetoric of private property with public funding of irrigation, the federal government found itself drawn into long term reclamation projects. Realizing the economic and political importance of the irrigation issue, Theodore Roosevelt boasted that his first priority upon accession to the Presidency "was [to be] the work of reclamation."[7]

Irrigation was not new to the American west.[8] But in 1902 the presidentially supported Newlands Bill passed through Congress allotting public funds for irrigation projects to benefit both selected public and private lands on a scale never before undertaken. In the long term irrigation work did not prove as successful as had been initially anticipated – more placebo than panacea – but the immediate result of projected irrigation schemes was to create the prospect of new and inexpensive areas opening to prospective settlers.[9] Thus, land-hungry farmers might look hopefully to reclamation projects for a resurrection of the farm frontier.

Unfortunately for many Indians, the land hunger which erupted in the late nineties did not confine itself to unclaimed land. Between 1890 and 1918 approximately eighteen and a quarter million acres of Indian reservation lands were thrown open under pressure of would-be settlers. Indian protests were cast aside as farmers swept in to stake their homesteads.[10]

The Immigration Branch argued that its promotional operations were perceived as a threat in some American quarters and resulted in heightened interest in domestic settlement schemes. Even before the passage of the Newlands Bill in 1902, the Department claimed that renewed attention on the American public domain was, in large measure, a response to ever increasing success of Canadian immigration activities. William J. White, Inspector of Agencies in the United States, suggested that the new American public land offerings represented Washington's attempt to create an attractive alternative to Canadian migration for land-hungry American farmers.

103

> I especially desire to direct . . . attention to the fact that
> owing doubtless of the active propaganda carried on by
> our immigration branch in the United States, an agitation
> has begun in some of the states putting forth great efforts not
> only to retain the people which they now have but inducing
> new settlers to occupy their vacant lands, which they now
> have opened for settlement. In line with this, legislation has
> been recently passed in the House of Representatives and
> Senate at Washington, opening up several Indian and
> military reservations in Wisconsin, Minnesota, the Dakotas
> and Montana, also in Oklahoma Territory, which has been
> idle for some time.[11]

The subsequent passage of the Newlands Bill tended to confirm Departmental fears. The author of the bill, Senator Francis G. Newlands of Nevada, emphasized that his bill was designed, in part, to offer an alternative to Canadian lands. If irrigation did not make vast expanses of territory available for settlement, the United States, he warned, would continue "losing the brawn and muscle which ought to be utilized in building and extending this great country."[12]

The progress of irrigation work was closely watched from Ottawa. White observed with some concern that "the United States government has spent . . . millions of dollars in ditches, reservoirs, and whatever else was needed in the reclamation of lands considered barren."[13] But, in actual fact reclamation work lagged while land values in areas designed for irrigation rocketed. The prime beneficiary of this land boom was not the land-seeking farmer. Although the attraction of irrigated lands might draw potential settlers away from exploring Canadian lands, quick-moving speculators and promoters were first on the scene laying out claims to homestead sites or investing in tracts of private land. Investment of a little time and capital while waiting for water and settlers to arrive brought rich financial rewards. The average increase in all land values for the eleven western states in which reclamation work was undertaken rose by 110.3 per cent between 1905 and 1913. The value of reclaimed lands in these same states jumped by 759.2 per cent during the same period.[14] Profits preceded crops.

It is difficult at best to distinguish statistically between the American farmer and the small speculator. However, the *bona fide* settler reaped little initial benefit from irrigation. As a former Assistant Commissioner of Reclamation later confirmed, "The settler was the victim." Not all land was gobbled up by speculators but enough to eventually "come very close to ruining" the reclamation programme.[15] A land-hungry farmer not fast enough to file a desirable homestead claim eventually had to negotiate a sizeable loan in order to acquire lands from a speculator. If, as was often the case, productivity of the land could not match the demands of the debt payments, foreclosure ensued. As a result cautious farmers seeing others fail or having failed once themselves shied away from lands where the potential return on investment was less than that offered elsewhere, particularly in Canada. Nevertheless, the appeal of public domain lands in the United States and the promotional tactics of local real-estate agents and speculators did tempt enough buyers to disconcert Canadian immigration officials.

Renewed land hunger, partially fed by the newly opened irrigation lands, also focused new attention on marginally productive tracts of land still in the possession of railroads or other private interests.[16] Though the emphasis upon agricultural development had been gradually reduced in the long-term planning of many American railroads, the sale of lands by land grant railroads or their agents continued to be actively promoted after the turn of the century.[17]

In northern Wisconsin and Michigan land cleared by the commercial lumberman's axe was "wishfully assigned to agriculture."[18] Land pockmarked with tree stumps may not be beautiful but the transition from cut-over to cultivation, from forest to farm, was a familiar part of the American agricultural tradition. In this case, the lumberman had already taken both the trouble and profit from clearing out the trees. Addressing the Wisconsin State Historical Convention at Madison in 1899, the judge of the 17th Judiciary Circuit, reminded the gathering that the shift from axe to plough was a welcome indication of movement down the evolutionary road toward progress with stability. As the judge put it, "With the decline of lumbering has come the development of agriculture and dairying, which ensures a more permanent and abundant prosperity."[19] From the Canadian perspective, however, the sale of cut-over lands appeared as simply a sly case of land promoters and tract owners unloading unwanted real-estate in direct competition with Canadian lands.

Thus, in spite of a growing American fear that land, a traditional backbone of American growth, was no longer available for settlement, the opposite was proving to be the case. The increased demand for land following the 1897 economic upswing spurred re-examination of marginal lands, irrigation and marketing of previously ignored railroad and stump lands. Perhaps the sale of good farm land could not always keep up with demand, but the less cautious farmer could and did find land. He was openly courted, especially by the southwest, mountain and northern prairie states. In regions where ranchers had lost their battle to retain the open range, states made new and organized efforts to attract settlers. It was not uncommon for public and private interests to join forces in land promotion. Like the Canadian government, they too had access to the best promotional techniques available to exploit existing land hunger.[20]

Railroads servicing under-developed areas, for instance, not only pushed the sale of their own lands but also the sale of all lands from which they would receive the "haul."[21] Local businessmen joined, often reluctantly, to assist in promotional schemes. They regarded an inflow of population (or in some areas, a reduced outflow of population) as crucial to continued prosperity. However, the emergence of close intra-regional co-operation led to the development of inter-regional competition. The continued availability of land in separate areas of the United States, as well as in Canada, made co-operation in land promotion difficult between competing regions.

The position of the Canadian Immigration Branch regarding the presence of marketable farm land in the United States was generally to wait patiently for the well to dry. Compared to the seeming boundlessness of available Canadian lands, it was believed that American lands would eventually reach their saturation point. White initially argued that newly opened areas of the American public domain could only remain a competitive factor "during the period it would take to occupy them, and judging from the number of people who [were] in a state of unrest, this [would] not be long."[22]

Superintendent of Immigration, Frank Pedley, also assumed that demand would shortly outstrip supply in the United States. Appearing before the Commons Committee on Agriculture and Colonization in April, 1901, he suggested that any setbacks the Department might face from American competition would be temporary. Indeed, as land seekers would soon overrun available American land, Canada would be the natural beneficiary of continued land hunger.

> . . . there is no doubt that [dissatisfaction] is a reason [for immigration] and the land pressure is so great, also. All or nearly all the desirable free land has gone, and whenever an Indian reservation or a new piece of land is thrown open you find a large number of American citizens flocking in there and camping around it for months before it is open. Then

taxes are high, and conditions of life are not as favourable as with us, and they want to move along the line of least resistance.[23]

The Oklahoma land rush of 1902 verified the Department's optimism. The Immigration Agent in Chicago observed that the opening of land for settlement on the Kiowa-Comanche Indian reservation expected on Independence Day had attracted far more farmers than could possibly file homestead claims. Many of those turned away disappointed, he suggested, would be ripe for Canadian picking.[24]

The Department was fully aware of the overflow that Oklahoma fever was producing. The salaried agent in Kansas City was instructed to go to Oklahoma and promote Canadian lands among settlers unlikely to receive one of the fourteen hundred homesteads to be offered. He found that Oklahoma land was in such demand that ten to twelve settlers arrived for each parcel of land. As the agent correctly pointed out, local railroad agents had actively encouraged an excessive influx of land-hungry farmers, thus inadvertently assembling his prospective clientele. Setting up an agricultural exhibit in a tent, the agent reported that settlers "express themselves surprised at [Canadian] products, and . . . declare that on failure to secure homes [in Oklahoma] they will at once go to Western Canada."[25] As a result of his work, about three hundred families were plucked out of Oklahoma and resettled in Alberta.[26]

In spite of the Oklahoma episode the supply of American land showed no signs of disappearing from the market. Rather than fill up as the Immigration Branch anticipated, continued promotion and sale of American lands plagued the Canadian programme throughout the Liberal ministry. As late as 1909 White offered the observation that Canadian lands might be cheaper and more productive than lands of the United States, but American lands held one distinct advantage: they were within the farmer's homeland. In spite of the best efforts of the Department "the desire to keep within one's own country is something that is hard to overcome." The most productive tactic available to Canadian agents in countering an American settler's patriotic reluctance to look northward was, White contended, a firm personal belief in the "superior advantages and opportunities afforded in Canada." But this did not always prove enough.[27]

One of the major regions in which the Department suffered the full brunt of American competition was northern Wisconsin. Here competition quickly reached a state of open hostility. Canadian agents working to promote migration out of northern Wisconsin confronted local lumber interests and railroads selling cut-over timber lands not just in the hope of turning a quick profit, but in an effort to guarantee the area a viable economic future as the lumbermen moved on. By actively encouraging out-migration no Canadian agent could be a welcome addition to the community.

The Wisconsin Central Railway, working in conjunction with the Great Northern and Northern Pacific Railroads tried "everything in their power to keep their people at home." If a prospective farmer could not find lands in northern Wisconsin to his liking, the railroads guided him towards available railroad lands in the Dakotas, Minnesota or Montana. Turning its guns against agent Thomas Currie, Stevens Point, Wisconsin, the Wisconsin Central undermined his fledgeling sub-agent organization. He charged the railroad with deliberately and systematically buying off his sub-agents, as he put it, "by offering them better inducements than it is possible for us to offer."[28] Some of Currie's sub-agents later reappeared selling cut over timber lands. The Canadian agent reassuringly clung to his one advantage. Currie informed his superiors, the "up hill work" was made much lighter by the recognizably superior quality of the lands he could offer in Canada.[29]

In 1901 Currie was transferred from Stevens Point to the larger centre of Milwaukee. But here too he faced stiff competition from railroad and lumber interests. He informed the Immigration Branch, "We still receive in this state strong opposition from railroad land owners, who feel somewhat hurt at every settler we send away." Nevertheless, the Canadian agent remained optimistic: "The more they give us the more we appreciate the effort and the prospects for the future are much brighter than ever before."[30] Some years later Currie would look back upon his arduous battle with private land interests of northern Wisconsin as a great personal victory.

> I took hold of this state eleven years ago without a friend in it, a stranger among strangers. I met the strongest opposition that was possible for a man to receive. Millions of acres of land in the northern part of this state being owned by wealthy lumbermen who wanted to sell those lands to citizens of Wisconsin. They did everything to battle against me but I succeeded in overcoming the strongest opponents . . . .[31]

Currie did not remain alone on the Wisconsin firing line. In 1902 James MacLachlan opened an office in Wausau, northern Wisconsin.[32]

Immediately he too ran headlong into bitter opposition from local land interests who would continually plague his operations. Assessing his situation, MacLachlan pleaded for a transfer.

> If there is any chance of my securing a better field of operations I would be pleased. There is so much land in the North here still unoccupied and they are fighting so hard for settlers themselves here that it makes work difficult. I have worked hard but am still not satisfied with results, altho [sic] not discouraged. If there is any chance to be moved I would be pleased to get a large city and better populated state [like Indiana] where people are looking for new homes.[33]

MacLachlan's request was denied. In its place the Immigration Branch promised MacLachlan all possible assistance and assurance that, in view of the conditions under which he operated, his efforts would get special notice in Ottawa.[34]

Unfortunately for MacLachlan the Department was far away while the competition was his neighbours. Like a prohibitionist in a saloon, the Canadian agent had set up office in the town which was both headquarters for major lumber companies and terminal of the Wisconsin Central Railway.[35] The lumber companies, aided by railroad interests, were busily converting their local cut-over holdings into dairy farms.[36] As the lumbering industry moved out, railroad and local businessmen welcomed each settler as a new recruit in the battle to stave off economic depression. With high priority set on local placement of settlers and land sales, every possible obstacle was placed in the way of MacLachlan's work.

In 1903 local business and real-estate interests in northern Wisconsin pressured county fair officials to reject all MacLachlan's applications to exhibit at fairs in the area. The boycott was effective. The Canadian agent reported himself barred from county fair after county fair within his assigned territory. In one notable instance, after sending fair officials three letters and two telegrams on the abrupt change in policy, MacLachlan was incorrectly informed that the fair had been cancelled even though advertising for the annual event was still underway.[37]

Excluded from setting up a display booth at another county fair, MacLachlan took the initiative; he exhibited Canadian goods in a rented store near the fairgrounds. He informed the Department, that "by a liberal distribution of hand bills, large crowds were attracted to our exhibits during the days and evenings of the fair." Such a manoeuvre, however, proved less effective and more costly than exhibiting within the fair itself.[38]

MacLachlan's scramble to collect settlers among the limited number of farmers in northern Wisconsin was further complicated by the unceasing hostility of the local press. The Wausau newspaper accepted no Canadian advertising and ran periodic features on local farmers who returned from Canada disappointed with what they had found and disillusioned with allegedly unfulfilled promises of Canadian immigration agents.[39] White laid responsibility for such press reports at the door of competing land promoters. It was more than possible, he proposed, that persons masquerading as settlers were cleverly sent to Canada by northern Wisconsin land and railroad interests just so they could return with slanderous stories of personal hardship and government trickery. Far-fetched perhaps, but, White reasoned, such tactics should be interpreted as an indication that interest in Canada was growing and business circles in the area sought stronger measures to ensure the movement to Canada would be halted.[40]

It was agent MacLachlan, however, who had to face the brunt of local opposition, especially when it manifested itself in abusive personal attacks. His life in Wausau was made as disagreeable as the local competition could arrange for it to become. In a letter to the Inspector of United States Agencies, MacLachlan reluctantly related an incident which revealed both the intensity of ill-will which MacLachlan's work generated and the gutter level to which personal attacks had stooped by the summer of 1903. The Wausau agent was concerned, angry and nervous.

> About six weeks ago, in arriving at my office one morning, I found a small package tied to the knob of my door. Upon opening it I found it contained a "French safe" filled with cotton battin [sic], and a card attached to it with the following, "suck this, its good enough for a canuck – why cant [sic] you work in your own country?" It was very disgusting and I felt it, but said nothing about the matter, thinking it was better not to notice it. I have as much pluck as the average man, but it was rather trying, as well as discouraging to live in a small place like this where everyone gives you the cold shoulder, and you are the recipient of such contemptible things as the above.[41]

By the end of 1903 the Immigration Branch was forced to concede; its operations in northern Wisconsin had completely collapsed under the weight of local opposition. Appearing before the Commons Committee on Agriculture and Colonization, James A. Smart, Deputy

Minister of the Interior, admitted that the Department was considering the removal of its northern Wisconsin agent to more fruitful grounds.[42] Soon thereafter MacLachlan closed down operations in Wausau and gladly accepted a transfer to Watertown, South Dakota.[43]

The opposition faced by MacLachlan in northern Wisconsin was unusual only in the intensity and extent of its success. An extreme case, it contained many elements commonly found in the situations of other immigration personnel across the United States. As early as 1898 many complained of work being hampered by the unscrupulous tactics employed by their rivals. The agent in St. Paul explained, for instance, that he was forced to maintain a protective vigil over settlers who had already committed themselves to Canada. "It is imperative," he wrote the Department, "that [Canada-bound settlers] should be closely looked after, taken to my office and guarded every moment they spend in this city, as land companies of this state have their agents everywhere looking after just such men, and use every power in their means to induce those passing through to their lands."[44] In 1900 an agent in South Dakota accused his opposition of using every possible manoeuvre to pirate settlers. As he stepped up his own efforts to divert land-hungry farmers toward Canada, he found himself in direct conflict with promoters from North Dakota, Washington and Colorado who "swarmed" into South Dakota armed with wild claims about the desirability of their particular state's available land. No man's work was sacred. Settlers committed to one agent were openly courted by all the others, presumably including the Canadian. He confessed to having lost fifteen families in this way. With some alarm he informed the Department, "Had I not carefully looked after [settlers committed to Canada] the number [lost] would have been doubled or trebled. Everything in the way of misrepresentation on the one side and glittering inducements on the other, was made use of to turn people west and south."[45]

Organizing farmers in Illinois, the Chicago agent complained that American land peddlers were making it difficult to hold public meetings for fear of identifying those local farmers considering the purchase of lands elsewhere. Not wishing to do his competitors' spade work, the Canadian was forced to rely on personal house calls in response to letters of inquiry to make new contacts. When possible such a visit was enlarged to include neighbouring farmers as well. However time-consuming, he recommended this tactic as the best method of denying competing land promoters "the chance to find out where [local agents] are working."[46] Another agent advised "constant vigilance and personal contact with the people" as the dual priorities in overcoming opposition attempts to impede emigration.[47]

It is possible, of course, that some immigration personnel exaggerated the impact of the competition to cover their own deficiencies, but, in general, agents seemed to have honestly appraised and confronted their rivals. Agent M. V. McInnes, Detroit, explained to the Department that any evaluation of an individual agent's efforts in the United States had to account for the handicap he suffered as a result of battling a well organized competitive machine. During the first years of work in the United States, he remembered, agents had little experience in dealing with American colonization or land-sale programmes long in existence. Patience and understanding, he assured Ottawa, had been required and rewarded.[48]

The Immigration Branch was concerned lest its American competitors form a united front against Canadian immigration activity. In reality no such coalition proved possible. Although Canadian lands held a singularly strong magnetism for land-hungry farmers, an organization designed to oppose the Canadian movement required a degree of co-operation perhaps possible within a state or region, but practically impossible between states. Thus, in spite of fears to the contrary, the Department was inadvertently protected by inter-state rivalry and inter-land company mistrust which rendered any anti-Canadian coalition unlikely.

Nevertheless, one such coalition was unsuccessfully attempted in 1902 as a number of American land companies organized a publicity bureau in St. Louis to initiate an anti-Canadian propaganda drive. Though the bureau at first seemed to be well funded, it dissolved after only a few months of operation. Its influence was negligible. White suggested that the bureau's early demise resulted from American newspapers, long courted by the Department, refusing "to open their columns to the attacks that were made in an organized way."[49] Equally important, the group's cohesion, dependent upon common antagonism to Canadian Immigration Branch activity, was not strong enough to overcome already existing rivalry between the independently competing members.

The prospect that railroads selling or supporting land sales would eventually unite against Canadian migration was also viewed as a potential threat. Those American railroads with a vested interest in population increase had separately opposed Canadian activity in the past. As early as 1900 the agent in Kansas City warned against "private corporations" disseminating anti-Canadian propaganda, even though they were having "doubtful results."[50] But competition did increase. With rising demand for farm land, land grant railroads turned to unloading marginal or semi-arid land previously considered unfit for agriculture. Low prices were asked in order to keep sales brisk. Through a successful bargain basement price policy, by 1905 the Burlington and Missouri River Railroad, for example, was able to divest itself of all lands tagged for settlement. The end of the Burlington's formal land sales, however, did not close the door on its association with colonization activities. The company was astutely aware of profits to be made by increased carrier trade from newly settled areas. Consequently they supported local land companies or homestead operations with low cost excursions for potential settlers interested in the western reaches of Nebraska, eastern Colorado, Wyoming and Montana. The Burlington maintained a Homesteaders Information Bureau which averaged fifteen thousand inquiries per year from persons interested in lands from which the railroad received the "haul."[52]

Canadian agents were well aware that their numerically small organization could not match that assembled by railroads. Railroads had advantages that the Department was denied. It was pointed out "These railroads have agents at all cities and towns on their line, who have annual passes; also at northern and eastern centres, from which they draw immigration; any person taking two prospective buyers over their line to examine country can get free transportation."[53]

Those facing direct competition from railroads continually complained that the companies discriminated against Canada-bound settlers by granting lower rates to those travelling to railroad-backed land settlement. "Working up" settlers in Montana, one agent claimed in 1905 that in competing with railroad promoters for the same settlers he could not quote the lower freight rates his competition offered. To circumvent the alleged discrimination he advised settlers bound for Canada from points near the border to drive their goods overland to Lethbridge thereby saving money at the expense of time.[54] Another agent, working temporarily out of Spokane, Washington, advised prospective settlers to take the same action. This money-saving tactic would not be needed, he contended, when railroads realized that the stream of immigration was unalterably set on the Canadian prairies. By discriminatory freight rates railroads were losing business rather than stemming the tide for settlement. Reason and profits would eventually dictate a reduction in freight rates "and thus put an end to the prairie schooner."[55]

While the railroads would not act, the Interstate Commerce Commission inadvertently did. The Hepburn Act of 1906 gave the I.C.C. power to annul excessive rates and to substitute reasonable rates for those it had condemned. Attacking railroad use of dual tier rates to undermine their real-estate competition, the I.C.C. ruled special rates to settlers bound for railroad-endorsed land schemes illegal. The Immigration Branch naturally welcomed the new ruling.[56]

The 1906 decision of the I.C.C. may have outlawed a major advantage the railroads had in land promotion, but it would not restrict them from promoting lands in which they had an interest. Only the gradual filling up of these lands removed them as rivals to Canadian efforts. In 1908 agent MacLachlan, now comfortable in Watertown emphasized the need for greater effort by the Department to overcome the colonization activities of railroads in his new region.

> I feel it is necessary to put forward all the efforts we can in order to hold our own in this state owing to the great energy being displayed on the part of the Chicago [and] Northwestern and Chicago and Milwaukee Railways in directing people, not only from this state but also other western states to the new lands opening up for settlement west of the Missouri River.[57]

A few years earlier, in 1904, the railroads of the northwest attempted to form a united front to promote land settlement. The Immigration Branch claimed that the sole purpose of this organization, the American Immigration Association, was to divert migration away from Canada and toward American lands. This was not the case. The organization had been set up as much to stop the outflow of farmers to southwestern states as it was to impede the continued movement into the Canadian northwest. An article outlining the group's formation published in the *Daily Pioneer Press* of St. Louis in March, 1904, did not even mention the Canadian migration as a factor for bringing the association into being. Rather, the newspaper pointed to the danger emerging from a growing interest among farmers of the midwest and northwest in the newly opened lands of the southwest, especially Texas and Oklahoma as the new group's prime target.[58]

Canada was not ignored. Delegates from Iowa, Illinois, Minnesota and the Dakotas and six other northwestern states who formed the

American Immigration Association were aware that a settler who migrated northward to Canada was as much lost as one who moved southward to Texas. During the Association's short life (it remained active for only a few months) Canadian immigration activities became a target for the group's attack. The Department was especially displeased when a few newspapers gave editorial support to an Association demand that the American government halt the alleged stealing of citizens of one country by another. As the *Kansas City Star* put it, while there could be no objection to agents of private land companies operating in the United States, "when . . . the government itself seeks to attract citizens of other countries the matter is one which calls for official remonstrance."[59] The Association's campaign came to nought and the Department was relieved to see the opposition disintegrate in short order.[60] The demise of the railroad Association, like that of the publicity bureau before it, was likely hastened by the internal friction between competing land and railroad interests.[61] Individual railroads might well have judged their money better spent on promoting their own interests rather than attacking the interests of others. Co-operation with groups within the states of a railroad's carrier operation and geared to local needs appeared a far better investment.

Important publicly funded state organizations were assigned to combat the outflow of population or encourage population increase. The Commons Committee on Agriculture and Colonization was informed, for instance, that in 1903 Minnesota appropriated a large sum for the activities of a Commissioner of Immigration. Working in much the same fashion as the Department, the Minnesota organization was publishing "documents and authentic information regarding lands belonging to the federal government open to homestead, and otherwise praising the advantages of the state of Manitoba [Minnesota?] which had been opened."[62]

Minnesota was not alone. Organized as much to compete with one another as with Canada, other states also created immigration commissions to retain or recruit population.[63] Especially active were the under-populated states of the southwest, each with major tracts of free homestead land to offer farmers. They sent personnel throughout the midwest and northwest to scout for would-be settlers. An irate agent complained that on arriving in Indiana in 1905 to organize a Canadian Immigration Office, he discovered the state already had "been thoroughly and systematically worked over by agents of western states, aided by an army of local real-estate men and farmers."[64] Like protective parents afraid their children could be seduced into leaving home, Iowa, Oregon, the Dakotas, Wisconsin and other more settled states followed Minnesota in organizing programmes to stop the outflow.[65] But newer states with homestead lands to offer were not always at an advantage. Entering the field late, the State Board of Immigration of Wyoming, organized in 1911, had a lot of catching up to do. "Neighbouring states [had] been carrying on strong publicity campaigns for twenty years or more."[66] The competition between states, even in the campaign to populate federal government lands, once again prevented any united front against Canadian activity from taking shape.

In spite of the opposition's fragmentation, the Department was concerned lest any region which was losing population to Canada might lash out with legislative restrictions on Canadian activity. Clifford Sifton was specifically cautioned that Minnesota might attempt to restrict Departmental activity. Opening the 1905 Minnesota legislative session, Governor John Albert Johnson announced that he envisioned "special measures being taken to prevent the exodus [of settlers] and secure [increased population] for his state."[67] Whatever schemes the governor might have envisioned beyond increased appropriations for the state's Immigration Commission were shelved in the excitement of the 1906 election. During the Minnesota state election the Department's activities became a minor political issue. The *Nation,* prophesying the election of Republican Albert L. Cole as governor long before a single vote was cast, applauded his call for an active campaign to nullify the impact of Canadian immigration work in Minnesota. The *Nation* noted with approval that "Mr. Cole regards it as a lack of enterprise to permit a Canadian Immigration bureau to exist in St. Paul while the state makes no effort to stop and hold the stream of people bound from Nebraska, Iowa, Wisconsin, and Illinois as well as Minnesota itself." Just what measures Cole would be prepared to take if elected were not indicated.[68] In spite of the *Nation's* predictions, Cole lost the election to incumbent Governor Johnson who had run harder against railroads than Republicans.[69] Following the election no new moves were made to restrict Canadian activities in Minnesota.

While no state actually took direct action to restrict the freedom of the Department directly, such action continued as a veiled threat. However, any one state taking direct action against Canada might soon find itself in difficulty. If Canadian immigration recruitment was attacked in conjunction with attacks against a state's other competitors, retaliation could be expected from the other states. If Canada alone was restricted, difficult questions might be raised as to the powers of the states to legislate in the areas of international affairs. In a more subtle move several states later barred the Canadian exhibit from state fairs on grounds that its appeal was "false and misleading." More a nuisance than a restriction, such action only points to the very real difficulty any one state had in attempting to prevent the outward migration of its citizens.[70]

In spite of scattered opposition, which at times undermined Departmental operations in some areas, the major threat to Departmental work continued to come from American federal support for settlement of the public domain and locally backed settlement schemes. The flash of excitement generated by the 1902 Newlands Act was felt again with the 1904 Kinkaid Act. The new legislation enabled settlers in a newly opened area of northern Nebraska to claim 640 acres of dry land for grazing homesteads. Eight million acres were opened and a series of similar bills were proposed to cover Colorado and South Dakota. Although the provisions of the Kinkaid Act were not extended to cover other areas, legislative lobbying and continued introduction of bills in Congress kept enlarged homestead schemes alive.[71] In 1909 Congress belatedly conceded the necessity of increasing the size of homestead allotments in semi-arid regions and passed the Enlarged Homestead Act granting 320 acres to those taking up farms in dry regions of Montana, Wyoming, Colorado, New Mexico, Utah and Nevada.[72] Congress also moved to shorten the time period from five to three years during which a homesteader had to wait for final title.[73]

There is no way of knowing how many farmers were drawn away from Canadian lands by the lure of private or homestead lands in the United States. Local agents continually complained that new homestead regulations, irrigation, opening of Indian reservations and local hostility to Canadian efforts were taking their toll in settlers who would otherwise have made their way to the Canadian prairie.[74] The reasoning of the agent in Watertown was typical:

> The opening of the Rosebud [Crow Indian] reservation in this state during the month of July [1904] was, in a large measure, one of the chief causes why the number going to the Canadian Northwest was not as large this year [as last]. Fully 115,000 registered at the opening when but 2,640 could get claims, that being the number available. It proved, however, a great advertisement for the State of South

117

Dakota, as well as the means of attracting people from all states of the union.[75]

As intimated, not only those who would get American lands but those who felt they *might* get these lands remained closed to solicitation by local agents, although disappointed land seekers became easy prey for Canadian agents. In his annual report of 1906-1907 White lauded the efforts of his personnel in the field but pointed out that their success was part of a wider movement of population taking place on the whole continent.

> As I write I have before me a report that in one day last week [August, 1906] one thousand homeseekers passed through Sioux City, South Dakota, on their way to vacant lands in that state. The information is also given that trains are being run in two sections, so great is the rush. It is stated that 1,000,000 acres of government land will be opening up there shortly. Then there are Texas, [New] Mexico, Colorado, Wyoming, and other western states with lands, whether good, bad or indifferent, upon which people can be asked to settle. Thus it will be seen that everything is not coming Canada-wards.[76]

White still had faith that American lands would gradually disappear from the market, raising the price of remaining land and turning the direction of population flow even more certainly toward Canada. As he put it, "as soon as prices advance, which in the natural order of speculation is sure to come shortly, the intrinsic value of Canadian land will demand as large (or larger) a share of attention as ever."[77] In the meantime the agent in Indianapolis advised that honesty and advertising were his best weapons in combating the activities of competitors. Only in this way "can we prevent many who . . . promised to locate in the Northwest from going [elsewhere]."[78]

During the years of Liberal administration, competition from American lands never disappeared. It only shifted. As the Department waited for lands to gradually fill, other lands opened. American farmers had a choice of lands available to them, but the quality, quantity and price of Canadian lands continued to work in favour of a steadily increasing movement toward Canada. Competition, which in 1911 White publicly referred to as " 'rivalry' not 'opposition' ", could also work to the benefit of Canadian activity by stimulating an insatiable desire for land. As he put it, competition would "assist the land hunger, and we are ready to do our part to assist in satisfying it."[79]

118

Nevertheless, Canadian agents and sub-agents in the United States were not operating in the complete seller's market that they wished for. The Department continued to be wary of the potential threat posed by the opposition to Canadian efforts and advised agencies to take care in overcoming any obstacles in their path. As late as the winter of 1912 White warned all local agents of an allegedly "well organized campaign to divert the movement from Canada," and advised them "to watch this, and meet it in every legitimate way."[80] The best the Department could offer was its propaganda campaign designed to keep the obvious advantage of Canadian prairie land in a prominent position for settler consideration.

Closing The Door
[THE ISSUE OF NEGRO IMMIGRATION]

As the Canadian government developed its American emigration programme, no social concern required a greater combination of legislative manoeuvrability and administrative resolve than the question of Negro settlers. Almost forgotten today, at the turn of the century the issue of Negro immigration into western Canada finds the Department of the Interior acting as midwife at the birth of a quasi-official policy of immigration restriction. The virtual sealing of the Canadian border to black Americans by 1911 was not a product of direct parliamentary action. Rather, it was an outgrowth of citizen agitation with which the Immigration Branch sympathized, agitation which fed on heightened fear of an anticipated tide of black immigration and resulted in demands for the erection of a firm colour bar to limit the admission of Negroes from the United States.

Throughout the years of the Laurier administration the Immigration Branch remained overtly hostile to black settlement. As William Duncan Scott, Superintendent of Immigration under Frank Oliver, observed, "At no time has the immigration of [Negroes] been encouraged by the Canadian government . . . ."[1] However, under increased pressure of constituent demands, the process of exclusions shifted over a ten-year period from haphazard stop-gap discouragement of black settlement to a well polished mechanism completely geared toward preventing Negroes from crossing the border into Canada.

The Immigration Branch's attitude toward the Negro was moulded by both Departmental pragmatism and domestic racism. Looking south, Canadians were well aware of the racial tensions plaguing post-Reconstruction America and had no desire to import these prob-

lems to Canada. The existing Negro population of Canada was very
small and concentrated in limited geographic pockets.[2] Undoubtedly
it was assumed that any influx of American blacks into areas without
a Negro population would create social problems far out of proportion
to any economic benefits Canada could derive from such settlement.[3]

Although Canadians may self-righteously have prided themselves
on their distance from American racial troubles Canadians proved as
racist as their American neighbours. In his widely read analysis of
Canada's new immigrant communities, James S. Woodsworth, Superintendent of All Peoples Mission in Winnipeg and a future father of
the Canadian social democratic movement, adopted an unflattering
American analysis of the Negroes potential as a citizen. Woodsworth's
book, *Strangers Within Our Gates,* quotes from an article in the
popular American magazine *Chautauquan* to the effect that the "very
qualities of intelligence and manliness which are essential for citizenship in a democracy were systematically expunged from the negro race
through two hundred years of slavery." It was argued that the
American Negro was still cursed with the burden of his African
ancestry. The Negro, Woodsworth allowed, had an "aversion to silence
and solitude, love of rhythm, excitability and lack of reserve. All
travellers speak of their impulsiveness, strong sexual passion and lack
of willpower."[4] Hardly a desirable settler.

A major mass circulation Canadian magazine of its day, *Canadian
Magazine,* contained few articles directly related to Negroes or the
Negro question. However, in one instance where the character of the
Negro was discussed, he was a Sambo, a playful if somewhat danger-
ous child. In an article describing Negroes of the West Indies, the
paternalistic author viewed the black as "intensely emotional, impul-
sive, polite, given to begging, very liberal [sexually], 'has no strict
regard for the truth, is affectionate . . ., when enraged does not reason,
and is ungovernable. This, of course, is the trait of an undisciplined
mind; yet his fury rarely ever lasts."[5] While this article dealt with a
topic seldom explored in *Canadian Magazine,* the process of stereotyp-
ing the Negro in the white mass media surely was not new to Canadian
readers. Of course, the Canadian did not rely solely on Canadian maga-
zines for his periodical reading. By the turn of the century he was
already accustomed to a diet of American publications, much of which
helped to reinforce his negative image of American blacks.[6]

Interest in lands of western Canada which developed among
American Negroes was rooted in a growing apprehension over their

deteriorating position in the United States. While it is not within the scope of this study to detail the plight of the American Negro at the turn of the century, it is relevant to note that 1896, a pivotal year for Canadian immigration, was also a turning point in the history of the American Negro.[7] After the collapse of Reconstruction in the southern states, whites gradually erected a legal framework to support the informal practices of segregation which had come into being. In 1890 Lousiana passed a law providing for "separate but equal" racial accommodations on public transit. A court case to test the constitutionality of the Louisiana legislation had slowly edged its way through the courts and on May 18, 1896, Justice Henry Billings Brown read the Supreme Court's decision in the famous case of *Plessy* vs. *Ferguson*. The court upheld the doctrine of separation of the races contending that the Louisiana law did not violate Negro rights. The law, it was claimed, merely gave legal recognition to the biological differences between the races. Rather than stamp the Negro as inferior, the Court declared that the "separate but equal" concept gave Negroes equality under the law. Social equality could not, the court argued, be legislated.[8]

In spite of these judicial gymnastics and the Court's assurances to the contrary, the 1896 ruling became a justification, not for equality, but for white racial supremacy. Moral as well as legal support seemed to have fallen in behind those already busily engaged in enacting segregationist statutes.[9]

To some Negroes the thought of moving to Canada as a possible escape from a rapidly decaying domestic situation was likely appealing. One cannot be surprised that such interest existed. Indeed, one wonders why immigration to Canada was not more attractive for blacks. The puzzle is not to difficult to solve. Most Negro farmers, poorly educated and often illiterate, had no direct way to become informed about Canada. The Negro population of the United States, geographically centred in areas of the south or in small urban pockets, was generally removed from the activities of most Canadian Government Agents. At the same time, lines of Negro migration from rural to urban areas and from south to north were being established. While the Great Migration north would not be fully underway until the eve of war, the Negro who found it possible to resettle was far more likely to have his eyes fixed on Atlanta than on Alberta, on Cincinnati than on Calgary.[10]

Though undoubtedly some blacks read the religious, agricultural and local press in which the Department placed advertisements, there was never a direct appeal made to them. No advertising was submitted to the Negro press nor were special promotional publications issued from Ottawa to engage Negro interest as was done with other American ethnocultural and religious groups.

Financial considerations also tended to prevent the American Negro from turning to Canada in large numbers. Reconstruction had not produced a radical redistribution of southern land. In its place a thinly veiled plantation system still held many Negroes in virtual serfdom. Changing agricultural technology robbed others of the small holdings they did possess leading them into still further economic servitude. As a result few Negroes could afford to move to Canada. If any migration was possible for the Negro, it was without a large store of capital. Thus, out of necessity, this migration was streaming to larger urban areas where there was hope of immediate employment and wages.[11]

Nevertheless, in spite of conditions which mitigated against it, there developed enough Negro interest in the lands of western Canada to pose a problem for the Immigration Department and to eventually force a systematically tight-fisted approach to the issue. The first indications of possible Negro interest in migration to western Canada came early in January, 1899, from the old border state of Missouri. Agent James Crawford, Kansas City, reported to the Superintendent of Immigration that the immigration office had been questioned several times on whether the Canadian government and people would respond positively to Negro settlers. Crawford indicated that the blacks who had visited his office appeared to have outside financial backing and were considering the formation of a work colony in the northwest. Requesting some sort of general directive or statement of Departmental policy, Crawford admitted having independently discouraged the questioners with tales of cold weather on the prairies and the likelihood of colour prejudice.[12]

The response from the Immigration Branch was simple and to the point. Answering for the Department, Assistant Secretary Lyndwode Pereira explained: ". . . it is not desired that any negro immigrants should arrive in Western Canada, under the auspices of our Department, or that such immigration should be promoted by our agents."[13] Thus, while the Negro was not yet being excluded from Canada, he was being excluded from promotional work. This decision of the Immigration Branch had no basis in legislative statute. It was the outgrowth of racism and a Departmental assumption that Canada would best be served by having little or no Negro settlement in the west.[14]

Throughout the next ten years the Department maintained an informal but constant vigil cautiously guarding against the possibility of Negro settlement. Under no immediate pressure to establish fixed procedural guidelines, the Immigration Branch dealt with each expression of interest in black migration quickly, quietly and firmly so as to undermine any practical settlement plans. In one instance a respected Toronto businessman, Alfred Burton, devised his own scheme for black colonization and immediately presented his settlement plan to the Department. As Burton explained, on the return leg of a European tour, he befriended the well-known American Negro clergyman, Bishop Abraham Grant of Indianapolis. Bishop Grant was himself on the way home from visits to Sierra Leone and Liberia where he made an inspection tour with an eye toward possible Negro settlement in Africa. Burton, it appears, interested Bishop Grant in the possibility of a Negro colony somewhere to "the Northwest near the Rockies." The Canadian subsequently requested the Department to supply information which would reinforce Bishop Grant's interest in the project.[15] Burton's personal initiatives were not appreciated. The Immigration Branch dismissed the project in a curt note stating, in part, that the government "would not be disposed to lend any active encouragement to the immigration of negroes to our North West."[16]

A somewhat more subtle problem for the Department was how to answer requests for advice and information on Canadian settlement from persons who identified themselves as Negroes. Such letters were often laced with comments on the deteriorating position of Negroes in the United States and the black's special historical and emotional relationship to Canada and the crown. References to the British abolition of slavery, the crusade against slave traders by the Royal Navy and the Canadian terminus for the underground railroad were not uncommon. A Canadian Negro student attending Lincoln University in Pennsylvania was certain that his personal scheme for black colonization would gain favour with his government because, as he put it, "our government has always been a friend of the coloured man especially is this true during the war of 1812 and later the underground railway system [sic]." By encouraging a Negro colony, he assured the Department, Canada was being offered an opportunity of "setting the civilized world an example that would live and bear fruit for untold ages to come."[17] But the Department was not interested in Negro settlers and he was informed only that his letter had been filed for later reference.[18]

Approaching the Canadian government, Director of the Afro-American Literary Society in Washington, Barney McKay, hypothesized a situation in which the black settler could become a staunch defender of the Empire. He assured Ottawa that American blacks "are home loving Christianized and make the finest soldiers in the world and above all every colored soldier has a warm spot in his heart for all that is English." Any Negro who became a British subject would, he contended, help maintain the "free institutions of the proud English government," and protect Canada as "a land free from prejudice, caste and social and political slavery."[19] He was promptly informed that "the Government of Canada is not prepared to take any action on the lines indicated."[20]

In two other noteworthy instances the Canadian government was advised that the Negro would prove an ideal settler because his negative experience in the United States would engender in him a degree of loyalty to Canada that other settlers might never match. Therefore, it was argued, the Negro could act as a check against the possible disloyalty of others. The problems of the United States were not just a result of race, advised a Negro student at Hiram College in Ohio, "but a problem of crime labor brought by the foreign European inhabitants." With loyal Negro subjects, Canada would have the opportunity to avoid the American error by balancing white Europeans with the American blacks.[21] The Department was not impressed and the student was informed that Canada had no desire to encourage Negro settlers.[22]

In 1906 a Negro clergyman in Galveston, Texas, who claimed to be a British subject, proposed yet another scheme for Negro settlement in the Canadian prairies. As an extra inducement to Canadian authorities he suggested that the Negro settler might act to "checkmate" the large number of white American settlers who would not give up their ties to the United States as readily as the black man. Negro settlers were potentially "more loyal to the flag of the British Empire, and the Dominion" than white settlers, thus, the Canadian government could successfully make good use "of the antipathy now brewing between [black and white]."[23]

While the Immigration Branch was not impressed with any vision of American Negroes defending the Union Jack against the onslaught of Uncle Sam, the historical mythology which gave rise to such Negro

126

images must be viewed as an indication of why Canadian settlement could appeal to some Negroes on purely emotional grounds. If a Negro could find the financial means to move and desired to maintain an agricultural way of life, his naive faith in a legendary British friendship toward the Negro might at least make Canada an attractive possibility. The Department, however, made perfectly clear the distance between myth and reality.

In answer to the Reverend the Department was willing, for some unexplained reason, to mail out literature on the Northwest. However, Departmental Secretary L. M. Fortier employed a tactic which had quickly become standard equipment in dealing with the Negro question — the climate. The Secretary claimed to have "observed that after some years of experience in Canada [Negroes] do not readily take to our climate on account of the rather severe winter."[24] The Department was beating the Negro bogey with the same stick that was then being used against potential white settlers by the Department's opponents in the United States. While on the one hand the Immigration Branch was doing all in its power to convince white Americans that the Canadian west did not have a climate too harsh for productive labour, in virtually the same breath, it was trying to convince the Negroes that, at least in their case, the opposite was true.

As its policy was not to encourage Negro settlement in the Canadian west, the Immigration Department was not disposed to co-operate in any private immigration schemes involving blacks, even when these schemes concerned white-owned land companies. Such proved the case with the German American Colonization Company of Calgary. The company's president, J. Steinbecker, had entered into negotiations with Z. W. Mitchell, a Negro leader from Minneapolis. A plan was devised whereby the German American Colonization Company would act as local agents in settling a well-financed Negro colony in Alberta. Steinbecker was of the opinion that a successful black settlement could be organized only if four to six newly opened townships were officially set aside for homesteading by the proposed Negro settlers. After touring Alberta with Steinbecker, Mitchell concluded that the best area for his colony was in the Nehill district, about seventy-five miles from Calgary. However, as the government land agent in Calgary advised, no programme for a Negro colony or reservation of several townships could be approved by him unless authorized by Departmental headquarters in Ottawa. Writing to the Deputy Minister, Steinbecker pointed out that "unless the Government will grant these people the right to select a certain number of townships for their colony, I do not see for my part how we can successfully colonize them."[25]

The Department was well aware of its power to set aside land. But it was far from pleased with the prospect of seeing a black colony organized on government or private lands regardless of financial backing. In a curt note to Steinbecker, Fortier informed him that "the Department is unable to entertain your proposal with references to reserving land for a colony of coloured people."[26] A letter from Mitchell was not answered. No more was heard from Mitchell or the German American Colonization Company about the scheme.

Turning to the activities of government agents in the field, it is difficult to estimate the amount of contact they had with Negroes interested in Canada. There were no Negro agents or sub-agents nor was there any white agent authorized to work among members of the black community. Indeed, agents were instructed to use their influence to prevent Negro settlement. On the only occasion in which the proposal for a Negro sub-agent was put forward, the scheme was, of course, rejected. James A. Strachan, a watchmaker from Atlanta, advised the Department that he could easily organize a "company of 1,000 of the most industrious negroes" to leave their home state of Georgia for the Canadian prairie. Strachan offered himself as a possible candidate for sub-agent in the undertaking.[27] The government's reply was predictable. While informing him that he would be mailed Departmental literature for himself, the government turned down his offer to assist in immigration work. The Superintendent of Immigration also dismissed any proposed move of blacks from Georgia to the west by informing Strachan that "this Department will give no extra encouragement in favor of their removal."[28]

Individual agents and sub-agents were not always clear as to the best tactics to use when faced with Negroes who applied for Settlers' Certificates. On occasion agents might refuse to take any decisive action themselves but solved their immediate problems by passing the issue on to Ottawa. Faced with the prospect of handing out Settlers' Certificates to a group of Negroes heading for Medicine Hat, the agent in Chicago telegraphed Ottawa for instructions.[29] The Superintendent of Immigration telegraphed back the reply, "We do not want these people."[30] Armed with the telegram, the immigration agent had no further need to consider the issue for himself and it is safe to assume that Certificates were not issued.

For the most part, however, agents appeared to have been ready to make decisions on their own. As the hostility of the Immigration Branch to Negro settlement became more apparent to local agents in the field, these agents not only felt more secure in their refusal to give information, assistance or Settlers' Certificates to Negroes, but they also felt obliged to do so. It would have taken a large dose of naiveté for anyone wishing to remain in the Department's employ to challenge his superiors by openly engaging in immigration work among Negroes.

The pressure on agents to avoid encouraging Negro settlers became so great that agent Crawford, Kansas City, felt compelled to defend his record with the Department. Evidence indicates that Crawford unknowingly issued Settlers' Certificates to a group of Negroes who used them to cross the border. The Immigration Branch was quickly informed by railway authorities that its Kansas City agent had been instrumental in sending Negro settlers into Canada. In his defence Crawford pointed out that many Certificates, including those in question, were issued through the mail as a product of indirect contacts from newspaper advertisements or literature sent out from Ottawa. Unless it was specified, he claimed, there was no way of knowing the race of the letter writer. When he was aware that a request came from a black, Crawford answered that no advertising was mailed out, let alone Settlers' Certificates. The only case in which he admitted to having knowingly issued Settlers' Certificates to Negroes was on an occasion when the following conditions existed: the Negroes had already obtained their railroad tickets through to the Canadian border, could prove they had sufficient capital to undertake migration, and, most importantly, refused under any circumstances to change their immigration plans even if denied the reduced railroad rates from the border as offered by the Certificates. As there seemed no way of discouraging the Negro immigrant, Crawford reasoned it was more valuable for them to spend their money in Canada on settlers' goods rather than on transportation.[31]

As if to verify Crawford's defence, a black farmer, S. J. Ligan of Fitzhugh, Arkansas, wrote the Immigration Board requesting direct assistance after he was given no aid in his immigration plans from the Kansas City office. Writing for himself and "sevel . . . friends and nabors [sic]," Ligan protested that he received no reply from Crawford after repeated requests for information and Settlers' Certificates. Ligan's attempt to bypass the rebuff from Crawford did elicit a reply from Ottawa, but of course, it was designed to discourage both Ligan and his friends from moving.[32] Ligan's letter, however, may have indicated an increased interest among Negroes of his state in the Canadian west. As he put it, "The Western Canada Fever is here [and I] want Information concerning the nationalities Allowed to settle their [sic] whether white only, or for every good moral [sic]."[33]

While Ligan took the trouble to reach beyond the initial rejection he received from a local agent, there is no way of knowing how many blacks passively accepted the negative treatment from the agents as final with no further appeal possible. While statistics remain unknown, one agent made it a point of pride that he had refused to deal with Negroes in any way. The local agent in Toledo assured the Department, "I have never issued certificates to that class of people and have generally evaded and turned them down, believing that Canada did not want to encourage that nationality."[34]

Agent Crawford, however, was not easily forgiven his sins in spite of his defence. Minister of the Interior, Frank Oliver, was advised that Crawford had continued to allow Negroes to slip through his office with Certificates.

> Over a year ago White advised Mr. Crawford, of Kansas City, that it was not in the interests [sic] of the work that he should issue certificates to coloured people from the South. They were a different class altogether from those who have been resident in Canada for a long time and they are not farmers in the way that we apply the term. The farming that they did was indifferent and careless and they were not desirable for Canada. I supposed that he had been living up to my verbal instructions. Notwithstanding this he has issued certificates right along and only as recently as a month ago.[35]

What disciplinary action if any taken against Crawford was not specified. Nevertheless, it is clear that the Immigration Branch was displeased enough with agents who dealt with Negroes to keep a close watch on their activities and to keep the Minister personally informed of developments.

While the attitude of the Immigration Branch generally filtered down to the agents in the field and found expression in their increasingly hostile stance with respect to Negroes of their districts, the actual Immigration Branch's position on Negro immigration was not as strong as the Department might have wished. In spite of the refusal

130

of most agents to deal with blacks, there was little to prevent blacks from crossing the border on their own if they so desired. When approached by prospective Negro settlers, local agents might continue to undermine black migration and the Immigration Branch could use its influence to frustrate proposed schemes for black settlement. The legality of these actions was, at best questionable. The immigration statutes did not distinguish between American settlers on the basis of race although the potential to do so existed in legislation, and there was no way for agents to legally prevent Negro settlers with independent means from crossing the border and taking up homestead lands.[36]

In 1909 William J. White, Inspector of United States Agencies, observed that Negro interest in Canadian lands was on the increase. Reporting from his inspection tour of the American agencies, White commented that "at almost every office I find applications from these people." In a letter addressed to the Minister, White requested greater ministerial leadership in instituting an airtight scheme for excluding Negro settlers who continued to find their way into the Canadian west.

> Notwithstanding our best efforts to guard carefully the class of people, who go to Central Canada, we find the case of the negro probably the most difficult to deal with. If given a free hand and the privilege to absolutely refuse to give a certificate entitling him to [reduced railway] settlers' rates, we could meet it. Whether it is advisable to refuse the coloured man this certificate is a question that bothers us considerably. There is a fairly large coloured vote in Eastern Canada, most of which is Liberal and if it comes to their notice that their people were discriminated against, it might lead to their opposition. On the other hand I know that the people in the West do not care to have them in their neighbourhood . . . In some cases where we have thought it safe, we have absolutely refused to give certificates; in other cases we have advised them of special rates which can be secured on special days and which they can take advantage of. This, however is only a makeshift and is likely to be resented . . . I wish you to bear in mind that the refusal of the Department to help them secure a rate will not keep them from coming.[37]

While the Minister of the Interior pondered what steps could be taken to restrict black entry into western Canada, the Negro immigration problem took on an added dimension. By 1910, there developed fear of a mass migration of Negroes out of Oklahoma into Canada and a consequent backlash among whites in the Canadian west. It was this issue of Oklahoma's blacks which finally crystallized

131

Departmental thinking on the black settler and resulted in the virtual sealing of the border to American Negroes.

The interest in western Canadian lands which emerged among Oklahoma Negro farmers was a product of the convulsive dislocation of a portion of that community under pressure of Oklahoma's rapidly shifting social and economic structure. Those blacks considering northward migration, Creek-Negroes, were concentrated in eastern Oklahoma, the counties of which had been carved out of lands previously granted the Creek Indians, one of the Five Civilized Tribes. The Indians lost their tribal lands as punishment for alleged support of the Confederacy during the Civil War. A post-war series of land treaties dispensed with communal land holdings and placed property into individual hands. Remaining land tracts reverted to federal government ownership and became part of the territory opened during the great Oklahoma land rushes at the turn of the century.[38]

The Five Civilized Tribes, including the Creeks, had been slaveholding Indians, and, when the Creeks were forced from their ancestoral homes into the Oklahoma Indian Territory in the 1820's and 30's, an estimated four to five thousand Negro slaves accompanied their masters. Compared to conditions of southern slavery, slavery within the Creek Nation was not nearly so oppressive. As ownership of slaves was more a status symbol than an economic factor within the Indian community, blacks were allowed a large measure of social equality. While tribal laws against intermarriage existed before the Civil War, inter-racial couples were not unknown and all offspring of such unions were freemen. Slaves could also hold personal property and for many the only mark of their slave status was the payment of a small annual tribute. A Negro slave might also serve the special social and political function of diplomat. Because he often spoke English and was better acquainted with the white man's world, the Negro was given the responsibility of handling whatever interaction with white society the Indians required. At the close of the Civil War the Indians' slaves were emancipated. In the Creek Nation the Negro was generally accepted and legally incorporated into the tribe, receiving a share in the redistributed Indian land holdings. A total of 6,807 Creek freemen received lands in severalty.[39]

Integration of the former Creek slaves with their past masters might have progressed smoothly were it not for the introduction into Oklahoma of new social elements which ruptured existing relationships. In the wake of new Indian treaties and the opening of Oklahoma lands to settlement, the territory witnessed an influx of many southern whites and former slaves who came to claim their share of the shrinking frontier. Included among the recent Negro arrivals were railroad construction workers who, having laid track across the territory, decided to stay. Friction between the Creek-Negro and the southern Negro developed quickly. The Creek-Negro had increasingly come to identify himself with the Indian community. His adoption of an Indian culture and his different experiences under slavery gave him little in common with the southern black. Creek-Negroes saw the southern blacks as interlopers and were in turn viewed as savages.[40]

Left to themselves, time might have allowed for the development of mutual accommodation and even union between the two Negro groups, but this possibility was denied them. The large white population which was flowing into Oklahoma territory during the land booms soon acquired all real political power, which was confirmed with statehood. Whites made little or no distinction between the Creek-Negro and the more recent black arrivals. The end to the land booms which brought stability and statehood, also brought the introduction of legally sanctioned discrimination patterned after the southern model. The black was quickly denied the vote as a grandfather clause and literary test effectively disallowed his franchise.[41] The Creek-Negroes were most affected. They found themselves squeezed out of a previous position of relative security as Indians into a new world of segregated facilities and second class Negro citizenship. Unlike the new Negroes in Oklahoma, the Creek-Negroes had little experience with a caste system governing relationships between racial groups. The Indians, now too weak to defend themselves, could render the blacks no assistance. As the position of the Creek-Negro became more and more untenable, the possibility of migration to Canada grew as an attractive alternative.[42]

In 1910 the Immigration Branch was suddenly confronted with evidence of the Creek-Negroes' interest in Canadian lands. The Department's Kansas City agent sent Ottawa a lengthy letter explaining the background of the expected exodus out of Oklahoma. As well as outlining the historical relationship between Negro and Creek, he informed the Department that Oklahoma's blacks had the financial means necessary to undertake migration. He noted that the former Indian slaves had farmed their allotted lands but now "on account of treatment by their State they have become discontented." Good prices for farms were easily acquired "since [these lands were] made more valuable by oil finds." So, with a good supply of capital in hand, Creek-Negroes were drawn toward Canada "where they look for better usage [sic], than in their opinion, prevails where they now live."[43]

Predictably, the prospect of a Negro movement from Oklahoma to the Canadian west was not welcomed by white settlers on the prairies. In response to a number of early protests from western Canada, the Minister, Frank Oliver, instructed the Immigration Branch to send Inspector White on a fact finding tour of Oklahoma. White was charged with exploring the state's black community and reporting any interest in the Canadian west generated among Negroes.[44]

The Inspector of United States Agencies lived up to the implications of his surname. White spent five days in Oklahoma, largely within the eastern counties of the state. He visited the growing white centres of Tulsa and Oklahoma City and the Negro towns of Muskogee, Okmulgee and Coweta. The White black report did little to allay growing fears of possible racial friction or loose morals among the would-be Negro migrants. Relations between the whites and blacks of Oklahoma, White observed, were firmly fixed along colour lines. He assumed that had no legal barriers been legislated, the blacks would still have found themselves in an inferior position resulting from a pronounced lack of individual ambition. Compared to the busy and thriving white towns he visited, White observed that in Negro towns "laziness is abundant and seems to have put its hall-mark everywhere."

In rural areas, among those Creek-Negroes who were reportedly considering migration to the Canadian west, the situation was even worse. The "negro-Indians" whom White saw "possessed . . . wealth much greater than most of the white settlers of the State." However, the possession of money did not seem to raise either their level of expectation or stimulate their economic acumen any more than was witnessed in Negro towns. In fact, White concluded, the prosperity of the whole region was "kept back and held back by the preponderance of the coloured people who [owned] most of the land."

As White saw it, at least one reason for such a degenerate style of life was a direct result of miscegenation. The "negro-Indian" was the product of the union of two races which in combination created a mongrel having acquired the worst elements of both groups to the total exclusion of the good.

134

The Indian has brought into the mixed race the cunning that the Indian is credited with, and has raised the lower and more harmless instincts of the negro, but only to a more brutal level, and with the combination he thus becomes a more undesirable person. He has worked alongside of the Indian until he has acquired a lot of that individual ['s] shiftless methods and added to his own indifference of surroundings to his own carelessness in everything that elevates [sic].

White contended that the Creek-Negroes were not leaving for Canada solely of their own volition. Rather, the migration was being encouraged by "the progressive element in Oklahoma," whites who wished to be rid of the black land owners. White also found that local railroads had a major interest in promoting such a migration. The railroads saw any programme which inspired Negroes to move out and be replaced by whites as a boon to the state's development. Consequently, the Creek-Negro could often command a price of forty or fifty dollars per acre for his land when sold to railroads or white settlers. The railroads, especially the Southern Pacific, proved more than willing to co-operate in moving the Negro almost anywhere so long as he got off the land.

White reported that those blacks who did not use their money to move out of Oklahoma tended to "move into the towns, drink and waste their capital, and often wind up in penitentiary . . . ." White doubted the wisdom of encouraging the black to better his position. The possibility of Negroes improving their lot through education, even in segregated facilities, was fraught with danger for whites. As one local white resident explained, the degree of black "menace" was directly proportional to the level of education attained by black leadership. "With a little learning and a little prestige they soon become first class agitators, and this was to be feared." One can only guess how White foresaw the impact of open education in the Canadian west on newly arrived blacks.[45]

Negro clergymen in Oklahoma had reluctantly watched their congregants slip off the land and into towns. In order to maintain their congregants' base in the rural communities, the clergymen played into the hands of railroad interests and joined in encouraging the movement toward the Canadian west. White made a point of holding conversations with several black clergymen during which he did all he could to satisfy them "that Oklahoma was a much better place."

Later the Immigration Branch was to fight fire and brimstone with fire and brimstone. Ottawa hired an itinerant black clergyman, G. W. Miller, to stump the Oklahoma blackbelt, preaching against any black migration to Canada.[46]

In concluding his report to the Minister of the Interior, White advised that "it would be wise to take such action as would prevent any more [blacks] making homes in Canada." If there was any possibility of the Creek-Negro making a good farmer in western Canada, White had once again failed to find it. "There is so much of the Indian blood in the coloured man of Oklahoma, carrying with it all the evil traits of a life of rapine and murder, that it will not easily assimilate with agrarian life." For the good of the Negro and the safety of the Dominion, it would be best that the Negro stay in Oklahoma, and accept a role which, White concluded, was best suited to his primitive state.

> If undesirable to Oklahoma why not undesirable to Canada? more so. In Oklahoma he has lived the life that suits him best. All the ties that have been since his birth are there, the climate is one to which he is best fitted. He has social relations, and he has the surroundings that he has partly created. In Canada he has a different climate, he is removed from all the things which to his not overactive mind are part of his being, and he will never be able to fit himself to the very changed conditions. He will not have the happiness and contentment he has enjoyed all his life. He will be called into greater activity than his system can meet.[47]

The White report by itself might well have been enough to frighten Oliver into taking the drastic step of closing the Canadian border to black settlers. However, the issue was becoming more acute. The prospects of any movement of Negroes out of Oklahoma into the Canadian west set off protests in the western Liberal heartland. With a federal election in the not too distant future, it would have been politically unwise to let voter discontent run unchecked without at least giving the appearance of concern for demands of constituents. Thus, as protest forced Oliver to commission White's report, so it forced Oliver to act on the report.

Prior to 1910 little notice had been taken of the few Negroes who made their way past local agents and took up homesteads on government lands. In 1908 the *Ottawa Free Press* ran a small article on Oklahoma Negro settlers under a colum heading of "Negro Settlers— Party From Oklahoma Has Located in Alberta." The article reported that seven black families had taken up residence on homestead land. The report did not mention any negative reaction from whites in the region.[48]

The same year the Immigration Branch was advised of a racial incident which occurred in Estevan, Saskatchewan. Six Negroes from Barbados who arrived in town without warning were quickly arrested and jailed on a charge of vagrancy. An investigation soon discovered that the men, sent as harvest workers by the Canadian Pacific Railway, had done little more than get off the train when local citizens began to panic. The Commissioner of Immigration in Winnipeg confirmed that "it appears that men's colour and the peculiar predicament in which they were placed were their only offences." When released, the men disappeared, and the incident was quickly forgotten in the area. Nevertheless, the Department was aware that this incident revealed the degree of tension which could develop under the pressure of expected Negro settlement.[49]

By 1910 it was not the number of Negroes already settled in the Canadian west that was receiving attention but rather rumours of an incipient invasion from Oklahoma. As the Oklahoma migration appeared headed toward northern Alberta, anti-Negro sentiment first erupted around Edmonton with press reports feeding local uneasiness. On one occasion the *Edmonton Capital* informed its readers that the Negro Press of Oklahoma was already referring to Alberta as "the home of the coloured race." The *Capital* warned that the editor of an Oklahoma newspaper was then in Edmonton arranging for the settlement of twenty-nine black farmers and would soon return to Oklahoma to "set the tide of coloured emigration in the direction of Edmonton."[50] Less dramatic than the *Capital,* but still opposed to continued entry of blacks into Canada, the *Edmonton Bulletin,* owned by Frank Oliver, Minister of the Interior, warned that increased Negro immigration could potentially serve to incite racial violence on a level yet unknown in Canada.[51]

Spokesmen for the western business community reacted to the feared influx of blacks from Oklahoma through local Boards of Trade. At their monthly meeting in April, 1910, the Edmonton Board urged "that such immediate steps be taken by the Dominion Government as will result in [the Negro] influx being stopped." The Edmonton business community was not alone. Under a column heading of "Negroes Not Wanted in Province of Alberta," the *Calgary Albertan* reported that its municipal Board of Trade endorsed the action of the Edmonton group. Winnipeg soon followed suit as did the Bordon, Saskatchewan Board. The Saskatoon Board of Trade sent their Member of Parliament, George E. McCroney, a resolution demanding that the government make it impossible for blacks to file on homestead lands in order to remove this major inducement to Negro migration. Other anti-Negro resolutions reached the Immigration Branch from business groups in Yorkton, Saskatchewan and Morinville, Fort Saskatchewan and Strathcona, Alberta.

Discussion of the issue in the eastern Canadian press was characterized by sensational headlines with loaded words and phrases carrying emotional overtones. The *Ottawa Free Press* warned, "Negro Settlers Troop Into West, Edmonton White People Complain to Minister of Interior of the Influx."[53] From the *Montreal Herald* came a report of "Negroes Ousting Whites in Alberta – Edmonton Board of Trade Calls Attention of Minister of Interior to Matter."[54] The *Port Arthur Evening Chronicle* reported on "An Invasion of Negroes, Edmonton Board of Trade Asks Government to Intervene."[55] In April, 1911 the *Toronto Mail and Empire* gave the Negro question both editorial and feature coverage. In a lead article the newspaper warned that "Negro Immigrant Influx Has Become Live Issue."[56] An editorial the following day came out squarely for exclusion of blacks.

> If negroes and white people cannot live in accord in the South, they cannot live in accord in the North. Our Western population is being recruited largely by white people from the United States [sic]. If we freely admit black people from that country, we shall soon have the race troubles that are the blot on the civilization of our neighbours. Canada cannot be accused of narrowness if she refuses to open up her west to waves of negro inmmigrants from the United States. The negro question is of the United States' own making and Canada should not allow any part of her territory to be used as a relief colony on that account.[57]

The Edmonton region, where it was rumoured that most black immigrants were heading, remained the centre of anti-Negro sentiment.[58] In the spring of 1911 a petition was organized by the local Board of Trade demanding exclusion of blacks. Copies of the petition were available for signature at Edmonton banks, hotels and other business establishments.[59] Over 3,400 persons, including two who made their mark with an X, placed their names on the list. Many identified themselves as members of the Orange Lodge or Imperial

Order Daughters of the Empire. Representing approximately fourteen per cent of the city's population, the petition urged "that such steps immediately be taken by the Government of Canada as will prevent any further immigration of negroes into Western Canada." The petition warned that Negroes were not good farmers and could never live side by side with whites without disorder.[60] A separate petition from the Edmonton chapter of the Imperial Order of the Daughters of the Empire was also sent to Ottawa. Playing on the myth of Negro sexual aggressiveness, the petition warned that white women of Alberta would become easy prey of black men.[61]

If the Immigration Branch required any further evidence of the political force of anti-black sentiment, it came when the Edmonton Municipal Council joined the outcry. In April, 1911, the elected body passed a resolution with only one dissenting vote, calling on the federal government to take all action necessary to prevent the expected influx of Negroes. Even more remarkable, the city fathers demanded that "such negroes as are now on homestead lands in the country be segregated in a certain defined area from which [white] settlers be removed."[62]

The sudden rise of an anti-black immigration protest, especially in the Edmonton area, helped reinforce the position of those immigration officials who wanted power to close the border to Negro settlers. It was not enough, some Immigration officials pointed out, to simply withhold the co-operation of government agents in the United States from individual Negroes or to use governmental influence to discourage private schemes for black settlement.[63] So long as the border remained open, blacks could and would cross it in spite of preventive measures the Immigration Branch had managed to institute thus far. From 1901 to 1911 the Negro population of the Canadian prairies had climbed from 98 to 1,524. While this number posed no great threat in itself, the fear ran high that, left unchecked, these Negroes would prove the advance guard of a black army.[64]

There can be little doubt that Oliver was sympathetic to the demand for restriction of immigrants. Before entering the Cabinet he had shown himself as a supporter of selective immigration and as early as 1901 he had voiced concern in Commons' debates over his predecessor's open immigration policy.[65] As the question of Negro immigration became more urgent, Oliver was faced with the necessity of deciding not whether but how to impose restrictions. Two programmes were considered; one official restriction, the other unofficial exclusion.

At the end of May 1911 Superintendent of Immigration Scott drew up a proposed Order-in-Council which would prohibit "any immigrant belonging to the Negro race, which race is deemed unsuitable to the climate and requirements of Canada" from landing in Canada for a period of one year. The request for an Order-in-Council was signed and submitted to the Governor General on June 2, 1911.[66] However, the order was never declared. It was likely vetoed by Laurier. Such an Order would have raised undesired diplomatic problems with the United States. It would also have upset Negro voters in Nova Scotia and Southwestern Ontario whose support had traditionally fallen to Liberal Party candidates. With an election pending, Laurier would be leery of irritating more liberal-minded Canadians, especially those removed from the heart of western discontent. Lastly, the Prime Minister may have judged the expanded informal restrictions already being instituted by the Immigration Branch as sufficient to bar Negroes from Canada. The proposed Order-in-Council would thus have been a symbolic political medication to soothe western voters, but one which was fraught with possible harmful side effects.

On the other hand, the informal exclusionary programme adopted by the Minister of the Interior and his Immigration Branch was equally effective in its simplicity. Rather than enacting new regulations, selectively strict enforcement of existing legislation provided sufficient leeway to deny Negroes access to Canada. At the core of the scheme lay a formal inspection of immigrants which had been routinely instituted at border crossing points on April 1, 1908. It was a simple matter to adapt the standard medical and character examination at frontier posts to reinforce a white-only admission policy. While officially claiming only to be applying existing regulations as was their duty, the Interior Department also undertook to inform American Negroes, especially in Oklahoma, that any border inspection would end in rejection of blacks. Thus, private interests were warned against solicitation of black settlers.

Medical and character inspections were perverted so as to prevent a Negro from entering Canada, but this ploy was to be a last resort. By allowing knowledge of this tactic to spread throughout the American Negro community, the would-be migrant could be discouraged before he made concrete plans to move. In spite of a veneer of public denial, largely for domestic consumption, the Immigration Branch

140

undertook to make it perfectly clear to blacks that they would not be permitted entrance into Canada.[67]

The American press was inadvertently co-operative in spreading the word. Conservative Member of Parliament for St. John City, John Waterhouse Daniel read the Commons a newspaper report dated Winnipeg, February 24, 1911. Under a column heading of "United States Negroes Barred," Daniel read, "The Dominion government has decided to prohibit the immigration of Negroes from the United States and stopped at the boundary a party that wanted to go to western Canada. The Negroes were turned back because they were regarded as undesirable citizens."[68] Although Oliver denied any knowledge of this case or that the government had authorized a policy for excluding Negroes on the basis of race, the article read by Daniel had already been picked up by the American press.[69]

Oliver's denial that race was being used as a criterion in rejecting Negroes may have been designed to placate liberal or Negro voters, but the Minister could not let the opportunity pass without informing his Edmonton constituents that border inspection could close Canada to any group as readily as any regulation. Indeed, without referring to a specific group, the Minister pointed out that desirable settlers were already being given the benefit of a more lax reading of the law. All immigrants had to jump the hurdle. The more desirable the immigrant, the lower the hurdle.

> The immigration policy of Canada to-day is restrictive, exclusive and selective as compared with the former policy of indiscriminate immigration . . . there are many cases where the admission or exclusion of an immigrant depends on a strict or lax interpretation of law, so that if the immigrant is of what we would call the desirable class they [sic] are administered laxly and if he is of presumably less desirable class then they [sic] were administered more restrictedly. Beyond that there are no instructions to immigration officers, but they are expected to act according to the instructions they have.[70]

Although the Minister of the Interior officially decried any attempt to brand immigration policies as racist, the Department's intent was soon clear. But, this was not enough. Policy rhetoric had to be so transparent that no prospective black immigrant could mistake its true message. The *Boston Post* clearly saw through ministerial speeches. The newspaper informed its readers that Canadian "law has not been changed to exclude negroes, but officials are more strictly interpreting the provision of the act which forbids the admission of persons not likely to make desirable citizens."[71]

In 1911 the widely read American magazine, *Chautauquan,* printed an editorial attacking Canadian immigration policy with regard to the Negro. Remembering Canada as an historic haven for runaway slaves, the magazine deplored Canada's break with its noble past. While implying that the rising anti-Negro sentiment in Canada may be a by-product of large American settlement of the west, the editorial contended that this was no excuse for the Department's double standard when applying inspection regulations to Americans. By giving more weight to pigmentation than to potential, Canada was denying itself good settlers. The article went on to note that immigration "laws have been very strictly construed against negroes, and even the possession of considerable capital, agricultural experience, intelligence and entire respectability" could not get a Negro into Canada. Though the black might yet have recourse to the Canadian courts, the *Chautauquan* lamented that in the "meantime Negro movement Canadaward has been checked." In any other such case involving its citizens the American government would have been expected to protest such discriminatory treatment of a group of its citizens "in violation of existing treaty rights." In this case Canada could and would deny that any anti-Negro legislation had been adopted, which the editorial concluded was technically true. But, more importantly to the American magazine, any such protest would seem like the proverbial pot calling the kettle black.

> . . . for our government to protest insistently and loudly would savor of hypocrisy. The world would ask why the American negro farmer or thrifty laborer should be driven to emigrate to Canada – and not only from southern states but from expanding and new western and northwest states that have barely scratched their natural resources and that profess advanced ideas of social and political organization. The question would be embarrassing, to put it mildly.[72]

The American government was aware of Canadian policy, but barring formal admission of a purely anti-Negro racial policy by the Canadian authorities, there was little the United States could do. In March, 1911 the *New York Tribune* reported that the American Consul-General at Winnipeg, John Edward Jones, had received deputations from American railroad interests complaining that their Negro passengers were denied permission to enter Canada. In one reported case a special corps of immigration officials was allegedly despatched from Winnipeg to deny entrance into Canada of 165 blacks from Oklahoma. The same article continued with a note that in response to an official inquiry by the American Consul in Ottawa, the Canadian government denied racial bias at the border crossing points.[73]

The following month, however, the American government was informed that Canada had stretched the provisions of immigration inspection legislation to possibly exclude blacks on the grounds that they "could not become adapted to the rigorous climate and consequently may become a public charge." An official memorandum to this effect was communicated by Jones to the American Assistant Secretary of State, Huntington Wilson, in Washington on April 26, 1911.[74]

Increasingly aware of the Canadian situation, leaders of the American Negro community also expressed concern over immigration restriction. The editor of *Crisis*, official organ of the National Association for the Advancement of Coloured People, the great black leader, W. E. B. Du Bois, wrote Canadian officials for policy clarification. Noting that the American press had reported changes in immigration regulations, Du Bois requested exact information on how these changes applied to blacks.[75] The Immigration Branch's answer, published in *Crisis*, informed Du Bois that the government had issued no specific instructions to its agents on the barring of blacks. Writing for the government, the Departmental Secretary in Charge of Immigration, L. M. Fortier dredged up the well-worn arguments about Canadian climate. However, he added a new shading to this red herring. Fortier pointed out that Negroes in eastern Canada had shown no interest in western lands. This proved "that western Canada will not be found very suitable as a field for settlement of coloured people from the United States when similar people from Canada do not want to go west to take up land." But the argument of climate was no longer the major feature of restrictive policy. What the Negro had to face, if he dared, was inspection at the Canadian border, and Fortier was not reluctant to make this point crystal clear to Du Bois.

> There is nothing in the Canadian Immigration law which disbars any person on the ground of colour, but since coloured people are not considered as a class likely to do well in this country all other regulations respecting health, money, etc., are strictly enforced and it is quite possible that a number of your fellow countrymen may be rejected on such grounds.[76]

Ironically, by publishing the secretary's letter and a few later articles concerning black exclusion from Canada, Du Bois was playing the role of propagandist for Canadian policy. The Immigration Branch could not have hoped for better publicity in the Negro community than a few months' notice in *Crisis*.[77]

As the American press, black and white, helped spread the word of black exclusion from Canada, the Immigration Branch took other steps to make it more difficult for Oklahoma's Negroes to reach the border. In a 1910 agreement with the Canadian Pacific Railway, which had its own immigration service in the United States, the government was able to deny blacks the co-operation of Canadian railway personnel in any proposed move into the Canadian west. The railroad also agreed to exclude Negroes from the organized tours of western Canada given prospective settlers and report any government agent who was found to be encouraging Negro settlement. What is more, no further reduced railway rates were to be granted Negroes irrespective of the validity of their settlers' status.[78] On being informed of the anti-black regulations issued by Canadian Pacific management to its personnel, White wrote the railway, "I think the action you have taken is a wise one and I believe it will help to keep out the class of people that to my mind are undesirable."[79]

It is understandable that the Immigration Branch and the Canadian Pacific would co-operate in excluding blacks. However, American railroads, profiting from any northward migration of Negroes, as was the case in Oklahoma, had no reason to assist the Canadian government's white-only policy. As noted, American railways complained to the American Consul-General in Winnipeg of black exclusion, although to no avail.[80] The Immigration Branch advised American railroads that the Canadian west would not serve as a depository for displaced blacks. White informed the Superintendent of Immigration: "The railroads in the South have been advised of the difficulties that lie before the negro on his arrival at the boundary points, and will not take any chances in having a large number of them rejected and then having to haul them back free." Thereafter, ready access to border crossing points was increasingly denied Negroes.[81]

As no actual statistics on blacks turned back at the border are available, one can only conjecture as to what actually took place at the crossing points. The number of Negroes reported by the government to have entered Canada in the year 1909-1910 was seven. It rose to twelve the following year. This was a far cry from the one hundred and thirty-six who reportedly entered Canada in 1907-1908.[82] On the other hand the period 1908-1912 was marked by a steady increase in the number of persons rejected at border inspection. In 1908-1909 only 4,580 persons were turned back at the check points. By 1911-1912 the number of persons rejected had climbed to 22,034. There is, of course, no way of telling how many of the rejected were blacks. But it would have been relatively simple to find a reason to exclude any individual on officially sanctioned grounds which could vary from suspicion that he carried one of many illnesses to such catch-all categories as lack of funds, bad character or physical disabilities. If a Negro did not fit into a small box it was not too difficult to find a bigger box into which he would fit.[83]

Presumably, as word spread of the discriminatory nature of Canadian border inspection, much enthusiasm for moving to the Canadian west which might have existed among Negroes of Oklahoma would dry up. Growing awareness that crossing the border was becoming an impossibility could not help but deter blacks from realistically considering a move to Canada. Thus, the Immigration Branch likely succeeded in making its border inspection both a prevention and cure. In either case the flow of Negro immigration, including that from Oklahoma, quickly evaporated.

In retrospect, black immigration into the Canadian west was never more than a trickle as compared to the flow of whites who crossed the border between 1896 and 1911. Nevertheless, there is no doubt that a greater influx would have taken place. Larger numbers of Creek-Negroes or even sponsored Negro colonies might have found their way into the Canadian west. But this was not to be.

Though the impact of the Oklahoma Negro on western Canada was kept marginal at best, his impact on the development of a racist immigration policy in Canada was great. The dangers represented by Creek-Negro settlement, real or imagined, forced the Department to adopt a racist double standard with respect to American immigrants. It forced the Immigration Branch to adapt administration of existing legislation to meet ends not perceived by those who had enacted that legislation. The continuation of covert anti-Negro immigration restrictions beyond 1911 and the extension of such restrictions to other "undesirables" is a subject deserving of further investigation.

Conclusion

Ideally, an evaluation of the success of the Immigration Branch in the United States during the Laurier years should balance the Department's programme against its productivity, effort against effect. While the Department's operations have been outlined in detail, it is unfortunately impossible to establish the number of American settlers who emigrated to Canada, let alone the number who came as a result of contact, direct or indirect, with Canadian Government Agents.

Somewhat reluctantly this study has employed Canadian government statistics which often owe less to hard fact than to creative fantasy. It proves easy to expose these discrepancies but quite another matter to correct them![1]

Periodically, charges of deliberate deception or calculated manipulation of immigration figures were properly laid at the door of government personnel. Individual agents wishing to inflate their numerical returns, or sub-agents surreptitiously attempting to increase their bonus receipts, succumbed to temptation and issued Settlers' Certificates to persons not legitimately entitled to receive the reduced settlers' rate. Consequently, when such a certificate was submitted at the border the result was not only an increase in an agent's work figures, but also an unjustified increase in total immigration returns. Among those who might illegally find their way onto immigration rolls were tourists, land speculators, Canadians who slipped across the border only to be issued a certificate, and even Americans already settled in Canada who had returned home on business or pleasure.[2]

147

TABLE I: Total Immigration Into Canada
From the United States 1897 to March, 1912

Year	Number of Settlers
Calendar year 1897	2,412
1898	9,119
1899	11,945
First six months 1900	8,543
Fiscal year 1900 - 1901	17,987
1901 - 1902	26,388
1902 - 1903	49,471
1903 - 1904	45,171
1904 - 1905	43,543
1905 - 1906	57,796
Fiscal period (9 months) 1906 - 1907	34,659
Fiscal year 1907 - 1908	59,312
1908 - 1909	59,832
1909 - 1910	103,798
1910 - 1911	121,451
1911 - 1912	133,710
Total:	785,137

While some non-settlers found their way into immigration figures, many *bona fide* settlers remained untallied. Immigration returns, calculated largely on the basis of information gleaned from Settlers' Certificates or records of customs and immigration inspectors at regular border crossing points, generally failed to account for persons who travelled overland, by-passing border stations. In 1903 the American magazine *Independent* observed that during the previous year 32,880 American residents were officially tabulated in the government's immigration records. Nevertheless, the magazine continued, "The number of American immigrants is believed to be considerably greater than indicated by official returns, because many whose names were not formally registered at the [border] towns trekked across the border and took up lands."[3] For many Canada-bound settlers the overland schooner, the legendary covered wagon, was a convenient method of overcoming obstructionist tactics and high transportation costs inflicted by anti-migration American railways.[4] A wagon train of forty prairie schooners left Nebraska in May, 1900 and completed the journey of over 600 miles to Alberta "with no sickness, not even an accident."[5] Settlers came by wagon from even further afield. While on a visit to his home of Brithe, Saskatchewan in 1902, an immigration agent observed that "three 'Prairie Schooners' arrived there labelled 'Oklahoma to Carrot River.' "[6] The irregularity of border patrol, the very length of the border and ease with which it could be crossed made it unlikely that the government was ever cognizant of this movement's exact dimensions. It has been claimed that the Immigration Branch compensated for overland migrants in collected returns by tagging a further twenty per cent figure onto their jumbled statistics. This tampering set another layer of unreliable calculations atop already admittedly untrustworthy returns without lessening the statistical confusion.[7]

Immigration figures also fell victim to unwitting distortion. When certificates or customs records were tabulated in Ottawa, it proved impossible to guarantee that all the information thus gathered (the basis of tabulating the Department's annual statistics) as to a settler's age, previous home, citizenship or even Canadian destination, had been honestly reported by that settler. For instance, a farmer with a young son might attempt to pass off his son as eighteen years of age in order to make him immediately eligible for homestead lands, thereby vastly increasing the family's potential for acquiring property. Similar errors on Certificates could also result from office pressures or the inadvertent neglect by settlers in filling out answers to all questions on their application for Certificates. On receiving complaints of negligence in completing Certificates issued by his office, agent William V. Bennett, Omaha, protested that many such errors could be traced to increased work loads at peak periods of immigration movement.

> . . . we often had a crowd in for certificates between Trains and have so little time that at least three have to make certificates at once in order to get them on their Excursion Train, this with the lost ones that must be re-issued, and changes made in plans of settlers mixes the numbers and dates very badly.[8]

When a question necessary for validation of a Settler's Certificate was left blank by a prospective migrant, agents might independently take the liberty of filling the gaps. In a classic illustration, the salaried agent in Grand Forks, South Dakota, admitted, "Nationalities given in my statement of certificates are not reliable so far as a large number who are classed as Americans, as where we have not [been supplied with the] country of their birth, we simply class them as Americans."[9] There is, of course, no way of knowing how many instant Americans were created in this fashion.

149

The question of the legal citizenship of those moving northward was further complicated by the Department's arbitrary classification of non-Americans as American citizens for immigration purposes if their point of departure for Canada was the United States. Appearing before the Commons Committee on Agriculture and Colonization in 1900, Frank Pedley, Superintendent of Immigration, explained that "the native born American will appear in that [immigration tally] statement as an American; the German who has lived in the United States for ten years perhaps will give his origin as Germany, but will be included as from the United States."[10] Called before the same committee the following year, the Superintendent was asked whether the Department could sub-divide the all inclusive designation of "American" into constituent ethnic or religious groupings. After consideration the Superintendent could propose no more scientifically reliable method for determining settlers' national origins "with a far degree of accuracy" than by guessing from the sound of settlers' names."[11]

To establish a roughly reliable figure for the northward migration, it would be helpful to determine the degree to which the influx was composed of non-American born persons, naturalized Americans or immigrants. With this information, immigration figures could be correlated with Canadian census reports based not on country of last residence, as were immigration statistics, but on nativity. Unfortunately, as 1921 census officials warned, this information remains unknown.

> The census figures classifying immigrants according to birthplace do not furnish a true picture of the extent of Canadian immigration or the sources from which it is drawn. For instance many persons who were born in the British Islands or in European countries may have come to Canada as immigrants from the United States, yet they would appear on the census records as immigrants from the country of last residence. Again, the census records rarely report repatriated Canadians.[12]

Of the estimates of foreign born American residents who moved into Canada during the Laurier administration, the most reliable appears to be that of political economist Jacob Viner who places the figure at just under 30 percent.[13]

Among the non-American-born entering Canada, a sizeable percentage were returning Canadians. In his annual report for 1898 William J. White, Inspector of American Agencies, observed that Canadian Government Agents had been issued specific instructions to search out and encourage Canadian-born residents of the American-prairie states and their families to return home. Agents reported interest among ex-Canadians running high as many Canadians approached local agents.[14] An agent in Reed City, Michigan, received a typical letter of inquiry from an ex-Canadian in Missankee County, Michigan, which read, in part, "Will you please send me a pamphlet on the North West Territories, as I formerly belong to Canada [sic], and I wish I had never left, and oblige one who is anxious to go back to the old Dominion."[15] Some agents found a major portion of their Canada-bound settlers composed of returning Canadians and their offspring. In 1898 another immigration agent wrote that he was "greatly pleased with the character of most of those going from [his] district both as to their moral and financial condition. If not mistaken they will make first class citizens. Indeed the greater portion of them are ex-Canadians."[16] Similarly, in 1903 the local agent in Milwaukee, observed that of the 1,126 settlers he sent northward the previous fiscal year, "the vast majority . . . [were] Canadians or the descendants of the grand old mothers and fathers who left Canada many years ago in hopes of bettering their condition here . . . ."[17]

The return of farmers from the United States apparently reaffirmed Canadian confidence in the domestic economic upswing. The self-styled "Poet of the Rockies", Cy Warman was so impressed by these "prodigals, homeward bound" that he was moved to the following effusion.

"There's a bustle on the border, there's a shuffling of feet
Where the shores of the Republic and the big Dominion
          meet;
For the sons of the Dominion, who have wandered far away
          Are coming back to Canada to-day,
True, their children sing "American," and "Hands Across
          the Sea,"
And they themselves have learned to love the land of liberty.
But it's feet across the border now, with toes the other
          Way –
          They are coming back to Canada to-day.

Now the sleeping North is waking, and their loyal hearts
          are thrilled,
They are hearing from the home-folks who have tarried
          there and tilled.
So, the Sons of the Dominion who have wandered far away
          Are coming back to Canada to-day.
They are coming back to Canada, new Empire of the West,
To the boundless fields and forests, to the land that they
          love best;

151

Aye, it's feet across the border now, with toes the other
    way –
They are coming back to Canada to-day.

They are coming back to Canada,
    Although there's nothing wrong
With the land of their adoption,
    But they've been away so long;
And some of them have soldiered there,
    And some of them are gray,
But they're coming back to Canada to-day."[18]

Once again, numerical estimates of returning Canadians differ. An American official offered a figure of 13.7 per cent for repatriates out of a total of 152,894 persons who moved northward in the two fiscal years ending June 30, 1911.[19] George Bryce, a professor at the University of Manitoba estimated that "Probably half of those who enter the country are expatriated Canadians, or their children, who are returning to their own land. These rejoice in their old institutions and freely express their preference for Canadian laws and customs."[20]

If the statistical picture is not blurred enough, one further fault must be noted. Canadian immigration figures only tabulate a one way traffic, taking no account of any backflow to the United States. A return drift always existed. In 1899 the agent in Mt. Pleasant, proudly boasted that very few American settlers had returned to his jurisdiction. Of the three families who did return, none spoke "harshly of the country, but they lacked what is necessary to endure pioneer life in the new countries, viz., 'backbone.' "[21] The ebb-tide, however, was to increase especially among victims of a prairie drought which set in during 1908.[22] Unfortunately, there are no Canadian returns relating to emigration, nor statistics for returning Americans in the American statistics prior to 1910.[23] However, Viner has estimated that between 1900 and 1913, 380,000 native Americans moved back to the United States, and 180,000 of these by 1911. The majority did not stay in Canada long enough to complete homestead obligations, returning before two and a half years had elapsed.[24]

As a result of this statistical nightmare, the exact dimensions of American migration may never be fully known. Official figures remain more useful as an indication of immigration trends than a conclusive statement of numbers. However, sweeping over calculations with the licence of "questimation" one can reasonably assume the number of Americans who stayed in Canada to be approximately half a million.[25]

Official statistics place the cost of American operations between

1897 and 1912 at over three million dollars. This figure must also be approached with caution.[26] As James Allan Smart, Deputy Minister of the Interior, advised Superintendent of Immigration, the Department was itself unable to compute reliable balance sheets.

> There are . . . difficulties in the way of making anything like an accurate statement as there are many items . . . which it is difficult to classify satisfactorily . . . It is also very difficult to say what proportion of the pamphlets, maps, newspapers, photographs and telegrams were distributed or chargeable to the States. You will therefore see that nothing but a theoretical division can be made and that it seems impossible to show the expenditures made on account of emigration from different countries.[27]

While the Conservative opposition supported increased American immigration into Canada, it attacked government spending as a bottomless slush fund used to employ worn Liberal Party hacks. A 1908 Conservative pamphlet entitled *Facts For the People* led an assault against immigration spending.

> Much of this enormous outlay is wasted in maintaining an army of officials in Canada and other countries, many of them inefficient, nearly all appointed as rewards for party services or to serve some political purpose, or because they are relatives of ministers and members. Some are still active campaigners both on and off duty, and very few in the outside service have been engaged because of any special fitness for the work.[28]

The Department, pointing to the increased number of American settlers in western Canada and a generally improving economic climate in the region, was prepared to accept the lion's share of credit for initiating and sustaining this period of growth.[29] However, without knowing absolute immigration returns or, more importantly, without knowing the degree of influence propaganda and agents had in fomenting this movement, a judgement as to Department success or failure remains open to debate. The impossibility of establishing an empirical gauge to measure achievement was recognized by William Ross, Liberal Member of Parliament for Victoria and member of the Commons Committee on Agriculture and Colonization.

> I think it is impossible . . . to state definitely the number [of settlers] that come in through the agents, and the number who come themselves. I think it would be almost an impossibility, perhaps. You might as well ask a clergyman if it was by the influence of his preaching that all these people come to church.[30]

TABLE II. Immigration from the United States, total movement, total costs, per capita cost and homesteads completed by American Citizens.

Year	Number	Cost $	Per Capita Cost $	Homesteads completed by American citizens
1897-98	9,119	87,000	9.54	581
1898-99	11,945	75,000	6.27	1,064
1899-1900	8,543	112,000	6.55	833
1900-01	17,987	144,000	8.00	2,026
1901-02	26,388	178,000	6.74	4,761
1902-03	49,473	161,000	3.25	10,942
1903-04	45,171	205,000	4.53	7,730
1904-05	43,543	325,000	7.23	8,532
1905-06	57,796	248,000	4.29	12,485
1906-07 (nine months)	34,659	151,000	4.36	6,059
1907-08	58,312	250,000	4.29	7,818
1908-09	59,832	277,000	4.68	9,829
1909-10	103,798	241,150	2.33	13,566
1910-11	121,451	233,636	1.91	13,038
1911-12	133,710	318-655	2.77	10,978

Immigration and homesteads for years 1898 to 1900 are based on calendar years. The other years are fiscal years.

The Department made no systematic attempt to collect and tally Settlers' Certificates for individual state agents. Rather it preferred to rely on periodic spot checks of agent results or, as the minister noted, judge the "work as a whole."

> It is impossible to give [exact figures for each agent] . . . as no attempt has been made to keep a record of the number of immigrants sent by individual agents. We know from careful and constant supervision that our agents in the United States are working hard and faithfully, and we can only look at the result of their work as a whole, which is extremely satisfactory.[31]

When immigration authorities were asked for a tabulation of Settlers' Certificates issued at each office, results proved embarrassing. In 1903 the Committee on Agriculture and Colonization requested an agent by agent breakdown of settlers sent.[32] Statistics were drawn from reports of agents for the fiscal year 1901-1902. The agents cumulative result of 23,721 alleged settlers, supplemented by yet another 3,822 Americans sent into Canada by commissioned agents, totalled 27,543 persons.[33] As the Conservative opposition was only too ready to point out, this final figure represented 1,155 more American settlers than claimed by the Immigration Branch in officially released returns.[34]

Had the discrepancy in figures not existed, had the figures issued by the Immigration Branch been verifiably correct, one could still know only how many immigrants came into direct contact with Canadian Government Agents, not how much influence was exerted by individual agents or the Immigration Branch in fostering their movement. Nevertheless, while the impact of the Department's American operations cannot be measured with statistical accuracy, operational analysis leaves much room for conclusions.

Agents did not work in a vacuum. Within the context of rural America's shifting concerns, the agent was the potential supplier of a desired commodity, good free or cheap land. The socio-economic climate which generated land hunger and a search for alternate paths of parallel social mobility within the American farm community forced the Canadian agent and the programme he personified into the mainstream of rural life before the First World War. In spite of the competition from American lands, the agent had a ready and interested constituency in which to carry on operations.

The government's programme, both propaganda and agency activities, was not original. It relied heavily on previous land promotion experience, most of it imported from the United States. The Department's propaganda machine, relentlessly whirring away, was but an adaptation of previously tried and proven publicity techniques moulded to fit Canadian needs. However, one major difference existed between the Canadian government's campaign and that of other Canadian and American land settlement schemes. The government programme was based on a public policy dedicated to long-term national development through immediate stimulation of immigration. It was essentially a playing out of the government's role as neutral catalyst in national growth. Canadian Government Agents were the spokesmen of expansion, not profit, nation building, not land promotion. No private land scheme, no private land company could imitate the neutral yet authoritative image generated by the Immigration Branch.

Given the special tone of the government's activities and the milieu in which agents functioned, the total programme of American migration encouragement must be judged by their terms, a general success. Problems such as those raised by the sub-agent failure, the Negro question and misuse of Departmental funds for political purposes were further complicated by the ineptitude of individual agents in the field. But, on the whole, efforts to promote Canadian lands were rewarded by increased settlement. The government had succeeded in harnessing business techniques to meet the needs of national development.

Difficulties implicit in assessing the Immigration Branch's success on the basis of immigration or census returns, at best an inconclusive numbers game, leaves the security of concretely measurable conclusions beyond reach. Nevertheless, the non-tangible sense of national optimism which was bred to some degree, in the wake of an immigration boom in the Canadian west, cannot be denied. From the perspective of the Laurier years the twentieth century might well have belonged to Canada. Only looking back over the passage of time was Franklin Wicher Burton in 1936 able to remark, "The twentieth century was once supposed to belong to Canada, but it seems more and more likely that only the first quarter of the century was really ours."[35]

Success must not be measured solely by the standards of those involved. However, the long-term effects of the American migration into Canada, the results of a narrow agriculturally based immigration policy will only be understood in the wake of immigration studies yet to be undertaken.

Of the Immigration Branch it is fair to concede that as an organization it achieved its goals. Immigration of farmers from the United States mushroomed, land settlement flowered and farm production boomed. On the dark side, the Branch successfully destroyed black settlement prospects and, perhaps, retarded diversified economic growth by confining its work to agricultural settlers.

What of the individual within the civil service? For him security and loyalty were identical, the chance to unite policy and person tempting. Yet, for these immigration officials, products of patronage though they were, their relation to government employment was more an affair than a marriage. Individuality, with all its flaws, prejudices and idiosyncrasies, dominated action. Personnel might prostitute themselves to immigration policy, and often did, but they never became immigration policy. Furthermore, far too little is known about the American settler or his integration into Canadian society. Nevertheless, it is surely safe to assume that such a large migration significantly touched not just the course of western Canadian development, but all Canadian history. As the American magazine *Cosmopolitan* observed in 1903, this influx of population, so welcomed by the Canadian government, was having vast social and economic repercussions. "It is not only the Northwest of Canada which is being invaded by American settlers and American capital, but the entire Dominion is becoming Americanized, though the inflow is naturally more marked in particular localities."[36] The implications of this reality continue as crucial factors in the process of Canadian nation building.

Notes

NOTES TO CHAPTER I

Anxiety and Change

1. Increased interest in Canadian immigration history and ethnic studies has been reflected in official government publications. See *The Cultural Contribution of the Other Ethnic Groups* (Ottawa, 1969); *The Canadian Family Tree* (Ottawa, 1967); *Notes on the Canadian Family Tree* (Ottawa, 1960). Four volumes prepared to date by the Canadian Department of Citizenship and Immigration, entitled *Citizenship, Immigration and Ethnic Groups in Canada: A Bibliography of Research* (Ottawa, 1960-1969), and Andrew Gregorovich, editor, *Canadian Ethnic Groups Bibliography* (Toronto, 1972), prove excellent sources for further information on ethnic groups and immigration.

2. Clifford Sifton, "The Immigrants Canada Wants," *Maclean's* 35 (1922), 16.

3. Canadian immigration in the United States has received scant attention. The few published exceptions include: Paul Frederick Sharp, "The American Farmer and the Last Best West," *Agricultural History* 21 (1947), 65-74; "When Our West Moved North," *American Historical Review* 55 (1950), 286-300; James B. Hedges, *Building the Canadian West* (New York, 1939), 126-141; Marcus L. Hansen and John Bartlett Brebner, *The Mingling of the Canadian and American Peoples* (New Haven, 1940), 219-240; Karel Denis Bicha, "The North Dakota History 29 (1962), 297-302; "The American Farmer and the Canadian West, 1896-1914: A Revised View," *Agricultural History* 38 (1964), 43-46; "The Plains Farmer and the Prairie Province Frontier, 1897-1914," *Proceedings of the American Philosophical Society* 109 (1965), 398-440. The last article cited has been republished as a book, Karel Denis Bicha, *The American Farmer and the Canadian West 1896-1914* (Lawrence, 1968).

4. Dominion of Canada, *Sessional Papers* are hereafter cited as *Sessional Papers*.

5. The collection is housed as Public Archives of Canada, Ottawa, Record Group 76. Material from this collection is hereafter cited by box and file numbers.

6. *New York Times,* January 1, 1900, 6.

7. Robert H. Wiebe, *The Search for Order 1877-1920* (New York, 1967), 67.

8. Richard Hofstadter, "Manifest Destiny in the Philippines," *America in Crisis*, Daniel Aaron, ed. (New York, 1962), 173-200. This article considerably revised, is republished in Richard Hofstadter, "Cuba, the Philippines, and Manifest Destiny," *The Paranoid Style in American History and Other Essays* (New York, 1965), 145-187.

9. Henry Adams, *The Education of Henry Adams* (Boston, 1918), 328.

10. For an analysis of the Populist decline see Robert F. Durden, *The Climax of Populism: The Election of 1896* (Lexington, 1966).

11. Josiah Strong, *Our Country: Its Possible Future and Its Present Crisis* (New York, 1885), 153.

12. Thomas Jefferson as quoted in Richard Hofstadter, *The American Political Tradition* (New York, 1948), 27, 18. An excellent discussion of the evolution of agrarian mythology is available in Henry Nash Smith, *Virgin Land* (Cambridge, 1950).

13. Mark Twain, *The Adventures of Huckleberry Finn* (Harper edition, New York, 1912), 405.

14. C. W. Sutter, Lexington, to W. J. White, Ottawa, November 6, 1609. 302/806149-1. All agents are identified by the local centre out of which they were operating at the time of the reference.

15. W. C. Ford, "Turning the Industrial Tide," *North American Review* 161 (1895), 188.

16. Anthony Higgins, *Our Manifest Destiny* (Washington, 1893), 7.

17. Robert M. Hamilton, ed., *Canadian Quotations and Phrases Literary and Historical* (Toronto, 1952), 69. See also Hansen and Brebner, *The Mingling of the Canadian and American Peoples*, 182-218.

18. Canadian economic historians have recognized the pivotal importance of wheat as the prime developmental factor for this period. The chapter title of "Wheat" was chosen to cover this period by Mary Qualye Innis, *An Economic History of Canada* (Toronto, 1935), 235-292, while William Thomas Easterbrook and Hugh G. J. Aitkin, *Canadian Economic History* (Toronto, 1956), 476, contend "that wheat was the keystone in the arch of Canada's National Policy."

19. Archibald William Currie, *Canadian Economic Development* (3rd edition, Toronto, 1960), 178.

20. Easterbrook and Aitkin, *Canadian Economic History,* 483-484; Chester Martin, *Dominion Land Policies* (Toronto, 1938), 355-380.

21. Vernon Clifford Fowke, *Canadian Agricultural Policy: the Historical Pattern* (Toronto, 1947), 233-237.

22. A. W. Currie, *Economic Geography of Canada* (Toronto, 1945), 173-244.

23. Mabel F. Timlin, "Recent Changes in Governmental Attitudes Toward Immigration," *Transactions of the Royal Society of Canada* 49, series III, section II (1955), 95-105; "Canada's Immigration Policy, 1896-1910," *Canadian Journal of Economics and Political Science* 26 (1960), 517-532.

24. *Official Reports of the Debates of the House of Commons of the Dominion of Canada* are hereafter cited as *House of Commons Debates*, 57, April 17, 1902, 2991.

25. *House of Commons Debates* 50, July 26, 1899, 8501.

NOTES TO CHAPTER II

Machine and Personnel

1. Henry James Morgan, ed., *The Canadian Men and Women of the Time* (Toronto, 1912), 1023.

2. *Personnel of the Senate and House of Commons* (Montreal, 1898), 35.

3. John W. Dafoe, *Clifford Sifton in Relation to His Times* (Toronto, 1931), 95-96, 102-103.

4. Karel Denis Bicha, *The American Farmer and the Canadian West 1896-1911* (Lawrence, Kansas, 1968), 53-54.

5. Mabel F. Timlin, "Canada's Immigration Policy, 1896-1910," *Canadian Journal of Economics and Political Science* 26 (1960), 517-519.

6. *Montreal Standard,* July 30, 1910. 83/33175-1.

7. *Report of the Saskatchewan Royal Commission on Immigration and Settlement* (Regina, 1930), 43.

8. James R. Conn, "Immigration," *Queen's Quarterly* 8 (1900), 130-131.
9. Robert W. Sloan, "The Canadian West, Americanization or Canadianization," *Alberta Historical Review* 16 (Winter, 1968), 1-7.
   For a contemporary analysis of the dangers of "Americanization" see William R. Stewart, "The Americanization of the Canadian Northwest," *Cosmopolitan* 34 (1903), 603.
10. Charles Alexander Magrath, *Canada's Growth and Some Problems Affecting It* (Ottawa, 1910), 85.
11. William D. Scott, "Immigration and Population," *Canada and Its Provinces* 7, Adam Shortt, ed. (Toronto, 1914), 555-556.
12. *Ibid*, 556-557.
13. *House of Commons Debates* 111, May 31, 1906, 4270.
14. Vernon Clifford Fowke, *Canadian Agricultural Policy, The Historical Pattern* (Toronto, 1946), 177-183.
15. *House of Commons Debates* 111, May 31, 1906, 4319.
16. Narcisse Omer Côté, *Political Appointments Parliaments and Judicial Bench in the Dominion of Canada 1896 to 1917.* (Ottawa, 1917), 70.
17. Robert MacGregor Dawson, *The Civil Service of Canada* (London, 1929), 67-68.
18. *Sessional Papers* 1907-1908, no. 29, a, 27.
19. Dafoe, *Clifford Sifton*, 107-113.
20. *Sessional Papers* 1897, no. 57T., 34-35.
21. Dawson, *The Civil Service of Canada*, 170.
22. Morgan, *The Canadian Men and Women of the Time*, 1031; John F. Kennedy, ed., *Who's Who and Why in Canada* (Ottawa, 1912), 412; Dafoe, *Clifford Sifton*, 134; *Brandon Weekly Sun*, April 28, 1904. 76/86/34478.
23. *Classification of the Civil Service of Canada* (Ottawa, 1919), 612.
24. Côté, *Political Appointments*, 79.
25. *Sessional Papers* 1901, no. 25, ii.
26. Norman Macdonald, *Canadian Immigration and Colonization 1841-1903* (Toronto, 1966), 265-266.
27. *Classification of the Civil Service of Canada* (Ottawa, 1919), 610.
28. Morgan, *The Canadian Men and Women of the Time*, 893; Circular, Lyndwode Pereira, Ottawa, to All Agents in the United States and Canada, September 8, 1897. 97/41527; biographical material noted on the folder cover of file 97/41527.
29. Hector Charlesworth, ed., *A Cyclopaedia of Canadian Biography* (Toronto, 1919), 106.
30. *House of Commons Debates* 47, January 10, 1898, 7749-7750.
31. *Sessional Papers* 1898, no. 13, pt. 2, 106-112.
32. *Sessional Papers* 1898, no. 1, pt. H, 3.
33. Dafoe, *Clifford Sifton*, 277-302.
34. W. S. Waddell, "Frank Oliver and the Bulletin," *Alberta Historical Review* 5 (1957), 7-12.
35. *House of Commons Debates* 54, April 12, 1901, 2939.
36. *House of Commons Debates* 60, July 14, 1903, 6566.
37. *Report of the (U.S.) Immigration Commission, Vol. 40, The Immigration Situation in Other Countries* (S. Doc. No. 761, 61st Cong. 3d. sess), 41-59; W. G. Smith, *A Study in Canadian Immigration* (Toronto, 1920), 92-113; Mabel F. Timlin, "Recent Changes in Government Attitudes Toward Immigration," *Transactions of the Royal Society of Canada* 49, Series III, section II (1955), 95-96.
38. L. M. Fortier, Ottawa, to W. E. B. Du Bois, New York, March 17, 1911. 115/72552-2. This letter was reprinted in *Crisis,* 1 (April, 1911), 11.

39. Smart entered the passenger booking and land business, opening offices in Montreal and Winnipeg. Morgan, *The Canadian Men and Women of the Time*, 1031.

40. *Ibid*, 260. It is interesting to note that a later biographical source, Hamilton's *Prominent Men of Canada* lists Cory's earlier civil service positions by their later classification titles. See Ross Hamilton, ed., *Prominent Men of Canada* (Montreal, 1932), 54.

41. Dawson, *Clifford Sifton*, 78-89.

42. In one area a case can be made that merit did have an impact on the Inside Service even before 1908. Relative responsibility and work load assumed within the Inside Service was reflected in salary sales. The salary of the Minister remained pegged at $7,000. The Deputy Minister received substantially less although his salary greatly exceeded that of any other Departmental employee. White's salary is of special interest. While he began as Inspector of United States Agencies at a lower salary than the Departmental Secretary, the relative importance accorded his work, the responsibility and respect it demanded and the energy with which it was carried out soon brought him a salary close to that of the Superintendent of Immigration. The relationship of wages to Departmental pecking order was significant as salaries were common knowledge. The wage scale for top civil servants was published annually in the *Canadian Almanac* and for all government employees in the *Sessional Papers*. *The Canadian Almanac, 1898* (Toronto, 1898), 110; *1899*, 115; *1900*, 123; *1901*, 234; *1902*, 248; *1903*, 259; *1904*, 259; *1905*, 277; *1906*, 274; *1907*, 270; *1908*, 299; *1909*, 305; *1910*, 307; *1911*, 310; *1912*, 303.

43. W. J. White, Watertown, South Dakota, to L. Pereira, Ottawa, June 14, 1897. 84/33918.

44. M. V. McInnes, Detroit, to L. Pereira, Ottawa, July 20, 1897; L. Pereira, Ottawa, to M. V. McInnes, Detroit, July 30, 1897 [copy]. 42/5146-2. In personal or intra-Departmental correspondence, agents were often referred to by an assortment of names including: agents, salaried agents, local agents, state agents, immigration agents and American agents. Used freely and interchangeably by Department personnel, this assortment of nomenclature is also reflected throughout this study.

45. *Sessional Papers* 1898, no. 13, pt. 4, 69-71.

46. Statement giving place of office, date opened, name of agent, salary, letters received and sent and number of interviews in fiscal year 1904-1905. 41/5146.

47. *Sessional Papers* 1907-1908, no. 29a, 27-28.

48. M. V. McInnes, Detroit, to J. A. Smart, Ottawa, March 9, 1897. 83/3374-1.

49. J. Keith Johnson, ed., *The Canadian Directory of Parliament 1867-1967* (Ottawa, 1967), 246.

50. *House of Commons Debates* 47, June 2, 1898, 6819.

51. *Ibid, Journal of the House of Commons* 33, Appendix III, May 25, 1898, 243.

52. B. Davies, St. Paul, to C. Sifton, Ottawa, June 23, 1897. 76/53/9679-1.

53. *House of Commons Debates* 92, May 18, 1909, 7005.

54. *House of Commons Debates* 33, June 11, 1900, 7200.

55. Letter to the Editor of the *Scotsman*, signed "Vindex," Balmoral, Manitoba, March 13, 1897 as printed in the *Glasgow Scotsman*, March 29, 1897; L. Pereira, Ottawa, to T. Duncan, Mordon, Manitoba, February 11, 1897 [copy]; Telegram, J. A. Smart, Ottawa, to T. Duncan, London, November 24, 1904 [copy]; T. Duncan, Syracuse, to W. D. Scott, Ottawa, March 8, 1905. 84/33958; *Canadian Almanac* 1893 (Toronto, 1893), 75.

56. *House of Commons Debates* 53, June 11, 1900, 7200.

57. W. H. Rogers, Watertown, to J. A. Smart, Ottawa, November 24, 1897; H. McKeller, Winnipeg, to C. Sifton, Ottawa, December 17, 1897; L. Pereira, Ottawa, to W. H. Rogers, Watertown, December 24, 1897 [copy]. 94/40043-1.

58. W. D. Scott, Ottawa, to W. Scramlin, Halbrite, Saskatchewan, March 11, 1909 [copy]. 303/806477.

59. Johnson, *The Canadian Directory of Parliament 1867-1967* (Ottawa, 1967) 582; Morgan, *The Canadian Men and Women of the Time,* 1119.

60. J. G. Turriff, Ottawa, to W. D. Scott, Ottawa, March 25, 1909. 303/806477.

61. W. D. Scott, Ottawa, to William Scramlin, Halbrite, Saskatchewan, March 26, 1909 [copy]. 303/806477.

62. M. V. McInnes, Detroit, to All Agents in U.S., January 26, 1898. [copy]. 42/5146-2.

63. *House of Commons Debates* 47, June 10, 1898, 7747.

64. *House of Commons Debates* 55, May 9, 1901, 4852-4853.

65. Robert MacGregor Dawson, *Constitutional Issues in Canada 1900-1931* (London, 1933), 287.

66. *Canadian Almanac* 1893 (Toronto, 1893), 75; *House of Commons Debates* 53, June 11, 1900, 7200; Memorandum for the Establishment Book of the Department of the Interior. 136/130979; P.G. Keyes, Ottawa, to J. M. MacLachlan, Winnipeg, January 24, 1901. 140/138303-1.

67. C. Pilling, Grand Forks, to W. D. Scott, Ottawa, June 27, 1903; C. Pilling, Grand Forks, to W. D. Scott, [n.d.], 1908. 136/130979.

68. L. Pereira, Ottawa, to W. H. Rogers, Watertown, December 24, 1897 [copy]. 94/40043-1.

69. M. V. McInnes, Detroit, to J. A. Smart, Ottawa, March 7, 1897. 83/33674-1.

70. Memorandum for the Establishment Book of the Department of the Interior. 83/33674-1.

71. W. D. Scott, Ottawa, to R. Kerr, Montreal, January 14, 1904 [copy]. 113/69678.

72. L. Pereira, Ottawa, to M. V. Bennett, Omaha, December 6, 1897 [copy]. 72/23605-1; *Journal of the House of Commons* 38, Appendix 2, May 29, 1903, 51.

73. Memorandum for the Establishment Book of the Department of the Interior; G. Aird, Ottawa, to D. W. Scott, Ottawa, December 16, 1908; Memorandum, W. W. Cory to L. M. Fortier, August 12, 1909. 301/-806091-1.

74. C. W. Sutter, Indianapolis, to W. D. Scott, Ottawa, February 19, 1909. 302/806146-1.

75. Memorandum, W. J. White, to F. Oliver, March 16, 1909. 302/806146-1.

NOTES TO CHAPTER III

In the Field

1. J. A. Smart, Ottawa, to D. McNicoll, Montreal, June 22, 1897 [copy]. 84/33917.

2. *House of Commons Debates* 50, July 27, 1899, 8654.

3. Aubrey Fullerton, "The Lure of the Best West," *Canadian Magazine* 26 (1905), 127.

4. Allan Johnson, ed., *Dictionary of American Biography* 3 (New York, 1936), 510.

5. Frank George Carpenter, "Progressive Canada Adopts Live Methods to Attract the Go-Ahead American Farmer," *New York Herald,* April 15, 1906. 211/502634.

6. D. McNicoll, Montreal, to J. A. Smart, Ottawa, June 26, 1897. 86/33917.

7. *House of Commons Debates* 60, June 17, 1903, 6876.

8. *House of Commons Debates* 60, June 14, 1903, 6593.

9. *House of Commons Debates* 72, June 19, 1905, 7712.

10. *House of Commons Debates* 81, April 15, 1907, 6759.

11. "Immigration Selection Illustrated," *Outlook* 97 (1911), 805.

12. *Sessional Papers* 1899, no. 13, pt. 2, 268.

13. Instructions for State Agents, Ottawa, February 12, 1897. 42/5146-2.

14. F. Pedley, Ottawa, to All Agents in the United States, July 7, 1898. 42/5146-2; Frank Gilbert Roe, "The Alberta West Cycle of 1899-1903: A Climatic Interlude," *Agricultural History* 28 (1945), 112-120.

15. Karel Denis Bicha, *The American Farmer and the Canadian West, 1896-1914* (Lawrence, 1968), 85, 9-31.

16. *Sessional Papers* 1898, no. 13, pt. 4, 82.

17. Clarence H. Danhof, "Farm-Making Costs and the 'Safety Valve': 1850-60," *Journal of Political Economy* 49 (1941), 317-359; Fred A. Shannon, "A Post Mortem on the Labor-Safety Valve Theory," *Agricultural History* 19 (1945), 31-37.

18. *Sessional Papers* 1898, no. 13, pt. 4, 108, 109.

19. W. H. Rogers, Watertown, to F. Pedley, Ottawa, July 14, 1900. 94/40043-1.

20. C. Pilling, Grand Forks, to J. A. Smart, Ottawa, October 6, 1903. 136/-130979. One agent found that twelve families he had planned to move northward in the spring of 1903 were unable to do so after a flash flood carried off their livestock they had expected to sell in financing their move. As a result "they had not the means to enable them to get away." W. J. White, St. Paul, to J. A. Smart, Ottawa, June 16, 1903. 42/5146.

21. W. J. White, Watertown, to J. A. Smart, Ottawa, June 14, 1897. 84/33918; *House of Commons Debates* 100, March 13, 1911, 5168.

22. *Sessional Papers* 1900, no. 13, pt. 2, 178. *Journal of the House of Commons* 37, Appendix I, February 27, 1902, 324.

23. *Journal of the House of Commons,* 36, Appendix I, April 26, 1901, 306.

24. *Sessional Papers* 1902, no. 25, pt. 2, 143.

25. See for example James B. Hedges, *Building the Canadian West* (New York, 1939), 161-162.

26. W. H. Rogers, Indianapolis, to W. D. Scott, Ottawa, April 2, 1910 [copy]. 95/40043-4.

27. In lieu of a finite appraisal of each settler's goods and capital an arbitrary value of $1,000 per settler was often given in evaluations of settler wealth. See for example *Monthly Consular and Trade Reports,* no. 354 (Washington, 1910), 174.

28. W. V. Bennett, Omaha, to F. Pedley, Ottawa, July 18, 1898. 72/23605-1.

29. While proof is lacking, it is interesting to conjecture that renting rather than selling of farms in the United States would not only insure a migrating farmer a continuing income from the United States and act as an insurance policy should the Canadian venture fail, but also tend to increase the growth of tenancy in the United States. The increase in tenancy as an outgrowth of the Canadian bound migration is noted in Theodore Saloutos and John D. Hicks, *Twentieth Century Populism, Agricultural Discontent in the Middle West 1900-1939* (Lincoln, 1951), 16.

30. Gilbert F. Fite, "Flight From the Farm," *Nebraska History* 40 (1959), 159-176.

31. *Census of the United States* 1910, Population 1 (Washington, 1913), 327.

32. Marcus Lee Hansen and John Bartlett, *The Mingling of the Canadian and American Peoples* (New Haven, 1940), 223-224; Conrad Taeuber, "Rural-Urban Migration," *Agricultural History* 15 (1941), 159-160; T. Lynn Smith, "Levels and Trends in Rural Migration," *Rural Sociology* 19 (1954), 79.

33. Cy Warman, "Migration to the Canadian Northwest," *American Review of Reviews* 26 (1902), 295.

34. *Sessional Papers* 1897, no. 13, pt. 4, 48.

35. *Sessional Papers* 1898, no. 13, pt. 4, 109.

36. Emerson Hough, *The Sowing* (Winnipeg, 1909), 171.

37. *Sessional Papers* 1900, no. 13, pt. 2, 194; 190, no. 25, pt. 2; 1905, no. 25, pt. 2, 45; 1910, no. 25, pt. 2, 83; 1911, no. 25, pt. 2, 91-92; *Journal of the House of Commons* 36, Appendix I, April 26, 1901, 299.

38. J. Baril, Pierpoint, to J. M. MacLachlan, Watertown, April 26, 1908 [copy]. 140/138202-1.

39. *Sessional Papers* 1899, no. 13, pt. 2, 274.

40. *Sessional Papers* 1900, no. 13, pt. 2, 178; see also *Monthly Consular and Trade Reports,* no. 357, pt. 1 (Washington, 1910), 137.

41. For a discussion of the international migration of "group colonies" see C. A. Price, "Immigration and Group Settlement," Wilfred David Borrie, ed., *The Cultural Integration of Immigrants* (Paris, 1959), 267-287.

42. For examples of groups not discussed in this study see Carl Addington Dawson, *Group Settlement* (Toronto, 1936); John A. Hosteller, "Hutterite Separation and Public Tolerance, *Canadian Forum* 41 (1961), 11-13; Bicha, *The American Farmers*, 99-109.

43. J. A. Koehn, Mountain Lake, to Department of the Interior, Ottawa, April 3, 1899. 114/70386-1. A Mennonite source has noted that "When Saskatchewan invited settlers in its pioneer days, 157 families from Mountain Lake accepted the invitation." *Mennonite Encyclopedia* 3 (Scottsdale, 1957), 707-708, 760-761. The Mennonite colonies are also discussed in Dawson, *Group Settlement*, 95-171; Emerich K. Francis, *In Search of Utopia* (Altona, 1955); Leo Driedger, "Saskatchewan Old Colony Mennonites," *Mennonite Life* 13 (1958), 63-66; Margaret Heinricks, "Hague in Saskatchewan," *Mennonite Life* 13 (1958), 18-19; Ferdinand P. Schultz, *The Settlement of German Mennonites from Russia at Mountain Lake, Minnesota* (Minneapolis, 1938), 68.

44. W. J. White, Lincoln, Nebraska, to F. Pedley, Ottawa, May 21, 1899. 116/76054-1. The story of Mormon migration into southern Alberta is interwoven with the history of dry farming and irrigation in the region. "Proposal for the Settlement of Land in Alberta Territory, Canada, Northwest, Belonging To The Albertan Immigration Company," Alberta Irrigation Company File, Manuscript Collection, Church Historian's Office, Salt Lake City, Utah; "Re John W. Taylor," C. A. Magath Papers, M.G. 30 B.Z., File 51, Public Archives of Canada, Ottawa; Dawson, *Group Settlement*, 175-272; David W. Buchanan, "The Mormons in Canada" *Canadian Geographical Journal* 2 (1931), 255-270; Lawrence B. Lee, "The Canadian-American Irrigation Frontier, 1884-1914," *Agricultural History* 40 (1966), 271-283; H. G. Cochrane, "Irrigation in Alberta," *Alberta Historical Review* 16 (Spring, 1968), 14-18; Lawrence B. Lee, "The Mormons Come to Canada, 1887-1902," *Pacific Northwest Quarterly* 59 (1968), 11-22.

45. *Sessional Papers* 1897, no. 13, pt. 2, 50-51.

46. Memorandum, W. D. Scott, to L. M. Fortier, December 12, 1908. 302/806149-1. Dawson, *Group Settlement*, 175-332.

47. J. L. Doupe, Montreal, to W. Bonnotyne, Winnipeg, December 30, 1910 [copy]; W. J. White, Ottawa, to J. L. Doupe, Montreal, January 9, 1911 [copy]. 115/72552-2.

48. *Sessional Papers* 1901, no. 25, pt. 2, 173; 1902, no. 25, pt. 2, 151.

49. *Statistical Review of Immigration 1820-1910 — Distribution of Immigrants 1850-1900* (Washington, 1911), 373, 380-381. The United States only began collection of data on aliens leaving the country on July 1, 1907. *Abstracts of Reports of the Immigration Commission* 2 (Washington, 1911), 735.

50. *Immigration Facts and Figures* ([n.p.] 1913) 2. Approximate figures are used as Canadian and American fiscal years do not correspond with one another. However, the discrepancies are likely minimal and do not alter the conclusions drawn. It is also interesting to note that American citizenship was not recognized as a nationality in Canadian statistics. *Ibid,* 7-10.

51. *Sessional Papers* 1898, no. 13, pt. 4, 111; 1904, no. 25, pt. 2, 126. See also Marcus Lee Hansen and John Bartlet Brebner, *The Mingling of the Canadian and American Peoples* (New Haven, 1940).

52. *Sessional Papers* 1898, no. 13, pt. 4, 69-71; Statement giving place of office, date opened, name of agent, salary, letters received and sent and number of interviews in fiscal year 1904-1905. 41/5146.

53. *Sessional Papers* 1898, no. 13, pt. 4, 112.

54. W. V. Bennett, Omaha, to W. J. White, Ottawa, August 8, 1898; Memorandum, W. J. White, to F. Pedley, April 18, 1898. 72/23605-1.

55. *Sessional Papers* 1901, no. 25, pt. 2, 176.

56. C. Pilling, Grand Forks, to W. D. Scott, Ottawa, March 18, 1903. 136/130979.

57. J. Grieve, Reed City, to J. A. Smart, Ottawa, July 2, 1897. 84/33917.

58. G. A. Hall, Pittsburg, to W. J. White, Ottawa, February 28, 1907. 113/69678.

59. W. J. White, Ottawa, to G. A. Hall, Pittsburg, April 3, 1907. 113/69678.

60. F. Pedley, Ottawa, to B. Davies, St. Paul, December 19, 1900 [copy]; Telegram, F. Pedley, Ottawa, to C. Pilling, St. Paul, June 10, 1902 [copy], 136/130979; W. J. White, Milwaukee, to F. Pedley, Ottawa, April 12, 1901 [copy]. 140/138303-1.

61. Memorandum, W. J. White to W. D. Scott, February 14, 1904. 42/-5146-2. Available statistics seem to verify the need for assistance. During the fiscal year 1904-1905 government figures show that 43,543 American settlers crossed into Canada. During the same period, the seventeen salaried agents reportedly received 70,948 letters, mailed out 102,132 replies and granted 105,901 personal interviews. *Immigration Facts and Figures* ([n.p.], 1913), 2. Statement of office activity for fiscal year 1904-1905, April 2, 1900. 42/5146-2.

62. Agents spent 2,781 work days in the field as compared to only 1,762 work days in their offices, or approximately sixty-three per cent of their time on the road. Statement showing the number of days the salaried agents in the U.S. were in their offices, and number they were travelling during the fiscal year 1901-1902. 42/5146-2.

63. Instructions for State Agents, Ottawa, February 12, 1897. 42/5146-2; *Sessional Papers* 1898, no. 13, pt. 4, 69.

64. *Sessional Papers* 1899, no. 13, pt. 2, 285.

65. Of these, nearly 10,000 came from the list of county auditors, over 2,000 from agricultural fairs, 12,000 from local farmers who supplied the Department with likely prospects and the remainder from returned clip-out coupons in local newspapers. During this same year, before the lists would become subject advertising, only 300 Minnesota farmers moved into Canada. *Sessional Papers* 1898, no. 13, pt. 4, 85.

66. *Sessional Papers* 1904, no. 25, pt. 2, 123.

67. T. Duncan, Syracuse, to W. J. White, Ottawa, September 21, 1907. 84/33958.

68. *Sessional Papers* 1898, no. 13, pt. 2, 70.

69. L. Pereira, Ottawa, to M. V. McInnes, Detroit, March 17, 1897 [copy]. 53/9679-1.

70. *Sessional Papers* 1903, no. 25, pt. 2, 129.

71. *Sessional Papers* 1908, no. 25, pt. 2, 87.

72. L. Pereira, Ottawa, to M. C. McInnes, Detroit, March 17, 1897. 53/9679-1. The failure of the sub-agent system is the topic of the following chapter.

73. Memorandum, W. J. White, to W. W. Cory, Ottawa, April 11, 1911. 113/69678-2.

74. *House of Commons Debates* 57, May 6, 1902, 4249.

75. Statement giving place of office, date opened, name of agent, salary, letters received and sent and number of interviews in year 1904-1905. 41/5146.

76. *Sessional Papers* 1904, no. 25, pt. 2, 125.

77. W. J. Bennett, Omaha, to F. Pedley, Ottawa, August 21, 1901. 72/-23605-2.

78. W. V. Bennett, Omaha, to F. Pedley, Ottawa, October 3, 1910. 72/-23605-2.

79. Agent Benjamin Davis, St. Paul, flatly denied all Bennett's charges. He claimed by way of explanation, that the settlers in question had approached his office for Certificates never mentioning that they had been issued Certificates elsewhere. B. Davies, St. Paul, to W. J. White, Ottawa, December 26, 1901. 72/23506-2.

80. W. V. Bennett, Omaha, to F. Pedley, Ottawa, January 2, 1902. 72/-23605-2.

81. J. M. MacLachlan, Wausau, to W. J. White, Ottawa, December 27, 1903. 140/138303-1.

82. C. Pilling, Grand Forks, to W. J. White, Ottawa, May 7, 1904. 113/-69678.

83. C. Pilling, Grand Forks, to W. D. Scott, Ottawa, November 28, 1904. 113/69678.

84. W. V. Bennett, Omaha, to W. J. White, Ottawa, February 26, 1903; W. J. White, Ottawa, to W. V. Bennett, Omaha, March 24, 1903 [copy]. 72/23605-3.

85. W. H. Rogers, Watertown, to B. Davies, St. Paul, February 2, 1900 [copy]. 114/70386-1.

86. J. C. Koehn, Mountain Lake, to Department of the Interior, Ottawa, September 18, 1900. 114/70386-1.

87. F. Pedley, Ottawa, to W. H. Rogers, Watertown, October 10, 1900 [copy]. 114/70386-1.

88. P. G. Keyes, Ottawa, to J. C. Koehn, Mountain Lake, November 2, 1900 [copy]. 114/70386-1.

89. W. D. Scott, St. Paul, to J. C. Koehn, Mountain Lake, December 1, 1903. [copy]. 114/70386-2. The Koehn problem arose again in 1907. Agent James M. MacLachlan, Watertown, found his four most populous counties, Clay, Turner, Lincoln and Union removed from his jurisdiction and given over completely to Koehn. This reduced MacLachan's population base by almost one eighth. J. M. MacLachlan, Watertown, to W. J. White, Ottawa, December 6, 1907. 114/70386-2.

90. C. E. E. Ussher, Montreal, to W. D. Scott, Ottawa, March 28, 1905. 83/83679-2; F. S. Longworth, Detroit, to W. D. Scott, Ottawa, April

1, 1905; M. C. McInnes, Detroit, to W. D. Scott, Ottawa, April 3, 1905. 83/3374-2; C. E. E. Ussher, Montreal, to W. D. Scott, Ottawa, May 30, 1906; T. Duncan, Syracuse, to W. D. Scott, Ottawa, June 11, 1906. 89/33958; *Journal of the House of Commons* 37, Appendix I, February 27, 1902, 319.

91. C. E. E. Ussher, Montreal, to W. D. Scott, Ottawa, March 28, 1905; Statement signed by Robert Adams, Toronto, March 21, 1905. [copy]. 83/33674-2. It is interesting to note that the first reports of such frauds were made to the Immigration Branch by Canadian agents accusing the railway's own personnel in the United States of inflating results by sending phoney American settlers north. The settlers were allegedly not Americans but Canadians issued with reduced-rate railroad tickets. Grieve, Reed City, to J. A. Smart, Ottawa, September 15, 1897. 84/33917; M. V. McInnes, Detroit, to F. Pedley, Ottawa, September 5, 1899. 83/33674-1.

92. F. S. Longworth, Detroit, to W. D. Scott, Ottawa, April 1, 1905; M. V. McInnes, Detroit, to W. D. Scott, Ottawa, April 3, 1950. 83/33374-2.

93. C. E. E. Ussher, Montreal, to W. D. Scott, Ottawa, May 30, 1906; T. Duncan, Syracuse, to W. D. Scott, Ottawa, June 11, 1906. 84/33958.

94. For a detailed account of Canadian Pacific immigration activities as they related to land sales see Hedges, *Building the Canadian West.*

95. Extract from the Inter-State Commerce Law Defining the Liability of Shippers Thereunder. 86/3460.

96. W. C. Van Horne, Montreal, to W. J. White, Ottawa, November 29, 1897. 86/34360.

97. J. A. Smart, Ottawa, to C. A. Shaw, Chicago, December 19, 1900 [copy]. 113/17152.

98. M. V. McInnes, Detroit, to J. A. Smart, Ottawa, December 14, 1898; L. Pereira, Ottawa, to M. V. McInnes, Detroit, December 30, 1898. [copy]. 115/34360.

99. Circular, P. G. Keyes, Ottawa, to All Agents, August 3, 1900. 42/5142-2.

100. F. Pedley, Ottawa, to J. M. Lyons, Moncton, January 20, 1900 [copy]. 84/34360.

101. J. M. Lyons, Moncton, to D. Pottinger, Moncton, February 1, 1900 [copy]. 86/34360.

102. J. M. Lyons, Moncton, to F. Pedley, Ottawa, February 15, 1900. 86/34360.

103. Extract from the Deputy Minister of the Immigration Branch, re work to be performed by Mr. White [1897]. 86/3460. The full report was filed under 86/37884.

104. Unpublished research paper for 1938 Alberta Government Report, *The Case for Alberta,* compiled by R. E. English, Calgary, 1937, 184. Longman Papers, Glenbow — Alberta Institute Archives, Calgary. D 630.- 97123.L 8566.

105. *Sessional Papers* 1898, no. 13, pt. 2, 111.

106. Evidence indicates that during the initial stages of its American operations, the Immigration Branch knowingly gave preference to the Canadian Pacific and Soo Lines. On one occasion agent James Crawford, Kansas City, was advised to send settlers over the Soo Line rather than the Great Northern where possible "unless it can be shown that there is a practical advantage from it." Memorandum, L. Pereira, to L. M. Fortier, October 11, 1897. 42/5146-2.

107. W. J. White, St. Paul, to J. A. Smart, Ottawa, December 9, 1897. 86/34360.

108. W. R. Callaway, Minneapolis, to W. D. Scott, Ottawa, March 7, 1906. 210/488060.

109. W. A. Pinkerton, St. Paul, to H. M. Louis, St. Paul, March 3, 1906. 210/488060.

110. Memorandum, W. J. White, to W. D. Scott, March 26, 1906. 210/488060.
111. W. J. White, Ottawa, to E. T. Holmes, St. Paul, March 26, 1906 [copy]. 210/488060.
112. G. H. Shaw, Toronto, to W. D. Scott, Ottawa, May 12, 1911, 84/33919-3.
113. L. M. Fortier, Ottawa, to J. Crawford, Syracuse, May 23, 1911 [copy]. 84/33919-3.
114. *Sessional Papers* 1899, no. 13, pt. 2, 276.
115. J. Grieve, Mt. Pleasant, to F. Pedley, Ottawa, January 6, 1899. 84/-33917; *Sessional Papers* 1900, no. 13, pt. 2, 179.
116. *Sessional Papers* 1901, no. 25, pt. 2, 163.
117. *House of Commons Debates* 47, June 10, 1898, 7746; Circular to prospective agents, from M. V. McInnes, Detroit and Ottawa, July 27, 1897. 53/9679-1.
118. Report, W. J. White, to F. Pedley, September 13, 1910 [copy]. 115/-72552-2.
119. W. V. Bennett, Omaha, to F. Pedley, Ottawa, March 19, 1902. 72/-23605-3.
120. F. Pedley, Ottawa, to W. V. Bennett, Omaha, March 24, 1902 [copy]; W. J. White, Ottawa, to W. V. Bennett, Omaha, April 16, 1902 [copy]. 72/23605-3.
121. E. T. Holmes, St. Paul, to T. J. Atkinson, Clarinda, Iowa, October 3, 1902; E. T. Heyden, Omaha, to T. J. Atkinson, Clarinda, June 20, 1903; B. R. Hastings, Omaha, to T. J. Atkinson, Clarinda, July 31, 1903. Glenbow-Alberta Institute Archives, CG. 787.
122. E. A. Stewart, Milwaukee, to Imperial Development Company, Winnipeg, November 11, 1909. 113/69678-2.
123. C. J. A. Dalziel, Winnipeg, to J. B. Walker, Winnipeg, November 19, 1909. 113/69678-2.
124. In 1902 the Immigration Branch was confronted with a similar case in which the Haslam Land and Investment Company of St. Paul, charged an unidentified agent with using his agency office as a front for land promotion of a competing firm. The Department denied that this was the case although it conceded that sub-agents could be doing this. However, sub-agents were beyond the direct control of the Immigration Branch. Haslam Land and Investment Company, St. Paul, to F. Pedley, Ottawa, October 22, 1902; F. Pedley, Ottawa, to the Haslam Land and Investment Company, St. Paul, October 28, 1902 [copy]. 113/117152.
125. G. A. Hall, Milwaukee, to W. D. Scott, Ottawa, November 23, 1909. 113/69678-2.
126. W. J. White, Ottawa, to J. Grieve, Spokane, July 6, 1911 [copy]. 84/33917-7.
127. J. Grieve, Spokane, to W. J. White, Ottawa, June 19, 1911. 84/33917-7.
128. The Western Canadian Immigration Association should not be confused with the short-lived Western Canada Immigration Association founded at Winnipeg, February, 1896. Bicha is mistaken in alleging the Winnipeg-based organization was active in later years, and is most likely a victim of the similarity in names of the two groups. Bicha, *The American Farmers*, 45-46; *Winnipeg Free Press*, March 30, 1896, 4. For details on the founders and members of the Association see: *Western Canadian Immigration Association, Proceedings of the Second Annual Convention, Winnipeg, January 5, 1905* (Minneapolis, 1905), 49; *Manitoba Free Press*, January 26, 1904, 1; January 29, 1904, 9; *Toronto Globe*, January 29, 1904, 7.
129. *Proceedings 1905*, 3.
130. Among the more important promotional articles the Association was responsible for publishing were: Theodore Macfarlane Knappen, "Western Canada in 1904," *American Review of Reviews* 30 (1904), 578-585; "Winning the Canadian West", *World's Work* 10 (1905), 6607-6613.

169

131. *Manitoba Free Press,* January 30, 1904, 4.

132. Hedges, *Building the Canadian West,* 164; *Proceedings 1905,* 21-22; *Manitoba Free Press,* January 26, 1904, 1; *Minneapolis Journal* [n.d.] 1904. 76/181/294612-2; Memorandum, J. A. Smart, to W. J. White, January 8, 1904. 181/294612-1.

133. Sifton's approval of a $10,000 grant to the W.C.I.A. for 1904 and another for 1905 was largely influenced by his working relationship with David Wesley Bole, president of the Western Canadian Immigration Association. Bole was also the Liberal Member of Parliament for the Manitoba riding of *Winnipeg* and past president of the Manitoba Liberal Association. J. Keith Johnson, ed., *The Canadian Directory of Parliament, 1867-1967* (Ottawa, 1968), 55; Hector Charlesworth, ed., *A Cyclopaedia of Canadian Biography* (Toronto, 1919), 221-222.

134. Memorandum, W. J. White, to W. D. Scott, December 20, 1905. 181/29435-2.

NOTES TO CHAPTER IV

Unknown Failure

1. Circular, Instructions to Agents in the United States re Commission to Local Commission Agents, Ottawa, February 12, 1897. [copy]. 53/9679-1. Agents paid on a commission had been employed in immigration work in the United States as early as 1894 and in Europe from 1890. However, the programme adopted in 1897 was so different in scope and operation as to make it virtually a new scheme for the Department.

2. M. V. McInnes, Detroit, to J. A. Smart, Ottawa, March 9, 1897. 53/9679-1.

3. Memorandum, L. Pereira, to J. A. Smart, March 11, 1897. 53/9679-1.

4. L. Pereira, Ottawa, to D. L. Craven, Bad Axe, Michigan, March 17, 1897. [copy]. 53/9679-1.

5. B. Davies, St. Paul, to F. Pedley, Ottawa, December 12, 1898. 114/-70386-1.

6. Memorandum for the Establishment Ledger of the Department of Immigration and Colonization, January 12, 1923. 114/7086-9.

7. J. W. Taylor, Salt Lake City, to W. J. White, Ottawa, March 30, 1900. 116/76054-1; J. W. Taylor, Magrath, Alberta, to Lorrenzo Snow, Salt Lake City, July 23, 1901, John W. Taylor file, Manuscript Collection, Church Historian's Office, Salt Lake City.

8. L. Pereira, Ottawa, to M. V. McInnes, Detroit, March 17, 1897. [copy]. 53/9679-1.

9. In at least one case a salaried agent requested that he be granted an amount of money equal to that he would have received had he been a sub-agent. Agent Davies, St. Paul, argued that the money could be used to pay persons, who though not officially registered as sub-agents, would direct him to prospective settlers. Davies' request was turned down. B. Davies, St. Paul, to J. A. Smart, Ottawa, June 11, 1897; L. Pereira, Ottawa, to B. Davies, St. Paul, June 17, 1897 [copy]. 53/9679-1.

10. Memorandum, L. Pereira, to J. A. Smart, February 27, 1897. 53/9679-1.

11. W. J. White, Ottawa, to J. W. Taylor, Cardston, Alberta, June 12, 1899 [copy]. 116/76054-1.

12. *House of Commons Debates* 47, June 10, 1898, 7746.

13. Circular to prospective agents, from M. V. McInnes, Detroit and Ottawa, July 27, 1897. 53/9679-1; *House of Commons Debates* 45, June 14, 1897, 4065.

14. M. V. McInnes, Detroit, to J. A. Smart, Ottawa (March ?) 19, 1898. 53/9679-1.

15. J. Grieve, Reed City, to J. A. Smart, Ottawa, May 1, 1897. 53/9679-1.

16. L. Pereira, Ottawa, to M. V. McInnes, Detroit, May 3, 1897 [copy]. 53/9679-1.
17. M. V. McInnes, Detroit, to L. Pereira, Ottawa, April 30, 1897. 53/9679-1.
18. J. H. M. Parker, Duluth, to F. Pedley, Ottawa, April 15, 1902. 80/-32972-5.
19. J. Grieve, Reed City, to J. A. Smart, Ottawa, April 16, 1897. 84/33914.
20. J. Grieve, Reed City, to J. A. Smart, Ottawa, March 4, 1897. 84/33914.
21. List of Local Commission Agents in the United States, July 16, 1898. 53/9679-1.
22. List of Local Commission Agents in the United States, October 3, 1900. 53/9679-2.
23. List of Local Commission Agents in the United States, November 1, 1901. 53/9679-2.
24. List of Local Commission Agents in the United States, March 4, 1902. 53/9679-2.
25. J. Oliver Curwood, "The American Invasion of Canada," *Overland Monthly and Out West Magazine* 41 (1903), 392.
26. Number of persons sent to Canada by Local Commission Agents in the United States upon whom a bonus was paid. 53/9679-2.
27. *Immigration Facts and Figures* ([n.p.], 1913), 2.
28. *Sessional Papers* 1898, no. 13, pt. 4, 82-83.
29. W. H. Rogers, Watertown, to P. G. Keyes, Ottawa, September 22, 1900. 94/44043-1.
30. W. H. Rogers, Watertown, to L. Pereira, Ottawa, February 19, 1898. 94/40043-1.
31. *Sessional Papers* 1902, no. 25, pt. 2, 160; J. H. M. Parker, Duluth, to F. Pedley, Ottawa, April 15, 1902. 80/32972-5.
32. J. Oliver Curwood, "American Invasion of Canada," 392.
33. *Sessional Papers* 1899, no. 13, pt. 4, 69.
34. M. V. McInnes, Detroit, to All Sub-Agents, October 15, 1897. 53/9879-1.
35. L. Pereira, Ottawa, to D. McNicoll, Montreal, March 17, 1897 [copy]. 53/9679-1.
36. D. McNicoll, Montreal, to L. Pereira, Ottawa, March 22, 1897. 53/-9679-1.
37. J. R. Hall, Ottawa, to J. M. McDougold, Ottawa, March 27, 1897 [copy]. 53/9679-1. The early organization and co-operation of Canadian Pacific Railway agents in the United States with the Canadian government is dealt with in James B. Hedges, *Building the Canadian West* (New York, 1939), 94-125.
38. J. A. Smart, Ottawa, to C. A. Shaw, Chicago, December 19, 1900 [copy]. 113/17152.
39. Telegram, R. Kerr, Montreal, to P. G. Keyes, Ottawa, March 17, 1900. 53/9679-2.
40. P. G. Keyes, Ottawa, to R. Kerr, Montreal, April 5, 1900 [copy]. 53/9679-2.
41. M. V. McInnes, Report of Week Ending December 7, 1900. 83/833674-1.
42. P. G. Keyes, Ottawa, to M. V. McInnes, Detroit, January 22, 1901 [copy]. 53/9679-2.
43. *Sessional Papers* 1899, no. 13, pt. 4, 87.
44. W. H. Rogers, Toledo, to F. Pedley, Ottawa, December 14, 1901. 53/9679-2.
45. J. H. M. Parker, Duluth, to F. Pedley, Ottawa, April 21, 1902. 80/32972-5.
46. J. H. M. Parker, Duluth, to F. Pedley, Ottawa, July 16, 1902. 80/-32972-5.

47. L. Pereira, Ottawa, to D. McNicoll, Montreal, March 17, 1897 [copy]. 53/9679-1.

48. F. Pedley, Ottawa, to H. M. Williams, Toledo, December 23, 1901 [copy]. 53/9679-2.

49. *House of Commons Debates* 47, June 10, 1898, 7746. In 1900 Sifton again outlined the process for paying commissions and the methods employed to insure against irregularities in claims. *House of Commons Debates* 53, July 9, 1900, 9635.

50. C. E. E. Ussher, Montreal, to W. D. Scott, Ottawa, March 28, 1905. 83/83679-2.

51. Osler, Hammond and Norton, Winnipeg, to M. V. McInnes, Detroit, June 5, 1900 [copy]. 113/117152. For an outline of land sale activities by Osler, Hammond and Norton see Hedges, *Building the Canadian West*, 143-144, 153-155; Chester Martin, *Dominion Land Policy* (Toronto, 1938), 323-324.

52. M. V. McInnes, Detroit, to Osler, Hammond and Norton, Winnipeg, June 8, 1900 [copy]. 113/117152.

53. F. Pedley, Ottawa, to M. V. McInnes, Detroit, June 22, 1900 [copy]. 113/117152.

54. Haslam Land and Investment Company, St. Paul, to F. Pedley, Ottawa, October 22, 1902. 113/117152. For an outline of land sales activities of the Haslam Land and Investment Company see Hedges, *Building the Canadian West*, 162-163.

55. F. Pedley, Ottawa, to the Haslam Land and Investment Company, St. Paul, October 18, 1902 [copy]. 113/117152.

56. Memorandum, W. J. White, to J. A. Smart, December 17, 1902. 53/-9676-2.

57. Circular to J. H. M. Parker, Duluth, [n.d.]. 80/32972-5.

58. W. J. White, St. Paul, to J. A. Smart, Ottawa, May 18, 1903. 80/-32972-5.

59. Memorandum, W. J. White, to J. A. Smart, December 17, 1902. 53/-9676-2.

60. Memorandum, W. J. White, to J. A. Smart, December 22, 1902. 53/-9676-2.

61. Memorandum, W. J. White, to J. A. Smart, December 17, 1902. 53/-9676-2.

62. *House of Commons Debates* 60, July 14, 1903, 6556-6557.

63. W. H. Rogers, Watertown, to F. Pedley, Ottawa, March 14, 1899. 94/40043-1.

64. J. Grieve, Sault Ste. Marie, to W. D. Scott, Ottawa, April 6, 1903. 53/9679-2.

65. B. Davies, St. Paul, to W. J. White, Ottawa, [n.d.], 1901. 53/9679-2.

66. List of Local Commission Agents in the United States, July 16, 1898. 53/9679-1. List of Local Commission Agents in the United States, March 3, 1903. 53/9679-2.

67. Table I was compiled from "Bonuses to agents for settlers from the United States" as listed in *Sessional Papers* 1898, no. 1, pt. H, 14; 1899, no. 1, pt. H, 18; 1900, no. 1, pt. H, 17; 1901, no. 1, pt. L, 18; 1902, no. 1, pt. L, 17-18; 1903, no. 1, pt. L, 19; 1904, no. 1, pt. L, 23; 1905, no. 1, pt. L. 26. All calculations are made to the nearest dollar. No attempt has been made to adjust the figures to allow for advance payments or small costs listed as part of sub-agent commissions. Allowing for such small changes in figures would in no way alter the picture presented by the statistics.
It should be noted that in at least one case, John W. Taylor, commissions collected before 1902 have not been listed in the *Sessional Papers* if such payments were made.

68. Number of persons sent to Canada by Local Commission Agents in the United States upon whom a bonus was paid. 53/8676-2.

69. Memorandum, J. A. Smart, to W. D. Scott, June 11, 1903. 53/9679-2.

70. Memorandum, W. D. Scott, to J. A. Smart, June 23, 1903. 53/9679-2.

71. *Journal of the House of Commons* 32, Appendix 2, May 29, 1903, 55, 59.

72. *House of Commons Debates* 60, July 17, 1903, 6848.

73. For the fiscal year 1903-1904, the year of reorganization, the Immigration Branch expended $14,428 in payment of commissions. The next year decreased emphasis on the sub-agent system saw paid commissions fall off to $5,860. *Sessional Papers* 1905, no. 1, pt. L, 26; 1906, no. 1, pt. L, 26.

74. Table II was constructed from *Immigration Facts and Figures* ([n.p.], 1913), 24. See also *Reports of the United States Immigration Commission, The Immigration Situation in Other Countries,* 40, S.Dor. No. 761, 61st Cong. 3d sess. (Washington, 1911), 33 and *Journal of the House of Commons* 43, Appendix II, May 13, 1908, 370. Over the period 1904 to 1912 bonuses paid on European immigrants continued uninterrupted. Commissions paid accounted for between 13.47 and 20.39 of the total immigration. *Immigration Facts and Figures,* 24.

75. W. D. Scott, to E. T. Holmes, St. Paul, July 8, 1903 [copy]. 53/9679-2.

76. Memorandum, W. J. White, to J. A. Smart, October 13, 1903. 80/-32972-5.

77. Memorandum, J. A. Smart, to W. J. White, October 16, 1903; Telegram, W. D. Scott, Ottawa, to J. H. M. Parker, Duluth, December 30, 1903 [copy]. 80/32972-5.

78. J. H. M. Parker, Duluth, to W. D. Scott, Ottawa, December 19, 1903. 80/32972-5.

79. The whole of file 80/72972-6 is the record of letters dealing with Parker's activities in his self styled Canadian Land and Immigration Office and the Department's efforts to deal with him.

80. *St. Paul Globe,* December 18, 1903, 8.

81. M. V. McInnes, Detroit, to J. A. Smart, Ottawa, January 13, 1904. 80/32972-5.

82. W. V. Bennett, St. Paul, to W. J. White, Ottawa, December 31, 1903. 80/32972-5.

83. *House of Commons Debates* 67, January 21, 1904, 7275, 7276. *Toronto Telegram,* December 30, 1903. The Parker article was vigorously attacked in the *Manitoba Free Press,* December 31, 1903. 80/32972-5.

NOTES TO CHAPTER V

Selling a Country

1. *House of Commons Debates* 50, July 26, 1899, 8501.

2. *Sessional Papers* 1899, no. 13, pt. 2, 274.

3. *Sessional Papers* 1906, no. 25, pt. 2, 76.

4. William R. Stewart, "The Americanization of the Canadian Northwest," *Cosmopolitan* 34 (1903), 605.

5. Instructions for State Agents, Ottawa, February 12, 1897. 42/5146-2.

6. Western Newspaper Union, price sheet. 101/49515-1. In 1914 the question of the Western Newspaper Unions propriety in acting as agents for foreign advertising would be raised in the Senate's Committee on Lobbying. See, "The Canadian Lure," *The Literary Digest* 48 (1914), 308-309.

7. *Sessional Papers* 1903, no. 1, L-21.

8. James B. Hedges, *Building the Canadian West* (New York, 1933), 133.

9. *Sessional Papers* 1905, no. 25, pt. 2, 32.
10. Proof sheet, "Looking For a Home," dated March 19, 1904; in possession of the author.
11. *Sessional Papers* 1907, no. 25, pt. 2, 78.
12. *Ibid.,* 79; 1904, no. 25, pt. 2, 124; *House of Commons Debates* 347, June 10, 1898, 7748.
13. *Sessional Papers* 1903, no. 1, L-21-22.
14. *Sessional Papers* 1904, no. 25, pt. 2, 124.
15. *Sessional Papers* 1899, no. 13, pt. 2, 267; 1897, no. 13, pt. 4, 47.
16. Clippings, *Kalkaska Leader,* October 2, 1897 [n.p.];*Leroy Independent,* October 22, 1897 [n.p.]; *Clare Sentinel,* October 15, 1897 [n.p.] 84/-33917.
17. Hedges, *Building the Canadian West,* 133.
18. Statement giving place of office, date opened, name of agent, salary, letters received, letters sent and number of interviews, 1904-1905. 41/5146.
19. Paul W. Gates, "Official Encouragement of Immigration by the Province of Canada," *Canadian Historical Review* 15 (1934), 24-38.
20. Adam Shortt, "Some Observations on the Great Northwest," *Queen's Quarterly* 2 (1895), 183-197; "Some Observations on the Great Northwest, II," *Queen's Quarterly* 3 (1895), 11-22.
21. James B. Hedges, *Building the Canadian West,* 94-125.
22. Clifford Sifton as quoted in John W. Dafoe, *Clifford Sifton in Relation to his Times* (Toronto, 1931), 139.
23. Rudyard Kipling, "Our Lady of the Snows, 1897," *London Times,* April 27, 1895.
24. *Western Canada* (Ottawa, 1899), 11.
25. *Ibid.,* 29. Also see *The Resources of Western Canada, Timely Remarks and Useful Information* (Ottawa, 1899), 24.
26. *Delegates Reports and Settlers Experiences in Western Canada* (Ottawa, 1899).
27. *Symposium of Ideas and Prophecies on the Canadian West by the Members of the National Editorial Association, and What They Said in 1900* (Ottawa, 1901?).
28. *Reliable Information For Use of United States Newspaper Editors Visiting Western Canada* (Ottawa, 1904?).
29. Karel Denis Bicha, *The American Farmer and the Canadian West 1896-1914* (Lawrence, 1968), 76-77.
30. *Great Growth of Western Canada* (Ottawa, 1906?); *Prosperity Follows Settlement In Western Canada* (Ottawa, 1905); *The Canadian West, Strides That Have Been Made In Recent Years* (Ottawa, 1906?); *Canada Land of Opportunity* (Ottawa, 1906?); *1905 The Biggest Crop in the History of the Canadian West* (Ottawa, 1906?).
31. *Sessional Papers* 1898, no. 13, pt. 4, 70. An interesting sidelight of the Department's publishing of the *Atlas of Canada* was that it caused a small uproar in the Commons Committee on Agriculture and Colonization. In 1900 as the delicate Alaska Boundary talks were under way, committee member, Conservative M.P. Nicolas Flood Davin charged that the printing of the atlas in the United States has produced a government publication with the Alaska boundary marked according to U.S. claims. He feared this would be used by American negotiators to show *de facto* recognition by one Canadian government agency of American claims. *Journal of the House of Commons* 35 (1900) Appendix 375.
32. *Sessional Papers* 1902, no. 25, pt. 2, 3; 1905, no. 25, pt. 2, 31; 1906, no. 25, pt. 2, 79.

33. *The Last and Best West* (Ottawa, 1906); *The Last and Best West* (Ottawa, 1907).

34. *The Last and Best West* (Ottawa, 1906), 30. The same question and answer method was used in *Where and How and All About It: Information and Facts for the Prospective Settler* (Ottawa, 1906).

35. Bicha, *The American Farmer*, 78.

36. *Canada Land of Opportunity* (Ottawa, 1906?) 23; *Sessional Papers* 1911, no. 25, pt. 2, 90.

37. *The Canadian West, Strides That Have Been Made In Recent Years* (Ottawa, 1906?), 6.

38. C. Pilling, Grand Forks, South Dakota, to W. D. Scott, Ottawa, February 15, 1905. 136/130974. The issue of the *Manitoba Free Press* was raised in the House of Commons. In 1904 Conservative M.P. Richard Blain attacked the Minister of the Interior claiming that the $7,500 spent in purchasing the Harvest Edition for that year was but Liberal Party support of a Liberal Party newspaper "under the guise of immigration literature for the purpose of inducing people to come to Canada." *House of Commons Debates* 67, July 21, 1904, 7339.

39. For the purpose of this essay a state fair is considered one which is owned and operated by the state government or by a body authorized by the state government to operate a fair. Local, county or regional fairs may have state support, but are generally the product of initiative of local agricultural associations which determine their character and policy.

40. Wayne Caldwell Neely, *The Agricultural Fair* (New York, 1935), 234-235.

41. *Ibid.*, 113; *The American Year Book,* 1916 (New York, 1917), 188.

42. Neely, *The Agricultural Fair,* 249-250.

43. L. Pereira, Ottawa, to W. V. Bennett, Omaha, July 15, 1897 [copy]. 95/40280.

44. J. A. Smart, Ottawa, to T. Greenway, Winnipeg, July 15, 1897 [copy]. 95/40280.

45. J. A. Smart, Ottawa, to S. A. Fisher, Ottawa, October 20, 1897 [copy]. 99/44544-1.

46. W. V. Bennett, Omaha, to F. Pedley, Ottawa, November 12, 1898. 99/44544-1.

47. *Sessional Papers* 1898, no. 13, pt. 2, 107.

48. *Ibid.*, 108.

49. *Sessional Papers* 1899, no. 13, pt. 2, 281.

50. *Toledo Daily News,* August 23, 1899. 83/33674-1. Also see *Grand Rapids Daily Herald* as quoted in *Sessional Papers* 1899, no. 13, pt. 2, 270.

51. J. M. MacLachlan, Wausau, to W. J. White, Ottawa, July 28, 1903. 140/138303-1. *Sessional Papers* 1903, no. 25, pt. 2, 137.

52. *Sessional Papers* 1904, no. 25, pt. 2, 123-124.

53. W. J. White, Ottawa, to J. A. Smart, Ottawa, May 11, 1904 [copy]. 172/274010.

54. Memorandum, W. J. White, to W. D. Scott, March 24, 1904. 172/274010.

55. Memorandum, W. J. White, to J. A. Smart, June 25, 1904. 172/274010.

56. *St. Louis Republic,* October 16, 1904, 13.

57. *Sessional Papers* 1906, no. 25, pt. 2, 64.

58. Memorandum, W. J. White, to J. A. Smart, September 19, 1904. 54/5146-3.

59. *Sessional Papers* 1899, no. 13, pt. 2, 269.

60. *Sessional Papers* 1899, no. 13, pt. 2, 267, 277-278; Bicha, *The American Farmer,* 71-72; Hedges, *Building the Canadian West,* 134-135.

61. In 1906 a payment of $2,753.13 was made to the Canadian Pacific to cover costs of transporting the 175-member delegation of the Pennsylvania Editorial Association. *Sessional Papers* 1908, no. 1, 2-28.
62. W. J. White, Ottawa, to Arthur Hawkes, Toronto, May 23, 1908 [copy]. 97/41303.
63. Statement accompanying cheque to Canadian Pacific [copy] and statement accompanying cheque to Canadian Northern [copy]. 97/41303.
64. J. M. Page, Jerseyville, to W. J. White, Ottawa, July 16, 1906. 97/-41303-6.
65. A. E. McKinnon, Battle Creek, to W. J. White, Ottawa, May 8, 1908. 97/41303.
66. A. E. McKinnon, Battle Creek, to W. J. White, Ottawa, December 30, 1908. 97/41303.
67. *Sessional Papers* 1900, no. 13, pt. 2, 178.
68. J. B. Walker, Winnipeg, to W. J. White, Ottawa, June 24, 1909. 97/41303.
69. Report, C. N. Speers, Brandon, to W. D. Scott, Ottawa, August 11, 1906. 97/41303-2.
70. J. B. Walker, Winnipeg, to W. J. White, Ottawa, April 30, 1909; J. B. Walker, Winnipeg, to W. J. White, Ottawa, May 25, 1909. 97/41303.
71. *House of Commons Debates* 50, July 27, 1899, 8655.
72. Historian Karel Bicha has claimed that the negative reports of the Illinois delegation prevented later visits by the Illinois group. See Bicha, *The American Farmer*, 73. This is incorrect. Arrangements for a second visit were made in 1906. J. M. Page, Jerseyville, to W. J. White, Ottawa, July 16, 1906. 97/41303-6.
73. *Reliable Information For Use of United States Newspapers Editors Visiting Western Canada* (Ottawa, 1904?).
74. W. J. White, Ottawa, to C. E. E. Ussher, Winnipeg, August 6, 1908 [copy]. 97/41303.
75. Circular, W. J. White, Ottawa, to editors from Ohio on 1910 tour, August 17, 1911. 97/41303-2.
76. M. V. Sullivan, Shelbyville, to W. J. White, Ottawa, August 26, 1911. 97/41303-2.
77. See for example, *Symposium of Ideas and Prophecies of the Canadian West by Members of the National Editorial Association, and What They Said in 1900* (Ottawa, 1901?)
78. C. N. Speers, Brandon, to W. D. Scott, Ottawa, August 11, 1906. 97/41303-2. Clippings are available in file 97/41303.
79. *Sessional Papers* 1905, no. 25, pt. 2, 32.
80. Richard Cleghorn Overton, *Burlington West* (Cambridge, 1941), 335-336, 343; Lawrence Leslie Waters, *Steel Rails to Santa Fe* (Lawrence, 1950), 222-223.
81. Hedges, *Building the Canadian West*, 137.
82. *Sessional Papers* 1899, no. 13, pt. 2, 274.
83. W. H. Rogers, Watertown, to L. Pereira, Ottawa, February 19, 1898. 94/40043-1.
84. Report, M. V. McInnes, Detroit, June 30, 1899, 5. 83/33674-1. *House of Commons Debates* 50, 8650, July 27, 1899.
85. *Sessional Papers* 1899, no. 13, pt. 2, 284.
86. See for example, *Delegates Reports and Settlers Experiences in Western Canada* (Ottawa, 1899).
87. *Sessional Papers* 1900, no. 13, pt. 2, 186.
88. *Sessional Papers* 1899, no. 13, pt. 2, 285.
89. *Ibid.*, 281, 1900, no. 13, pt. 2, 90.

90. W. H. Rogers, Watertown, to P. G. Keyes, Ottawa, September 22, 1900. 94/40043-1. *Sessional Papers* 1905, no. 25, pt. 2, 133; 1906, no. 25, pt. 2, 79.

91. *Sessional Papers* 1903, no. 25, pt. 2, 111.

92. *Sessional Papers* 1904, no. 25, pt. 2, 131.

93. *Journal of the House of Commons* 38, Appendix II, May 29, 1903, 44.

94. *Ibid.*, 45.

95. *Reports of the [U.S.] Immigration Commission, volume 40. The Immigration Situation in other countries: Canada - Australia - New Zealand - Argentina - Brazil,* S.Doc. No. 764, 61st Cong. 3d. sess. (Washington, 1911), 30.

96. *Sessional Papers* 1906, no. 25, pt. 2, 79.

NOTES TO CHAPTER VI

The Other Lands

1. Frederick Jackson Turner, "The Significance of the Frontier in American History," *Annual Report of the American Historical Association* (1893), 199, 227.

2. *New York Herald,* September 24, 1891 as quoted in *Literary Digest* 3 (1891), 642.

3. While it has been generally accepted that land was available for settlement in the United States after 1890, the impact of an allegedly widely accepted belief that the frontier had closed is still open to historical debate. Ray Billington has taken the position that the American public was aware of the frontier's closing and concerned for the process of national readjustment. Richard Hofstadter has integrated much of this argument into his discussion of the "psychic crisis," to explain the forces which propelled the United States into war in 1898. Challenging the frontier thesis and the Billington extension, Lee Benson contends that Billington has too easily accepted frontier mythology as fact and as a result has had to do major mental gymnastics in order to keep the frontier thesis alive. Ray Billington, *Western Expansion* (second edition, New York, 1960), 751-753; Richard Hofstadter, "Manifest Destiny and the Philippines," Daniel Aaron, ed., *America in Crisis* (New York, 1952), 174; Lee Benson, "The Historian as Mythmaker: Turner and the Closed Frontier," David M. Ellis, ed., *The Frontier in American Development* (Ithica, 1969), 3-19.

4. *Annual Report of the [United States] Department of the Interior* (Washington, 1900), 1, 20.

5. E. Louis Peffer, *The Closing of the Public Domain: Disposal and Reservation Politics, 1900-1950.* (Stanford, 1951), 134. Paul Gates has pointed out that much of the land homesteaded after 1890 fell not into the hands of individual farmers but of larger land interests as a result of abuses of the law. But development of farm ownership, especially in states extending from North Dakota to Oklahoma, moved forward in spite of the abuse. Paul W. Gates, "The Homestead Act: Free Land Policy in Operation, 1862-1935," Howard W. Ottoson, ed., *Land Use Policy and Problems in the United States* (Lincoln, 1963), 41.

6. Paul W. Gates, *History of Public Land Law Development* (Washington, 1968), 495.

7. Theodore Roosevelt, *Theodore Roosevelt, An Autobiography* (New York, 1911), 429.

8. Roy E. Huffman, *Irrigation Development and Public Water Policy* (New York, 1953), 18-24 and John A. Widtsoe, "A Century of Irrigation," *Reclamation Era* 33 (1947), 99, 102.

9. Benjamin Horace Hibbard, *A History of Public Land Policies* (Madison, 1924), 444.

10. Mary Wilma H. Hargreaves, *Dry Farming in the Northern Great Plains* (Cambridge, 1957), 364-372.

11. *Sessional Papers* 1901, no. 25, pt. 2, 168.

12. As quoted in Arthur B. Darling, ed., *The Public Papers of Francis G. Newlands* (2 vols., Boston, 1932), 1: 72.

13. *Sessional Papers* 1910, no. 20, pt. 2, 82.

14. William E. Warne, "Land Speculation," *Reclamation Era* 33 (1947), 178-179. Also, see Samuel P. Hayes, *Conservation and the Gospel of Efficiency* (Cambridge, 1959), 19-22.

15. Warne, "Land Speculation," 176.

16. *Sessional Papers* 1910, no. 25, pt. 2, 83.

17. Hargreaves, *Dry Farming*, 402-412; Lawrence Leslie Waters, *Steel Trails to Santa Fe* (Lawrence, 1950), 152-153.

18. James Willard Hurst, *Law and Economic Growth, The Legal History of the Lumbering Industry in Wisconsin*, 1836-1915 (Cambridge, 1964), 127.

19. James O'Neill, "The Future of Northern Wisconsin," *Proceedings of the State Historical Society of Wisconsin* (1899), 208. The transition from forest to farm was not always as smooth or productive as O'Neill seemed to suggest. The problems involved in the process are the topic of Vernon Rosco Curstensen, *Farms or Forests* (Madison, 1958).

20. Paul W. Gates, *History of Public Land Law Development,* 503.

21. The same reasoning was used by railroads which had no land to sell or promote in order to help the Canadian bound settler. In this case the railroad would receive the "haul" to the border by those moving to Canada while still continuing to service the new owners of land left by a settler. J. A. Grieve, Mt. Pleasant, Michigan, to F. Pedley, Ottawa. January 6, 1899. 84/33017.

22. *Sessional Papers* 1901, no. 25, pt. 2, 168. On one occasion when he was asked about the quantity of Canadian lands available for settlement Frank Pedley remarked, "There are several hundreds of millions of acres of land in the territories, and the chances are at the present rate of settlement, it will not be exhausted for 100 years." *Journal of the House of Commons* 37, Appendix I, February 27, 1901, 317.

23. *Journal of the House of Commons* 36 (1901), Appendix I, 306.

24. *Sessional Papers* 1902, no. 25, pt. 2, 153.

25. *Ibid.,* 158.

26. *Ibid.,* 145-146; 1903, no. 25, pt. 2, 128. White also noted that the agency office in Spokane, Washington, was also showing good results among disappointed land seekers. Memorandum, W. J. White, to W. D. Scott, July 7, 1903.

27. *Sessional Papers* 1909, no. 25, pt. 2, 88.

28. *Sessional Papers* 1899, no. 11, pt. 2, 280.

29. *Sessional Papers* 1900, no. 10, pt. 2, 188.

30. *Sessional Papers* 1901, no. 25, pt. 2, 188; 1902, no. 25, pt. 2, 145, 175.

31. T. O. Currie, Milwaukee, to W. D. Scott, Ottawa, July 13, 1909. 91/-36357-4.

32. *Sessional Papers* 1902, no. 25, pt. 2, 175; P. G. Keyes, Ottawa, to J. M. MacLachlan, Winnipeg, January 24, 1901. 140/138303-1.

33. J. M. MacLachlan, Wausau, to W. J. White, Ottawa, November 23, 1902. 140/138303-1.

34. W. J. White, Ottawa, to J. M. MacLachlan, Wausau, November 27, 1902 [copy]. 140/138303-1.

35. J. M. MacLachlan, Wausau, to W. D. Scott, Ottawa, April 9, 1903. 140/138303-1. Background on the lumbering industry in the Wausau area is available in W. H. Glover, "Lumber Rafting on the Wisconsin River," *Wisconsin Magazine of History* 25 (1942), 308-328.

36. The promotion of cut-over timber lands of northern Wisconsin is dealt with in Arlon Clayton Helgeson, "Nineteenth Century Land Colonization in Northern Wisconsin," *The Wisconsin Magazine of History* 36 (1953), 115-121 and D. O. Thompson and W. H. Glover, "A Pioneer Adventure in Agriculture Extension, A Contribution from the Wisconsin Cut-Over," *Agricultural History* 22 (1948), 124-128.

37. J. M. MacLachlan, Wausau, to W. J. White, Ottawa, July 28, 1903. 140/138303-1; *Sessional Papers* 1903, no. 25, pt. 2, 137.

38. *Sessional Papers* 1904, no. 25, pt. 2, 139.

39. W. E. Black, Crookson, Minnesota, to P. G. Keyes, August 20, 1910. 277/801543. J. M. MacLachlan, Wausau, to W. J. White, Ottawa, February 13, 1902. 140/138303-1. Arlon Clayton Helgeson, "The Promotion of Agricultural Settlement in Northern Wisconsin," (unpublished Ph.D. thesis, University of Wisconsin, 1951), 194, 204-205.

40. W. J. White, St. Paul, to J. A. Smart, Ottawa, May 23, 1903. 42/5146-3.

41. J. M. MacLachlan, Wausau, to W. J. White, Ottawa, July 20, 1903. 140/138303-1.

42. *Journal of the House of Commons* 38 (1903), Appendix II, 74.

43. J. M. MacLachlan, Wausau, to W. J. White, Ottawa, December 17, 1903. 140/138202-1.

44. *Sessional Papers* 1890, no. 10, pt. 4, 91.

45. W. H. Rogers, Watertown, to F. Pedley, Ottawa, June 30, 1900. 94/40043-1.

46. *Sessional Papers* 1901, no. 25, pt. 2, 174.

47. *Ibid.,* 179.

48. *Sessional Papers* 1898, no. 10, pt. 4, 69. The land settlement programmes of major American land grant railroads had closed or were in the process of closing during the period 1896-1911. However, the land promotion of remaining railroad lands or other land settlement schemes could call on a long tradition of salesmanship for precedence. Earlier railroad land settlement activity has been documented. See Paul W. Gates, *The Illinois Central Railroad and its Colonization Work* (Cambridge, 1934); Richard Overton, *Burlington West: A Colonization History of the Burlington Railroad* (Cambridge, 1941); James B. Hedges, "The Colonization Work of the Northern Pacific Railroad," *Mississippi Valley Historical Review* 13 (1926), 311-345; James B. Hedges, "Promotion of Immigration to the Pacific Northwest by the Railroads," *Mississippi Valley Historical Review* 15 (1928), 183-203; Edna M. Parker, "The Southern Pacific Railroad and the Settlement of Southern California," *Pacific Historical Review* 6 (1937), 103-119; Stanley N. Murray, "Railroads and the Agricultural Development of the Red River Valley of the North, 1878-1890," *Agricultural History* 31(1957), 57-66.

49. *Sessional Papers* 1905, no. 25, pt. 2, 32.

50. *Sessional Papers* 1900, no. 10, pt. 2, 196.

51. *Sessional Papers* 1906, no. 25, pt. 2, 63-64 and Overton *Burlington West,* 465-476.

52. *Ibid.,* 413-484.

53. *Sessional Papers* 1905, no. 25, pt. 2, 52.

54. *Ibid.,* 41.

55. *Ibid.,* 43.

56. *Sessional Papers* 1907-1908, no. 25, pt. 2, 64, 83; 1909, no. 25, pt. 2, 87. Agent William Rogers, Indianapolis, complained however, that some American land agents paid a portion of a settler's fare out of their own pockets but still were able to make a healthy profit from land sales. W. H. Rogers, Indianapolis, to W. D. Scott, Ottawa, May 12, 1906. 94/40043-2.

57. J. M. MacLachlan, Watertown, to W. D. Scott, Ottawa, May 2, 1908. 140/138303-1.

58. *Daily Pioneer Press,* March 17, 1904. It would seem from the priority given by the American Immigration Association to the movement of settlers to the southwest that Karel Denis Bicha is incorrect in assuming that organization was directed "solely" against Canada. Karel Denis Bicha, *The American Farmer and the Canadian West, 1896-1914* (Lawrence, Kansas, 1968), 118.

59. *Kansas City Star,* July 16, 1904, reprinted in *Manitoba Free Press,* July 18, 1904. 42/5146-3. Not all the American press joined in the Association's cry. *The Springfield Republican* pointed out that the American government had done the same type of recruitment in Europe while South Carolina, interested in white immigration, was doing so then. The paper argued, "The United States Government cannot ask other countries to desist from doing what States within that Government are permitted to do." The *St. Paul Dispatch* called not for a ban on Canadian immigration activity, claiming it was "rather late for such baby play." Instead they would prefer to see American authorities follow the successful Canadian model in an American campaign. *Springfield Republican* as quoted in *Manitoba Free Press,* July 26, 1904; *St. Paul Dispatch* as quoted in *Manitoba Free Press,* July 26, 1904. 42/5146-3.

60. W. J. White, Chicago, to J. A. Smart, Ottawa, July 19, 1904. 42/5146-3; *Sessional Papers* 1905, no. 25, pt. 2, 32. Karel Denis Bicha has pointed out that some of the farm press maintained open hostility to Canadian activities especially in areas where population or development seemed in danger as a result of the northward migration. It should be added that this opposition might well have been greater were it not for the influence of the Immigration Branch as a major advertiser in the local farm press. Bicha, *The American Farmer,* 120.

61. *Sessional Papers* 1905, no. 25, pt. 2, 32.

62. *Journal of the House of Commons* 38 (1903), Appendix II, 73-74.

63. *Sessional Papers* 1906-1907, no. 25, pt. 2, 79.

64. *Sessional Papers* 1906, no. 25, pt. 2, 77.

65. Theodore C. Blegan, "The Competition of the Northwestern States for Immigrants," *Wisconsin Magazine of History* 3 (1919), 26-28 and Helgeson, thesis 83-113, 234-242.

66. *Biennial Report of the State Board of Immigration of Wyoming 1911-1912* (Cheyenne, 1912), 4.

67. Memorandum, J. A. Smart, to C. Sifton, February 2, 1905 [copy]. 83/33674-2.

68. *Nation* 82 (1906), 523-524.

69. *Minnesota Historical Society Collection* 13 (1908), 446-447.

70. *Sessional Papers* 1914, no. 25, pt. 2, 104; Bicha, *The American Farmer,* 120.

71. Peffer, *Closing of the Public Domain,* 139-141.

72. Hargreaves, *Dry Farming,* 346-351.

73. Peffer, *Closing of the Public Domain,* 153-154.

74. *Sessional Papers* 1905, no. 25, pt. 2, 34, 40, 53.

75. *Ibid.,* 51.

76. *Sessional Papers* 1907-1908, no. 25, pt. 2, 82.

77. *Ibid.,* 83.

78. W. H. Rogers, Indianapolis, to W. D. Scott, Ottawa, July 4, 1907. 94/40043-2; *Sessional Papers* 1903, no. 25, pt. 2, 132.

79. *Sessional Papers* 1911, no. 25, pt. 2, 41.

80. Circular, W. J. White, Ottawa, to All Agents, January 3, 1912 [copy.] 113/69678-2.

Closing the Door

1. William Duncan Scott, "Immigration and Population," *Canada and Its Provinces,* vol. 7, Adam Shortt, ed. (Toronto, 1914), 531.

2. The total number of Negroes in Canada in 1901 was 17,347 with 8,935 in Ontario and 5,984 in Nova Scotia. "Origins of People by Provinces, 1901-1911," *Census of Canada, 1911,* 2 (Ottawa, 1913), 370-371. It is interesting to note that both in absolute numbers and percentage of population, the Negro population of Canada was in a process of decline. In 1871 the Negro population of Canada had stood at 21,496. James S. Woodsworth, *Strangers Within Our Gates* (Toronto, 1909), 15.

3. Among more recent works dealing with Negro immigration are Robin W. Winks, *The Blacks in Canada: A History* (New Haven, 1971); Trevor W. Sessing, "How They Kept Canada Almost Lily White," *Saturday Night* 85 (September, 1970), 30-32. Two submissions to the Royal Commission on Bilingualism and Biculturalism are, at the time of this writing, still restricted to public view. However, their release for public examination is expected in the near future. Norma E. Walmsley. "Some Aspects of Canada's Immigration Policy," unpublished essay prepared for the Royal Commission on Bilingualism and Biculturalism (April, 1966); Harold H. Potter and Daniel G. Hill, "Negro Settlement in Canada, 1628-1965: A Survey," unpublished essay prepared for the Royal Commission on Bilingualism and Biculturalism (April, 1966).

4. John R. Commons, "Racial Composition of the American People," *Chautauquan* (1903), as quoted in James S. Woodsworth, *Strangers Within Our Gates,* 92.

5. H. G. Le Lesser, "The West Indian Negro of To-day," *Canadian Magazine* 15 (1900), 120.

6. W. H. Kesterton, *A History of Journalism in Canada* (Toronto, 1967), 170-173; Norah Story, ed., *The Oxford Companion to Canadian History and Literature* (Toronto, 1967), 457.

7. Among the many studies of the Negro situation in the Gilded Age and the Progressive era especially useful are John Hope Franklin, *From Slavery to Freedom* (2nd ed., New York, 1956), C. Vann Woodward, *Origins of the New South, 1877-1913* (Baton Rouge, 1951), Raymond W. Logan, *The Negro in American Life and Thought* (New York, 1954), Raymond W. Logan, *The Betrayal of the Negro* (New York, 1965) C. Vann Woodward, *Strange Career of Jim Crow* (2nd ed., rev., New York, 1966) and Gwin Griffis Johnson, "The Ideology of White Supremacy, 1876-1910," *Essays in Southern History,* Fletcher Green, ed. (Chapel Hill, 1949), 124-156.

8. *Plessy* vs. *Ferguson,* 163 U.S. 537, *United States Reports* (1896).

9. *Plessy* vs. *Ferguson* was not overruled until the hallmark Supreme Court decision of *Brown* vs. *Board of Education of Topeka,* 347 U.S. 483 *United States Reports* (1954).

10. For an analysis of Negro migration patterns within the United States see Gunnar Myrdal, *An American Dilemma* (New York, 1944), 182-201.

11. *An American Dilemma* (New York, 1944), 200-250.

12. J. S. Crawford, Kansas City, to F. Oliver, Ottawa, January 17, 1899. 115/72552-1.

13. L. Pereira, Ottawa, to J. S. Crawford, Kansas City, January 23, 1899 [copy]. 115/72552-1.

14. The situation of Oriental immigrants was far different. At various periods from 1896 to 1911 the Chinese and Japanese entering Canada came

under a series of regulations or agreements designed to keep their numbers small. Control was maintained by federal and provincial statutes as well as agreements between the federal government and Japan similar to those between the United States and Japan. Joseph S. Roucek, "The Japanese in Canada," *The Study of Current English* 20 (1965), 55-58, and Charles H. Young and Helen R. Y. Reid, *The Japanese Canadians* (Toronto, 1938), 7-12.

15. A. Burton, Toronto, to the Minister of Agriculture, Ottawa, April 29, 1899. 115/72552-1. If Bishop Grant had been very committed to a back-to-Africa movement or a possible Negro colony in Western Canada, by 1908 he was singing a far different tune. As one of Booker T. Washington's closest advisers, Bishop Grant had by 1908 taken the position that 300 years of Negro history in the Americas had broken any tie the Negro had had with Africa except in areas of economic or missionary activity. The best path for the Negro to follow was that being laid out from Tuskeegee. August Meier, *Negro Thought in America, 1880-1915* (Ann Arbor, 1963), 218-319, 272.

16. L. Pereira, Ottawa, to A. Burton, Toronto, May 8, 1899 [copy]. 115/-72552-1.

17. S. Barrett, Chester County, Pennsylvania, to the Department of Agriculture, Ottawa, February 27, 1901. 115/72552-1.

18. P. G. Keyes, Ottawa, to S. Barrett, Chester County, Pennsylvania, March 7, 1901 [copy]. 115/72552-1.

19. B. McKay, Washington, to the Commissioner of Immigration, Ottawa, October 27, 1901. 115/72552-1.

20. F. Pedley, Ottawa, to B. McKay, Washington, October 31, 1901 [copy]. 115/72552-1.

21. S. Barrett, Hiram, Ohio, to the Department of the Interior, Ottawa, June 15, 1903. 115/72552-1.

22. W. D. Scott, Ottawa, to S. Barrett, Hiram, Ohio, June 22, 1903 [copy]. 115/72552-1.

23. Rev. W. A. Lamb-Campbell, Galveston, Texas, to the Prime Minister, Ottawa, September 6, 1906. 115/72552-1.

24. L. M. Fortier, Ottawa, to Rev. W. A. Lamb-Campbell, Galveston, Texas, September 20, 1906 [copy]. 115/72552-1. It has been noted by C. D. Corbett that the climate issue was used as late as the 1950's. C. D. Corbett, *Canadian Immigration Policy* (Toronto, 1957), 52-55.

25. J. Steinbecker, Calgary, to W. D. Scott, Ottawa, May 13, 1908 and Z. W. Mitchell, Calgary, to W. D. Scott, Ottawa, May 13, 1908. 115/72552-1. Z. W. Mitchell held the office of Principal and Founder of the Co-operative Education Council of the Loyal League of Labor U.S.A. Among those listed as members of the executive board of the Council was C. F. Dick of the Pillsbury and Wishburn Milling Company, Minneapolis. Mitchell's attempt to organize a Negro colony in Alberta was reported in the *Manitoba Free Press,* May 30, 1908. 115/72552-1.

26. L. M. Fortier, Ottawa, to J. Steinbecker, Calgary, May 22, 1908 [copy]. 115/72552-1.

27. J. A. Strachan, Atlanta, to C. Sifton, Ottawa, July 21, 1902. 115/72552-1.

28. F. Pedley, Ottawa, to J. A. Strachan, Atlanta, July 28, 1902 [copy]. 115/72552-1.

29. Telegram, C. J. Broughton, Chicago, to F. Pedley, Ottawa, January 31, 1902. 115/72552-1.

30. Telegram, F. Pedley, Ottawa, to C. J. Broughton, Chicago, February 1, 1902 [copy]. 115/72552-1.

31. J. S. Crawford, Kansas City, to W. D. Scott, Ottawa, March 26, 1910. 115/72552-1. On another occasion, Crawford claimed that if it were not for the fact that he had "stood in the way . . . there would have been

not just a few hundred but many thousands of them" in western Canada. J. S. Crawford, Winnipeg, to F. Oliver, Ottawa, December 2, 1910. 115/72552-2.

32. W. D. Scott, Ottawa, to J. S. Ligan, Fitzhugh, Arkansas, February 14, 1908 [copy]. 115/72552-1.

33. J. S. Ligan, Fitzhugh, Arkansas, to W. D. Scott, Ottawa, February 2, 1908. 115/72552-1.

34. H. M. Williams, Toledo, to W. D. Scott, Ottawa, March 26, 1904. 115/72552-1.

35. Memorandum, W. J. White, to F. Oliver, September 14, 1910. 115/-72552-2.

36. It is not possible to give an exact number of Negroes who came to Canada. The figures of the Immigration Branch show no Negro settlers from 1900 through 1905 and only 364 Negroes from 1905 to 1909. It would appear that the number was too low. It is possible that some Negroes who crossed the border were listed by citizenship, as Americans, rather than as Negroes. Other Negroes may have crossed without Settlers' Certificates and thus may not have been counted. However, one should not neglect the possibility that the figures for the number of Negroes entering the country were deliberately distorted in order to forestall any anti-Negro outcry. *Immigration Facts and Figures* ([n.p.], 1913), 8-9.

37. W. J. White, St. Paul, to F. Oliver, Edmonton, September 4, 1909 [copy]. 115/72552-1. Parts of this letter, incorrectly identified as being sent to W. D. Scott, are reprinted in Sessing, "How They Kept Canada Almost Lily White," 31. Sessing has also taken the liberty of capitalizing or italicizing words for emphasis where this does not appear in the original letter.

38. It has been pointed out that the Creek Indians remained largely loyal to the Union side during the Civil War. The alliance of a few Creek chiefs with the Confederacy was later used to discredit the whole tribe and, as a result, the Creeks were forced to sign a new treaty governing their land. Kenneth W. Porter, "Relations Between Negroes and Indians Within the Present Limits of the United States," *Journal of Negro History* 17 (1932), 352 and Wyatt F. Geltz, "The Relations of Negroes and Chactow and Chickosaw Indians," *Journal of Negro History* 33 (1948), 32.

39. *Sixth Annual Report of the Commission of the Five Civilized Tribes* (Washington, 1899), 13, 59-65; William E. Bittle and Gilbert Geis, *The Longest Way Home* (Detroit, 1964), 22. The number of slaves still held by the Creek Nation at the end of the Civil War has been estimated at 3,000. Porter, "Relations Between Negroes and Indians," ft. 357. This number would appear too small given the number of land holdings allotted freemen. Murial H. Wright, *A Guide to the Indian Tribes of Oklahoma* (Norman, 1951), 142-143; *Report of the Commissioner of Indian Affairs, 1907*), 178. The history of Indian ownership of slaves is the topic of Annie Heloise Abel's three volume study, *The Slave Holding Indians*. Annie Heloise Abel, *The American Indian as Slaveholder and Secessionist* (Cleveland, 1915); *The American Indian: Participant in the Civil War* (Cleveland, 1919); *The American Indian Under Reconstruction* (Cleveland, 1925).

40. The post Civil War migration of Negroes into Oklahoma and their attempts to build all Negro communities is dealt with in Mozell C. Hill, "The All Negro Communities of Oklahoma: The Natural History of a Social Movement," *Journal of Negro History* 31 (1946), 254-268; Edwin R. Redkey, *Black Exodus* (New Haven, 1969), 100-102.

41. Two Oklahoma Supreme Court cases, in 1910 and 1913, upheld the mechanism used to exclude blacks from voting. *Atwater* v *Hassett* (1910), 111 Pac. 802-814; *Colfield* v *Farrell* (1913), 134 Pac. 407-421; Frank A. Balyeat, "Segregation in the Public Schools of Oklahoma

Territory," *Chronicles of Oklahoma* 39 (1961), 180-192; Philip Mellinger, "Discrimination and Statehood in Oklahoma," *Chronicles of Oklahoma* 49 (1971), 340-378.

42. It is no coincidence that a back-to-Africa movement also found support among Negroes in Oklahoma prior to the First World War. Brittle and Geis, *The Longest Way Home,* 69-95.

43. J. S. Crawford, Kansas City, to W. D. Scott, Ottawa, April 11, 1910 [copy]. 115/72552-1.

44. Memorandum, W. W. Cory, to W. J. White, May 27, 1910. 115/72552-2.

45. Report, W. J. White, to F. Oliver, September 13, 1910 [copy]. 115/-72552-2.

46. Sessing, "How They Kept Canada Almost Lily White," 32.

47. Report, W. J. White, to F. Oliver, September 13, 1910 [copy]. 115/-72552-2.

48. *Ottawa Free Press,* April 20, 1908. 115/72552-1.

49. J. B. Walker, Winnipeg, to W. D. Scott, Ottawa, August 21, 1908. 115/72252-1.

50. *Edmonton Capital,* January 19, 1910, 1.

51. For an outline of the position held by the *Edmonton Bulletin* see Howard Palmer, "Responses to Foreign Immigration Nativism and Ethnic Tolerance in Alberta, 1880-1920," unpublished M.A. thesis (University of Alberta, 1971), 187-188.

52. "Copy of resolution unanimously passed at the Monthly Meeting of the Edmonton Board of Trade," April 26, 1910. 115/72552-1. *Albertan,* May 20, 1911; *Edmonton Evening Journal,* April 19, 1911; *Albertan,* April 20, 1911. Negroes-Alberta, Newspaper Clipping File, Glenbow — Alberta Institute Library, Calgary; F. M. Sclander to G. E. M. Mc-Graney, April 27, 1911; Resolutions from Fort Saskatchewan Board of Trade, April 25, 1911; Yorktown, Saskatchewan Board of Trade, May 1, 1911; Morinville, Alberta Board of Trade, April 29, 1911; Strathcona, Alberta Board of Trade, April 29, 1911; Strathcona, Alberta Board of Trade, May 3, 1911. 115/72552-3.

53. *Ottawa Free Press,* January 18, 1911. 115/72552-2.

54. *Montreal Herald,* January 18, 1911. 115/72552-2.

55. *Port Arthur Evening Chronicle,* January 21, 1911. 115/72552-2.

56. *Toronto Mail and Empire,* April 27, 1911, 1.

57. *Toronto Mail and Empire,* April 28, 1911, 6.

58. Ken Eric Liddell, "New Promised Land," *Saturday Night,* 65, (June 4, 1950), 11.

59. *Edmonton Evening Journal,* April 24, 1911, 1; April 25, 1911, 1.

60. Petition, Edmonton, April 18, 1911. 115/72552-3. The population of Edmonton in 1911 was 24,882 of whom 289 were Negroes. *Canadian Almanac 1912* (Toronto, 1911), 51; "Origins of People by Principal Cities, 1911," *Census of Canada 1911* 2 (Ottawa, 1913), 372-374.

61. Palmer, "Responses to Foreign Immigration," 189.

62. Resolution of Edmonton Municipal Council, April 25, 1911. 115/72552-3; *Edmonton Evening Journal,* April 26, 1911, 5.

63. W. J. Webster, Edmonton, to W. D. Scott, Ottawa, January 7, 1911. 115/72552-2.

64. Though the Negro population in western Canada had grown, the Negro population of Canada had fallen from 17,437 in 1901 to 16,877 in 1911. "Origins of People by Provinces," *Census of Canada 1911* 2 (Ottawa, 1913), 370-371.

65. *House of Commons Debates* 1901, 54; 2939.

184

66. Proposed Order-in-Council, F. Oliver to Governor General in Council, May 31, 1911. 115/72552-3. A photo-copy of the proposed order is reprinted in Sessing, "How They Kept Canada Almost Lily White," 30.

67. *House of Commons Debates* 1911, 100, 5915.

68. *House of Commons Debates* 1911, 100, 4470-4471.

69. The article read in the Commons appeared under a different headline, "Bar Negroes from Canada," in the *Boston Post,* February 25, 1911. 115/72552-2.

70. *House of Commons Debates* 1911, 100, 5915. Several weeks later Oliver made another statement in the Commons on the Negro question. He explained that the Negro was treated the same as any other immigrant at the border and this would remain the case until Parliament decided to amend the Immigration Act. However, the unstated implication remained that the law could be administered loosely for one man and severely for another. *House of Commons Debates* 1911, 101, 6524-6525.

71. *Boston Post,* February 25, 1911. 115/72552-3.

72. "The Negro in Canada," *Chautauquan* 63 (1911), 119-120.

73. *New York Tribune,* March 22, 1911, 6. For Consular and State Department reaction see Robin W. Winks, *The Blacks in Canada: A History,* 310-313.

74. *Lloydminster Times,* May 4, 1911, 3; *New York Times,* April 27, 1911, 4; *Toronto Globe, April* 27, 1911, 1; *Albertan,* April 27, 1911. Negroes-Alberta, Newspaper Clipping File, Glenbow-Alberta Institute Library, Calgary.

75. W. E. B. Du Bois, New York, to the Immigration Department, Ottawa, March 4, 1911. 115/72552-2.

76. L. M. Fortier, Ottawa, to W. E. B. Du Bois, New York, March 4, 1911 [copy]. 115/72552-2. Fortier's letter was reprinted in *Crisis* 1 (April. 1911), 11.

77. "Emigration to Canada," *Crisis* 2 (May, 1911), 13, 14; "The Northland Migration," *Crisis* 2 (June, 1911), 56. In both articles cited, the editor of *Crisis* quotes from a number of newspapers, including Negro newspapers, as to the Canadian anti-black immigration policy. This is yet another indication of the wide publicity the Canadian policy was receiving.

78. J. L. Doupe, Winnipeg, to W. Bonnotyne, North Portal, Saskatchewan, December 30, 1910 [copy]. 115/72552-2.

79. J. W. White, Ottawa, to J. L. Doupe, Winnipeg, January 4, 1911 [copy]. 115/72552-2.

80. *New York Tribune,* March 22, 1911, 6.

81. Memorandum, W. J. White, to W. D. Scott, January 22, 1912. 115/-72552-4.

82. *Immigration Facts and Figures,* ([n.p.], 1913, 9.

83. *Immigration Facts and Figures,* ([n.p.], 1913), 8.

NOTES TO CONCLUSION

1. Most often sighted in this study is *Immigration Facts and Figures* ([n.p.], 1913). While this paper deals almost exclusively with the inflow of population from the United States, and thus, the discussion which follows, relates most closely to this question, the merits of using official figures in dealing with total immigration during this period has also been examined. A. S. Whitely, "The Peopling of the Prairie Provinces of

Canada," *American Journal of Sociology* 38 (1932), 240-252; Nathan Keyfitz, "The Growth of Canadian Population," *Population Studies* 4 (1950-51), 47-63; Duncan M. McDougall, "Immigration into Canada, 1851-1920," *Canadian Journal of Economics and Political Science* 27 (1961), 162-175; James Pickett, "An Evaluation of Estimates of Immigration into Canada in the late Nineteenth Century," *Canadian Journal of Economics and Political Science* 31 (1965), 499-508.

2. C. E. E. Ussher, Montreal, to W. D. Scott, Ottawa, March 28, 1905. 83/83679-2; F. S. Longworth, Detroit, to W. D. Scott, Ottawa, April 1, 1905; M. V. McInnes, Detroit, to W. D. Scott, Ottawa, April 3, 1905. 83/3374-2; C. E. E. Ussher, Montreal, to W. D. Scott, Ottawa, May 30, 1906; T. Duncan, Syracuse, to W. D. Scott, Ottawa, June 11, 1906. 84/33958.

3. "Will the Canadian Northwest Be Americanized?" *Independent* 55 (1903), 810.

4. *Sessional Papers* 1905, no. 25, pt. 2, 41, 43.

5. *Sessional Papers* 1901, no. 25, pt. 2, 164.

6. *Sessional Papers* 1903, no. 25, pt. 2, 139.

7. Karel Denis Bicha, "The American Farmer in the Canadian West, 1896-1914: A Revised Review," *Agricultural History* 38 (1964), 44. As a source for the twenty per cent figure added to immigration returns, Bicha sights James Mavor, *Report to the Board of Trade in the Northwest of Canada with Special Reference to Wheat Production for Export, 1904* (London, 1905), 28. However, Mavor's report, published in the British *Sessional Papers*, makes no mention of the twenty per cent deliberate inflation. Rather, Mavor notes that the Canadian government was often unaware of 'Prairie Schooner' immigrants, noting their arrival only when they applied for homestead. *Ibid.*, 27-29.

8. W. V. Bennett, Omaha, to W. D. Scott, Ottawa, March 6, 1906. 72/-23605-4.

9. C. Pilling, Grand Forks, to W. D. Scott, Ottawa, March 6, 1906. 136/-130979.

10. *Journal of the House of Commons* 35, Appendix I, June 1, 1900, 442.

11. *Journal of the House of Commons* 36, Appendix I, April 26, 1901, 298.

12. *Census of Canada, 1921, Volume II, Population* (Ottawa, 1925), xiii.

13. Jacob Viner, *Canada's Balance of International Indebtedness 1900-1913*. (Cambridge, 1924), 45-50. Also see, Roland Wilson, "Migration Movements in Canada. 1868-1925," *Canadian Historical Review* 13 (1932), 165-168; Peter Henderson Bryce, "Some Phases of Canadian Immigration," *Journal of Social Science* 44 (1906), 168-169; W. W. Husband, "The Significance of Emigration," *American Economic Review* 2 (1912), Supplement, 79, 82; William Duncan Scott, "Immigration and Population," *Canada And Its Provinces* 7, Adam Shortt, ed. (Toronto, 1914), 558.

14. *Sessional Papers* 1898, no. 13, pt. 4, 111; 1904, no. 25, pt. 2, 126. For an outline of the background to the movement of Canadians into the American midwest and prairie states between 1880 and 1896 see Marcus Lee Hansen and John Bartlet Brebner, *The Mingling of the Canadian and American Peoples* (New Haven, 1940), 182-218.

15. *Sessional Papers* 1898, no. 13, pt. 4, 80.

16. W. H. Rogers, Watertown, to F. Pedley, Ottawa, May 6, 1898. 94/-40043-1.

17. *Sessional Papers* 1903, no. 25, pt. 2, 160.

18. Cyrus Warman, "The Building of the Canadian West," *Third Annual Report of the Canadian Club of Winnipeg* (Winnipeg, 1907), 47-48.

19. W. W. Husband, "The Significance of Emigration," 82.

20. *Manitoba Free Press*, July 31, 1902.

21. *Sessional Papers* 1899, no. 3, pt. 2, 274-275.

22. *Canadian Annual Review 1908* (Toronto, 1909), 500; *Canadian Annual Review 1910* (Toronto, 1911), 497, 518. Economic success in prairie farming was often dependent upon factors over which the individual had no control. The climate in general and rainfall in particular could play havoc with a farmer's dream. Dry periods, however, were not unusual. Indeed, a wet spell between 1899-1903 can be pointed to as a climatic exception. Frank Gilbert Roe, "The Alberta West Cycle of 1899-1903: A Climatic Interlude," *Agricultural History* 28 (1954), 112-120. See also Karel Denis Bicha, *The American Farmer and the Canadian West 1896-1914* (Lawrence, 1968), 138-144. The *New York Tribune*, March 27, 1905 claimed that many Americans returned home disappointed because the lands of Western Canada were over-rated and, as the paper advised, "The American farmer gets rid of a 'gold brick' as soon as he is made aware of its worthlessness." 54/5196-3. In part, however, the return flow might have resulted in the inability of Midwest corn farmers to adjust to different techniques required in wheat production. Theodore Saloutos and John D. Hicks. *Twentieth Century Populism. Agricultural Discontent in the Middle West* 1900-1939 (Lincoln, 1951).

23. Imre Ferenczi, *International Migrations* 1, *Statistics* (New York), 1929), 358, 376.

24. Viner, *Canada's Balance of International Indebtedness*, 49, 57.

25. For a more detailed outline of how this figure was reached see Harold M. Troper, "Official Canadian Government Encouragement of American Immigration 1896-1911", unpublished Ph.D. dissertation University of Toronto, 1971, 270-283.

26. *Immigration Facts and Figures*, 2, 25, 38; *Sessional Papers* 1905, no. 25, pt. 2, xxxi.

27. Memorandum, J. A. Smart, to F. Pedley, [n.d.], 1898. 42/5146-2.

28. *Facts For The People: Pages from the Record of the Laurier Administration from 1896 to 1908* ([n.p.], 1908?), 14.

29. *House of Commons Debates* 50, 8654, July 27, 1899.

30. *Journal of the House of Commons* 38, Appendix II, May 29, 1903, 45.

31. *House of Commons Debates* 48, 1979, April 24, 1899.

32. *Journal of the House of Commons* 38, Appendix II, July 11, 1903, 117.

33. *Immigration Facts and Figures* ([n.p.], 1913) 2.

34. *House of Commons Debates* 60, 6733, 6734, July 15, 1903. Assuming the honesty of the agents and the accuracy of their self assessment, there are two obvious explanations which might clarify the statistical discrepancies. While agents' reports listed the number of Settlers' Certificates they had authorized, agents had no way of knowing whether all those who were issued certificates migrated or how many had been issued a second certificate by another agent. Also, the distortion might have resulted, in part, from overland trekkers who travelled across the open border in a prairie schooner and, thus, never turned over their certificate to proper authorities.

35. F. W. Burton review of *Public Life* by W. H. Moore, *Canadian Journal of Economics and Political Science* 2 (1936), 598.

36. William R. Stewart, "The Americanization of the Canadian Northwest," *Cosmopolitan* 34 (1903), 610.

Index

Adams, Henry 3
Afro-American Literary Society 126
Alberta 6, 13, 21, 30, 34, 41, 53, 72, 107, 127, 137, 145
Alien Labour Act 7, 11
American Editorial Association 93
American Historical Association 101
American Immigration Association 114, 115, 154
American Interstate Commerce Law 49
American Press 79, 87, 89, 90-91, 92, 93, 94, 95, 98, 112, 141, 143
American Review of Reviews 40
Americanization 13, 157
Arkansas 129
Assiniboia East 28
Atlas of Canada 86

Banff 94
Barbados 137
Battle Creek Journal 93
Bennett, William J. 39, 47, 149
Boston Post 141
Brampton 21
Brandon 9, 10, 17, 30
Brandon Weekly Sun 20
Brithe 148
Brockville 17
Brown, Henry Billings 123
Bryce, George 152
Burton, Alfred 125
Burton, Franklin Wicher 156

Calgary 72, 127
Calgary Albertan 137
Canada: economic conditions 81; social conditions 80
Canadian Government Agents 25-26, 27, 28, 29-31, 34, 35-37, 38, 41, 50, 51, 53, 54, 55, 59, 79, 81, 82, 83, 89, 95, 96, 97, 107, 108, 109, 110, 111, 112, 113, 115, 117, 118, 119, 128, 129, 130, 139, 147, 151, 154, 156; duties 43-47; rivalry 46-48
Canadian Immigration Act 22
Canadian Magazine 33, 122
Canadian Nationalist League 12
Canadian Northern Railway 51, 52, 92
Canadian Pacific Railway 6, 19, 34, 49, 50, 51, 52, 65, 66, 67, 70, 92, 95, 137, 144
Carpenter, Frank George 33-34
Carrot River 149
Chautauquan 122, 142
Chicago Newspaper Union 81
Chicago Times 94
Civil Service 15, 26; appointments 21; Board of Examiners 16; Inside Service 15, 20, 24, 26, 31; Outside Service 15, 16, 24, 26, 27, 29, 31; party affiliations 16-17; patronage 16, 17, 24, 28
Civil Service Act 24, 29
Civil Service Commission 18, 24
Clarke, Edward Frederick 34
Climate 6, 79, 80, 85, 91, 97, 127, 143
Cole, Albert L. 116
Colorado 111, 113, 117, 118

Columbia World Exposition 101
Conn, James R. 12
Conservatives 18, 27, 29, 34, 69, 73, 78, 153, 154
Cory, William Wallace 24
Cosmopolitan 156
Country Fairs 87, 88, 89, 90, 91, 109-110, 117
Crawford, James 124, 129, 130
Creek-Negroes 132, 133, 134, 135, 136, 144, 145
Crisis 143, 144
Currie, Thomas O. 47, 108

Dafoe, John W. 10, 16
Daily Pioneer Press 114
Dalziel, C.J.A. 53
Daniel, John Waterhouse 141
Dauphin 41
Davies, Benjamin 27, 29
Davies, Louis Henry 27, 29
Davin, Nicholas Flood 27
Delegates Reports and Settlers Experiences in Western Canada 85-86
Democrats 3
DuBois, W.E.B. 23, 143, 144
Duncan, Thomas 27
Dunkards 42

East Grey 34
Economic expansion: western Canada 10
Edmonton 21, 30, 137, 138, 139, 141
Edmonton Bulletin 21, 137
Edmonton Capital 137
Emigration: American 152; Canadian 5
Enlarged Homestead Act 117 (*See also* Homestead Act.)
Estevan 137

Farm delegates 63, 64
Fisher, Sidney A. 89
Five Civilized Tribes 132
Ford, W.C. 5
Fort Saskatchewan 138
Fortier, L.M. 20, 23, 127, 128, 143
Fowler, George W. 35
Free Land Clubs 63

Gates, Paul W. 102
Georgia 128
German American Colonization Company 127, 128
German Americans 42
German-Baptist Brethren 42
Grant, Bishop Abraham 125
Greenway, Thomas 10, 19, 27, 88
Grieve, James A. 26, 27

Halbrite 28
Hall, John Richard 18
Haslam Land Investment Company, The 71
Hepburn Act 114
Higgins, Anthony 5
Hofstadter, Richard 3
Holmes, Edward T. 27
Holmes, Robert 27
Homestead Act 102
Homesteaders Information Bureau 113
Homesteads 14, 39, 45, 66, 80, 85, 96, 149
Hough, Emerson 40-41
Hutchinson, William 90

Illinois 101, 107, 111, 114, 116
Illinois Press Association 93, 94
Immigration: American aliens 42, 150; American Press 79, 87, 89, 90-91, 92, 93, 94, 95, 98, 110, 112, 115, 141; Anglo-Saxons 12; Asiatics 12; drought 37-38; eastern Canadians 42; Europeans 1, 11, 12, 14; ex-Canadians 150-52; farmers' sons 40-41; German-Mennonites 59; Hungarian 62; hyphenated Americans 41-42; Norwegian-Americans 65; pamphlets 84, 85, 86, 87, 88, 94; quality 11-12; race prejudice 29; Slav 22; testimonials 85; tour programme 91-98, 144; wealth 38, 39
Immigration Acts 24
Imperial Development Company 53
Imperial Order Daughters of the Empire 138-39
Independent 148
Indian Head 71
Indiana 30, 42, 48, 91, 109, 115, 118
Industrialization: European 5
Interstate Commerce Commission 114

Iowa 47, 88, 91, 114, 116
Jefferson, Thomas 4
Jerseyville Democrat 93
Johnson, John Albert 116
Jones, John Edward 142, 143

Kansas 37, 43, 52, 63, 89, 91, 107, 113
Kansas City Star 115
Kellogg Newspaper Company, A.N. 81
Kent West 98
Kentucky 30, 95
Keys, Perley George 18
Kings and Albert 35
Kinkaid Act 118
Kiowa-Comanche Indian 107
Kipling, Rudyard 85

Lake Louise 94, 95
Last Best West, The 86, 87
Laurier Wilfrid 1, 9, 10, 14, 15, 146
Leduc 41
Leeds 34
Lethbridge 113
Lexington-Addington 73
Ligan, S.J. 129, 130
Lincoln, Abraham 89
London Township 9
Louisiana Purchase 90, 123
Lumbering: U.S.A. 108, 109
Lyons, James M. 50

McCroney, George E. 138
McGill University 19
Magrath, Charles Alexander 12
McInnes, M.V. 28, 30, 61, 65, 78, 112
McKay, Barney 126
MacLachlan, James M. 47, 108, 109, 110, 111, 114
Manitoba 6, 9, 10, 17, 19, 20, 24, 30, 72, 88
Manitoba Frees Press 21, 54, 87
Manitoba School Question 10, 21
Martin, Joseph 10
Medicine Hat 12, 128
Mennonites 41, 59
Michigan 25, 26, 28, 30, 41, 43, 48, 49, 52, 60, 61, 62, 65, 70, 78, 79, 89, 93, 96, 105, 112, 151

Michigan Press Association 92, 93
Middlesex County 9
Miller, G.W. 136
Milwaukee Land Exchange 53
Minnesota 27, 41, 42, 45, 47, 48, 51, 59, 67, 71, 74, 78, 88, 89, 92, 108, 114, 115, 116, 127
Minnesota Editorial Association 91, 92
Missouri 90, 91, 112, 114, 124
Mitchell, Z.W. 127, 128
Moncton 50
Monk, Frederick Debartzch 27
Montana 108, 113, 117
Montreal Herald 138
Montreal Standard 11
Morinville 138
Mormons 41, 59
Mornington 26

Nation 116
National Association for the Advancement of Coloured People 143
Nebraska 30, 39, 47, 53, 88, 89, 91, 113, 116, 117, 148
Negroes 1, 23, 42, 121-45; American attitude (white) 122, 123; Canadian 125; farmers 123; immigration policy 121-22, 124-25, 126, 127, 128, 130-31, 132, 137, 138, 140, 141, 142, 144, 145; Indians 132, 133, 134, 135, 136, 137, 144, 145; Reconstruction 123, 124; underground railway 125
Nehill district 125
Nevada 104, 117
New Brunswick 50
New England 40
New Mexico 117, 118
New York 27, 48, 52, 79
New York Herald 33, 101-102
New York Times 2
New York Tribune 142
Newfoundland 19
Newlands, Francis G. 104
Newlands Act 103, 104, 117
North Dakota 28, 42, 47, 76, 108, 111, 114, 116
North West Council 21
North West Territories 89, 151
Norwegian-Americans 65
Nova Scotia 140

Ohio 48, 68, 89, 130
Oklahoma 52-53, 101-102, 107, 131, 133, 134, 135, 136, 137, 143, 144, 145
Oliver, Frank 21, 22, 23, 24, 31, 35, 121, 130, 134, 136, 137, 139, 141
Ontario 42, 60, 140
Orange Lodge 138
Oregon 116
Orientals 42
Osler, Hammond and Nanton 70
Ottawa Free Press 136, 138
Outlook 36
Overland Monthly and Out West Magazine 62, 65

Paris Exposition 20
Parker, J.H.M. 64-65, 68, 72, 77, 78
Patronage 27-28, 29, 35, 46; Civil Service 26
Pedley, Frank 19, 20, 37, 106, 150
Pennsylvania 43, 48, 94, 105
Pereira, Lyndwode 18, 124
Perth North 26
Pinkerton detective agent 51
Plessy vs. *Ferguson* 123
Populist movement 3
Port Arthur Evening Chronicle 138
Prairies, The 6, 9; agricultural economy 11

Queen's Quarterly 12

Railway 5, 13, 21-22, 48, 49, 50, 51, 52, 53, 58, 59, 60, 61, 65, 66, 70, 84, 92, 96, 112, 113, 114; American 49, 50, 51, 52, 53, 60, 61, 66, 67, 93, 105, 106, 108, 110, 112-13, 114, 115, 116, 135, 142, 144, 148; Ann Arbour 60; Baltimore and Ohio Railroad 60-61; Buckeye Route 60; Burlington and Missouri River Railroad 113; Canadian Northern 51, 52, 92; Canadian Pacific 6, 19, 34, 49, 50, 51, 52, 65, 66, 67, 70, 92, 95, 137, 144; Central Passenger Railroads 51; Cincinnati, Hamilton and Dayton 60; Columbus, Hoking Valley, Toledo Railroad 60; Detroit, Toledo and Cincinnati 60; Grand Rapids, Indiana and Michigan Central 61; Great Northern 51, 108; Intercolonial 50; land grants 14; Michigan Central and Flint and

Père Marquette 52; Northern Pacific 108; Ohio Central 60; Soo Line 51, 65; Southern Pacific 53, 135; Union Pacific 53; Wisconsin Central 108, 109
Reliable Information For Use Of United States Newspaper Editors Visiting Western Canada 86
Ritchie, William 76
Roosevelt, Theodore 103
Ross, William 153
Royal Canadian Mounted Police 87

St. John City 141
St. John's 19
St. Louis Exposition 90
St. Louis Republic 91
St. Paul Globe 77
Saskatchewan 6, 34, 41, 71
Scandinavian Americans 41-42
Scott, William Duncan 12, 19, 20, 28, 44, 121, 140
Scramlin, William 28
Sessional Papers 2
Settlers' Certificates 45, 47, 48, 49, 54, 59, 65, 66, 68, 69, 70, 71, 72, 73, 128, 129, 147, 148, 149, 154
Shelby Sentinel 95
Sifton, Clifford 1, 6, 7, 9-11, 13, 14, 15, 16, 17, 18, 19, 20, 21, 22, 24, 25, 27, 28, 29, 31, 33, 46, 55, 60, 69, 76, 84, 85, 87, 92, 94, 116; Attorney-General of Manitoba 10; civil servants 15
Sifton, John Wright 9
Significance of the Frontier, The (Frederick Jackson Turner) 101
Smart, James Allan 17, 24, 27, 33, 58, 110-116, 153
South Dakota 27, 38, 41, 42, 43, 48, 63, 73, 89, 96, 108, 111, 113, 114, 116, 117, 118, 149
Sowing, The (Emerson Hough) 40-41
Sproule, Thomas Simpson 34
State agents (*See* Canadian Government Agents.)
Stavely 72
Steinbecker, J. 127-28
Stephens, George 98
Strachan, James A. 128
Strangers Within Our Gates (James S. Woodsworth) 122
Strathcona 138

Strathroy 24
Strong, Josiah 4; *Our Country: Its Possible Future and Its Present Crisis* 4
Sub-Agents 56-78, 147
Symposium Of Ideas And Prophecies On The Canadian West By The Members Of The National Editorial Association, And What They Said In 1900 86

Taylor, George 34-35
Taylor, John W. 59
Technology: farming 5-6
Texas 114, 115, 118
Toledo Record News 89
Toronto 19
Toronto Board of Trade 1
Toronto Globe 21
Toronto Mail and Empire 138
Toronto Telegram 78
Toronto West 34
Tour programmes 91-98
Trans-Mississippi and International Exposition 89
Turner, Frederick Jackson 4, 101, 102
Turriff, John Gillanders 28
Twain, Mark 4

United States: farming 3-4; Indians 103, 107, 117, 132; irrigation 103, 104, 117; land expansion 4, 101-106, 107, 113, 115, 116, 118; lumbering 108, 109; urban development 4, 123, 124
University of Manitoba 152
Urban life: United States 40

Utah 59, 75, 82, 117

Van Horne, William 49, 50, 92
Victoria 153
Viner, Jacob 150, 152

Warman, Cy 151
Washington 54, 111, 113
West Huron 27
Western Canada 85
Western Canadian Immigration Association 54-55
Western development programme 10, 11; Clifford Sifton 10, 11
Western expansion: Canadian 5. (*See also* United States: land expansion)
Western Judicial Board 10
Western Newspaper Union 81
Wheat: Canadian 5; Marquis 6
White, William J. 20, 25, 36, 37, 40, 44, 45, 46, 51, 52, 55, 60, 71, 72, 73, 75, 77, 78, 82, 83, 90, 91, 92, 93, 95, 98-99, 103-104, 106, 107, 110, 112, 118, 119, 130, 131, 134, 135, 136, 144, 150
Wiebe, Robert 3
Wilson, Huntington 143
Wilson, Uriah 73, 78
Winnipeg 14, 19, 21, 24, 53, 78, 94, 122, 142, 143
Wisconsin 47, 53, 68, 72, 77, 105, 107, 108, 110, 111, 116
Wisconsin Editorial Association 92
Woodsworth, James S. 122
Wyoming 113, 116, 117, 118

Yorkton 138